OFF-SEASON

Discovering America on
Winter's Shore

KEN MCALPINE

THREE RIVERS PRESS • NEW YORK

Published by Three Rivers Press, New York, New York.
Member of the Crown Publishing Group, a division of Random House, Inc.

www.randomhouse.com

THREE RIVERS PRESS and the Tugboat design are registered trademarks of
Random House, Inc.

Printed in the United States of America

Design by Lauren Dong

Photograph on page iii: MILLENNIUM/NONSTOCK

Library of Congress Cataloging-in-Publication Data

McAlpine, Ken, 1959–
Off-season : discovering America on winter's shore / Ken McAlpine.
1. Atlantic Coast (U.S.)—Description and travel. 2. Atlantic States—
Description and travel. I. Title.
F106.M53   2004
917.504'44—dc22   2003023761

ISBN 1-4000-4973-3

10   9   8   7   6   5   4   3   2

First Edition   *4456887*

To my wife and best friend, Kathy;

she has shown me the meaning of love and belief.

And to my sons, Cullen and Graham,

who have shown me that anything is possible.

Acknowledgments

IN THE END one person gets credit for a book, but this is wholly misleading and unfair. This book would never have come about if not for the guidance and help of many.

First I would like to thank my wife and best friend, Kathy. I was gone from home for five long months, and we both know who did the real work. I never heard one complaint. I have never met anyone so selfless and giving. Your love and support are never taken for granted. I am the luckiest man alive.

I want to thank my father and mother, Harry and Betsy McAlpine, for instilling their love for the ocean in me. If we had vacationed in the mountains, this book would never have been written, and I probably would have gotten a conventional, respectable job.

I would also like to thank my in-laws, Allen and Dot McCart, first for raising a remarkable daughter, and then for helping her raise a family while her husband was away. Thanks, too, to my sister-in-law and brother-in-law, Pat and Tim McCart-Malloy, for their tireless help.

This book would never have seen print if not for my agent and friend, Stuart Bernstein, who found an editor who also believed. Heartfelt thanks, Stuart, for patiently guiding a neophyte through the whole Byzantine book-making process, and making me believe I could actually write a book. Thanks to my editor—Carrie Thornton—for taking a chance on me, and then editing my words with heart and care that went far beyond mere professionalism. You made me look better than I am.

And, last but not least, I want to thank from the bottom of my heart all the people I met during my trip, folks who, for no good reason other than human kindness, warmly welcomed a stranger—and his incessant questions—into their lives. I will never forget you. This book wasn't written by me. It was written by you.

Contents

OFF-SEASON

Introduction

No ONE CAN SAY, with absolute truth, what effect the ocean's shore has on the human soul. Too many souls are involved. But it has an effect, no doubt, and though I should be old enough to know better, I am certain it is a magical one. Others feel it. Our bodies, like our planet, are 71 percent salt water; our blood is precisely as salty as the sea. Take from that what you wish.

I have spent my own life at the ocean's edge. I was nearly born in the ocean, my mother, with the superb instincts of her sex, at the last minute reluctantly bypassing a beach outing for the hospital instead. My father instilled in me his own love of the ocean and taught me to bodysurf. I returned the favor by putting a good scare in him, working as an ocean lifeguard—in New Jersey and Florida—until I was nearly thirty. I fell in love with the woman of my dreams beside the ocean, asking for a first kiss on a moon-spackled jetty in Ocean City, New Jersey. Our two sons were born in a hospital that catches the Pacific Ocean breeze. We live two miles from the ocean now, farther than I'd like but as close as we can get, given the price of coastal real estate in California, or anywhere else for that matter. If a price tag can be affixed to magic, it has more zeros than reason can fathom. It doesn't matter. The ocean is free, and I still come to it several times a week, often just after dawn when no one is there, slipping into the cool Pacific to surf or kayak. For a few moments I slip away to a place beyond care or time. When the time comes, I want my two sons to scatter me across the water, beyond care and time forever.

The world, of course, is neither idyllic nor beyond care. At forty-three, I found my own outlook increasingly tainted. I woke, like the rest of the world, to days that couldn't be scrubbed clean. The world seemed to be sliding with exponential speed into a cesspool of trouble and inhumanity: terrorism, murder, corporate fraud, addict mothers, absent fathers, feral children with no ties and even less conscience. The woeful list is long and familiar to anyone who reads today's news.

I still believe most of the world isn't like this, only that the clamor and flash of mayhem and mistrust have drowned out the better behavior of the world at large. It is simplistic, but I believe it to be true. Harbors of upstanding conscience and intent still exist, vast anchorages actually, where people and communities are as good and right as people and communities can be, given our imperfections.

I wanted to see these places and meet these people, see the proof that the world still rested on a quiet foundation of hope and community. Led by my own bias, I went to the ocean's edge to look.

I went in winter, taking an off-season journey along the East Coast's beaches; over the course of five months, I drove hundreds of meandering miles from Key West, Florida, to Lubec, Maine. I chose winter for a reason. By traveling in the off-season, through hamlets like Ormond Beach, Florida, and Strathmere, New Jersey, I believed I would find people and their towns in their true form and best season, when life slows, and community and humanity reassert themselves. I hoped—no, I fervently believed—that I'd find a salty, small-town America, a place of substance with a unique stamp beyond the faceless suburbs and strip malls that are consuming this country, a place where people have time for themselves and their neighbors and possibly even a stranger.

Tourists know these beach towns in summer. Often loud, garish, and overrun, these swirls of boardwalk, sand, and coconut-scented skin are spread beneath a happy dome of sunshine. It's a season of gentle, frothy waves, when hooting kids bounce to shore, when fumbling teens find first love in dark dunes, when sunburned families play Crazy Eights around the dining room table at night and old couples sit on porches, picking through their memories on the sea breeze.

It's magic, certainly. But when the summer crowds leave and the last Indian summer withers, the tone changes, and the magic begins its real reign. Those who live beside the Atlantic Ocean in its off-season—the term, of course, is all wrong—know this. It was their story I wanted. Shrimpers, crabbers, drunks, and university zoologists, newspaper editors, bartenders, painters, poets, and postal clerks, social misfits and social pillars, I wanted a glimpse of their lives—funny, sad, selfless, petty, insular, enlightened—warts and all.

In setting out on this adventure, I believed I would discover a common thread, a human bond, and quite possibly a reassuring lesson in these trying times. I am not so naïve as to believe we can all get along—human beings are destined to clash. But for many the ocean is a link, and lives and people that at first glance seem impossibly distant—what could you have in common with a Chesapeake Bay crabber?—are really not so far apart after all. The ocean connects. Anyone who loves the water will recognize, in this journey and unspooling cast of characters, a piece of themselves.

Most Americans don't know winter's beaches. I now know this is both a blessing and a loss.

🌿

YOU WON'T DISCOVER anything until you go out and look. So in mid-October I left my home and family and drove to Florida in our Ford Windstar van. I had planned on starting earlier, but the actual leaving took longer than I expected. Preparing for a months-long road trip is no simple thing. For starters, there was the matter of winter clothing. Living in southern California, where cold-weather gear means a long-sleeved shirt and possibly a windbreaker, I owned none. Fortunately people in southern California ski, so I purchased several pairs of long johns and wool socks at a local sporting goods store. My in-laws, recent transplants to California from New Jersey, dug into their stock. My mother-in-law produced a down comforter to go with my sleeping bag. My father-in-law gave me his down jacket, unwittingly throwing in a plastic bag in the left pocket, a holdover from his last winter walk with his dog.

Another part of the preparation consisted of listening to plenty of advice. Almost everyone thought I should start in Maine and work my way south as fast as possible, so as to miss the worst of winter. No, I patiently explained, the worst of winter was a large part of the point. People who chose to live along the shores of February Maine must have a good reason for doing so. Right, mouthed my advisers, though their eyes regarded me sadly. One friend thought I was writing a travel guide to winter beaches, a sort of Lonely Planet triptik to beaches Jack London might enjoy. *Old Orchard Beach is a well-kept secret in January. You'll be charmed at how nothing is open, the sand cracks underfoot, and the bitter wind drives sand between your teeth.*

"Who is going to read a book about going to the beach in the winter?" he said testily, annoyed by my enthusiasm. "It's freezing cold, it's damp, and it's empty."

Precisely, I thought, and this trip will unveil these alluring enticements and others, glorious and unexpected.

I was traveling on a shoestring budget. A friend who had taken several long road trips advised me to sleep in my van to cut costs. Pull into a motel late at night, he said, and park in its lot. Chains work best. Private motel owners are apt to patrol their lots, but a sixteen-year-old making five dollars an hour at Motel 6 isn't likely to stray from watching *Sex and the City*. Peeing isn't problematic if you back up to a wooded area or a cement wall. Wake up early, he said, shower and shave at the nearest YMCA, and be on your sparkling way.

My friend showed me his pickup truck, the back cab rigged for the road. Mesh netting dangled neatly from the sides of his camper shell, storage for soft goods. Coolers held the perishables. Two padlocked strongboxes contained his valuables. The strongboxes weren't always effective. "The whole truck was stolen in Mexico," he said.

I went to a local business that specialized in outfitting campers. The owner was seated behind a desk littered with order forms. He was Japanese and emanated Zen calm. When I made my request, he folded his hands liquidly. "Certainly, we can put in a strongbox. What kind of truck do you want us to put it in?"

"It's a Windstar van."

His eyebrows arced, though only slightly. He said nothing.

"Have you ever put a strongbox in a van?" I asked.

"Noooo," he said slowly. "I don't believe we have. Most families keep their valuables in the house."

But he installed the box, or at least two of his employees did. It was white, about two feet deep and four feet long, and ran along one side of the van. I stuffed it with valuables—notebooks, a laptop computer, the down jacket, and a folder with drawings from my two young sons—and sent up a fervent prayer not to lose the thumbnail-sized key.

I realize it's odd to go out searching for trust toting a safe, but optimism and caution are not an odd couple. I believe in people, but even the most ardent social worker doesn't nuzzle Hannibal Lecter.

Crime was not something I hoped to find, though plenty of people thought it a distinct possibility. Several days before I left, my father-in-law presented me with a baseball bat. "In case," he said.

I accepted the bat, in case I stumbled on a winter softball league. It was sawed in half, which would sorely hurt my average.

One piece of equipment I knew I wanted to bring was my kayak. Kayaks, as anyone who owns one knows, are great for poking around. From dry land you are limited in what you can see. Set out in a kayak, and an entirely different world unfolds before you. In a kayak I have come within arm's reach of porpoises, explored sea caves and empty islands, and once, in an unnerving but memorable surprise, watched a gray whale breach almost directly under me: all difficult circumstances to experience on dry land. Viewed from the water, even the land you just left looks different.

With hundreds of miles of coastline to explore, the kayak addressed a critical need. Plus at roughly eight feet, it fit perfectly in the last available space in the back of the van. I had removed all the seats, except the driver and front passenger seats, to make room for my supplies. All that happy space was now filled. By shuffling items about, and placing the kayak on top of the strongbox, I found I could make enough room to roll out my sleeping bag. If the kayak didn't slide off the strongbox and crush me, I could spend a comfortable, though coffinlike, night.

Once you're packed, it's time to go. I had been dreading this moment for weeks. My parting with my wife, Kathy, was thankfully short. She was late for work, and with one half of our income taking a flier on a book, it wouldn't pay for her to get fired. We hugged, and she began to cry. We separated awkwardly, and she told me to be safe, and when she pulled out of the driveway, she nearly backed over my foot.

I walked our two boys around the block to their school. We had talked about the trip for months. Cullen, at nine, grasped the scope of our separation.

"I love you, Dad," he said. "I'll take care of the fish."

Graham, like many seven-year-olds, doesn't peer very far into the future. He regarded me calmly.

"On Friday I'm going to Rachel's."

I walked home feeling lonelier than I ever thought possible.

I started up the van, backed out of the driveway, swallowed, and turned east.

I

FORT LAUDERDALE, FLORIDA

No Barnacles in Heaven

IT WAS THE same bridge but a different memory, proving that everyone intersects with time differently,
though few more differently than Erik Jersted. On this fiery October evening, Fort Lauderdale's Las Olas Bridge arced steeply, as it
always does, over the Intracoastal Waterway. It has to, or the bridge
would be forever opening for the armada of sleek yachts that throb
down from the North in the fall, ferrying their owners away from the
season of brutish weather and nasty colds.

Twenty-one years ago, almost to this very day, I hired on to work
for a winter as a lifeguard on Fort Lauderdale's beaches. For seven
months I lived just across this bridge, riding a garage sale bicycle up
and over to get to a job no one would rightly call work. Each morning when I pedaled to the apex of this bridge, the breeze brought the
smell of the sea, cementing the promise of another idyllic day.

The ocean is like music. It resurrects memories, jumbling them
ashore on a flood tide.

As Erik's pickup labored up the bridge, my mind gathered memories. I remembered how the Atlantic gave up its night face as dawn
fired the horizon, morphing with ease, from darkness through lightening shades of blue to the palest green. The sun sent soft morning
rays, soon to be replaced by a harsh, urgent light. The elements all
gathered strength as the day progressed. The morning breeze, as
warm and delicate as a baby's breath, by afternoon created a steady,
white-capped beat. The sand that sifted between the toes, cool and
fine at dawn, attained skillet heat by squinty-bright afternoon, so that

inexperienced sunbathers started for the water with calculated ease and finished, mouth queerly puckered, with a knees-high sprint that would have done any track star proud. In the afternoon the squalls came off the ocean. The day's baking press seemed to crescendo in anticipation, and then came release, the air going cool, the first fat, warm drops and, without transition, rain running in sheets across the water and the beach, the tourists fleeing for the bars and hotel lobbies across Highway A1A. Many times I climbed down from the lifeguard stand and stood alone in the drumming rain. It was warm on my skin, and I liked the way the fat drops kicked up tiny coralline explosions and scrubbed the day clean. Looking back now, I realize I also liked the way the rain closed down time. There was no past and no future, only the moment's cocoon of salty-warm wet.

Everyone's memories are different, but the ocean remains the same. It is a happy gift.

I turned to Erik and smiled. "I remember riding across this bridge," I said.

"I remember jumping off this bridge on fire," he said.

Erik continued to look straight ahead, closely monitoring the surrounding traffic. These days he is a cautious driver, though that was not always the case.

I waited, but Erik offered nothing more. He doesn't see his own life as particularly interesting. He often needs prodding.

"You were on fire?" I asked.

"There were these clowns doing this exhibition in Fort Lauderdale, lighting themselves on fire, doing this diving thing," he said after a few beats. "My friend says to me, 'We can do that.' So we got some towels and doused them in gas and walked up on the bridge. We wrapped the towels around us and lit the towels on fire. He went first."

His companion's leap would have made the clowns proud, a flaming ball of linen and wild yowling summarily snuffed by the Intracoastal. Erik, on the other hand, experienced difficulties. Alarmed by the first human fireball, the bridge attendant was now sprinting up the bridge. Hanging over the side of the bridge, Erik applied a match to himself and flared brightly. The flame promptly went out.

Once motivated, Erik is not easily deterred. "I had to pull myself back up on the bridge and light myself again. The bridge attendant was running toward me, and I went up in this big ball of flame. Must have hit a wet spot on one of the towels."

Erik, I learned in the days I spent with him, has many unusual memories. When he talks about them, he speaks matter-of-factly, as if he's telling you how much soap to add to the laundry.

He is fifty-four and, for the moment, a professional lifeguard: three days a week in Lauderdale, two days a week up the coast in Pompano Beach. He is supremely capable: he can fix almost anything. He can save your life. He has plucked hapless swimmers from rips, jump-started stalled hearts, and tended to plane wrecks in the waters off his lifeguard stand and car accidents on A1A behind him. In Fort Lauderdale, where tropical heat and fruity mixed drinks turn vacationers toward self-destruction, lifeguarding extends far beyond developing a righteous tan. Erik has bellows for lungs, thickly muscled shoulders, and powerful hands. He twice rowed a dory from Bimini to Florida. The faster trip took fourteen and a half hours. He has spent his life in, on, and under the ocean—rowing, swimming, diving, surfing—and though the Fort Lauderdale Chamber won't tell you this, the ocean is a treacherous place. Erik once saw a man fall from a boat and disappear—as fast as you read this sentence—without a trace. Regarding water, Erik appears to fear nothing. He has fended off aggressive sharks, surfed enormous waves, and been dragged behind a fishing boat at night when one of the boat's trolling lines snagged his lobster bag, filled with a half-dozen plump lobsters.

"I wasn't about to let go of that bag," recalled Erik. "I don't know what that fisherman was doing, but it took him a while to notice he'd hooked a really big fish."

You would be lucky to walk down a dark alley with Erik. Yet he has the demeanor of a child. When he is thinking about something, he goes away. You speak to him, but he doesn't hear. Out of the blue spurt private thoughts, candid and unguarded. He is always losing the keys to his truck. He gives the last of whatever he has away. He used to bring homeless people home, until his wife, Sharon, finally requested an end to that.

Erik himself has not had an easy life. His father was in the merchant marine and rarely home. He and his brother ran wild. At twenty-four, with a wife and child, his brother simply disappeared. The accident report said he fell off a sailboat. Erik is not so sure. Erik is not school bright, but he is world wise. Anything he lacks in book smarts he makes up for in heart. He left the beach for twelve years and became a minister for a Baptist church in Fort Lauderdale. His official title was Minister to Senior Adults, but he also spent a lot of time ministering to dying AIDS victims. Fort Lauderdale has never been a bastion of chastity; few know this better than Erik. Some AIDS victims accepted the Lord in their last moments; others told God, and Erik, to fuck themselves. This Erik could handle. But then the church built itself a new and overly grand home and strayed away from ministering, focusing less on helping people and more on raising funds. Two months before I arrived, Erik left the church and came back to the beach. When he did so, he forfeited sixteen years of seniority and benefits. He returned to base pay—$12.75 an hour—and no benefits.

This isn't enough for Erik to live on, so he has to take odd jobs. One evening, the sun already low on the horizon, we were driving to a dock at Lighthouse Point, twenty minutes north, to scrape barnacles from the bottom of a ninety-foot yacht.

Through the windshield of Erik's Chevy pickup, ahead of the snaking lines of brakelights, the last pink light of day dissolved into the west.

Erik had been lost in thought, but now he suddenly perked up. "I don't know of any other boat-scrapers who work in the dark," he said brightly. "But you know what? It's beautiful down there. Serene. Real peaceful. I'll probably never own a boat like that. But to go underneath and clean the running gear, I really feel privileged."

The truck's air conditioning hummed. We turned into Lighthouse Point and drove past the sprawling, low-slung homes and well-tended yards of the wealthy.

"I don't make a lot of money, but it doesn't matter," said Erik. "When I was having a lot of stress at the church, I'd come out to the beach in the morning, and I'd go into work happy. I knew then it was time to come back. I was so unhappy at the church. I actually had so much stress, I went to the doctor and got on medication. I actually had a breakdown. I didn't have a balanced life. I went to the hospital and got treated for depression."

Inside the truck, sand on the floor, dive knife on the dash, it was almost dark. Ahead of us lay two hours of scraping in inky blackness under a stranger's yacht.

"I've realized that you have to make the most of your gifts. At fifty-four years old, I guess this is it. I wake up happy and go home happy."

I heard his words, soft, satisfied, and certain. And I knew both of us were doing the right thing.

⁂

I HAD PLANNED on starting in Key West, a logical beginning for a south-to-north traipse up the eastern seaboard. But journeys, at least good ones, don't proceed with sequential logic, which was why one of my first stops was Fort Lauderdale.

I headed to Fort Lauderdale looking for Erik. When I arrived in Lauderdale in 1981 for my own brief stint of lifeguarding, Erik was already a legend. Even then he looked out for others. I came down there with six friends, and Erik found us a home, which happened to be right next door to his. Living next door to Erik proved exciting. He rode a motorcycle. Some nights he would dress entirely in black, slap duct tape over his license plate, and then roar through the town with the police in hot pursuit, an orgasm of adrenalin that ended with Erik booming into his driveway and hiding in his dark home with minutes to spare. On the beach his workouts were both feared and renowned. He paddled and rowed until everyone else was all screaming nerve endings, then he paddled and rowed some more. Like some powerful black hole, he absorbed us into his lifestyle. We swam, rowed, paddled, and ran, and at night we drank and got thrown out of bars, though we never came close to exhibiting Erik's wanton disregard for pain or prison. We knew him simply as the Master. Others might have seen him in a similar light. Women streamed in and out of his house, which emanated screams of pleasure.

Erik lived so large that even after I left Fort Lauderdale and moved to California, rumors reached me, each one more unbelievable than the next. Erik had been arrested after doing pull-ups from the end of a crane. Twenty stories up. Naked. Erik had gotten married. Erik had become a minister.

The Fort Lauderdale Beach Patrol operates out of a small office at the International Swimming Hall of Fame. I exited I-95 onto Sunrise Boulevard, heading east past seedy storefronts hawking "Cash 4 Boats," "Cheap Beer," and "East Coast's Best Body Piercing and Tattoos." Sunrise spat me out at the beach. The ocean was a lovely expanse of blue, with nothing immediately visible for sale. Then a plane buzzed by towing a banner: "Your Ad Here."

I walked into the beach patrol office, the same small but blessedly air-conditioned box of twenty-one years ago. I asked the guard behind the counter if he knew where Erik ministered.

"Actually, he's back on the beach," he said. "He was working at the morgue or something. I think it got to be too much for him."

He regarded me curiously, with perhaps a touch of trepidation.

"You a friend of his?"

Erik, I knew, had gone through some hard times. I had heard that he had taken to proselytizing with the same vigor he had once applied to sinning. People don't always respond well to those who wish to save them—possibly some thought Erik had a screw or two loose. But I remembered the man who had found us a place to live and taken us under his wing. I smiled.

"We're old friends," I said, though truth was I wasn't sure he'd even remember me.

The guard nodded noncommittally. "He's at the tower right up the street."

It was a slower-moving Erik Jersted who came stiffly down the wooden walkway of the city's spiffy new $40,000 lifeguard towers. He remembered me, or at least he said he did, though the hundreds of guards who had come and gone since we last met might have made this a white lie. He squinted at me in the white-bright sun, shook my hand, and gave me a warm smile. After twenty-one years he looked exactly the same—leathery, lean, and muscled, though gray had crept into his hair.

I told him he looked great, which was true.

He didn't smile. "I'm fifty-four," he said. "When you're fifty-four, everything aches."

His partner Al called down from the stand. "Hey, Erik. One of us needs to work the phones in the office. You want to go?"

The office was cool and air-conditioned. Al obviously wanted to go, but Erik still commanded respect. Al looked to be half Erik's age.

"You go," said Erik. "I don't know how to work the phones, even though I've been here twenty-five years."

Al scurried off.

Erik nodded toward the tower. "Come on up," he said.

It is strange to suddenly confront my past, especially a past fat with happy memories. I worked for eight summers as a lifeguard in New Jersey, along with my brief Florida stint. At forty-three I still have dreams where I am back on the beach, dreams so vivid that I wake guiltily because I am sorry the dream is over.

For Erik, shuffling back up the walkway was just another trip. For me, it was nostalgia come to life. Imagine yourself thrust suddenly into the arms of an old lover, with nothing changed. You will have some idea how I felt.

We sat on plastic lawn chairs, cool wood beneath our bare feet. In my day the stand was a box with a bench just off the sand. This stand had sides with scalloped tiles and glass doors that opened to the water. It was far superior. Behind us A1A had experienced a face-lift, too. Where there had once been a string of raucous bars fronted by barfing collegians, there was now a squeaky-clean beach promenade with white serpentine walls and pretty flowers and no barf or collegians that I could see.

"The college kids don't come here anymore," said Erik when I mentioned the change.

Suddenly I remembered how, in the last few months of my tenure, Fort Lauderdale's city fathers had decided to put the kibosh on Spring Break. There was a police substation right next to the beach patrol office. Occasionally when we gathered in the office in the morning to get our beach assignment, we would hear the pleas and cries of frat boys who sorely wished they had remained behind in Michigan to bone up on their biochemistry.

Erik watched the water and talked about change. How Fort Lauderdale had changed. How he had changed. He reduced things to his own terms.

"When I was young, I was outside the rules. I didn't care. I just wanted to feel good and have a good time. The more lawless, the more immoral, the more selfish pleasure I had, the better. I operated way outside the rules. You see it on the beach all the time. If the people on the beach ignore the lifeguard's warnings and the signs, they go in these rips, and they're going to have to be rescued, and they're really going to be embarrassed or worse. As you get older, you realize the rules are good, they're not all bad. But it took fifty-four years. I joined the church because I wanted some type of moral restraint and discipline. The more you read the Bible, the more humble you get."

Erik bent to reposition a pair of swim fins.

"I'm not perfect, either," he said softly. "It's not easy being morally disciplined, especially working this job."

The palm trees rustled under a postcard-blue sky. Reggae music drifted over the hot sand. Below us perfectly proportioned women, bronzed and oiled, lay basting in the sun, clad in a postage stamp's worth of fabric.

The stand's smoked-glass doors opened to the Atlantic, small green waves lapping frothily. I looked to the north. An incessant string of high-rises marched off into the fuzzy distance.

Erik followed my gaze. "They're just overdeveloping everything," he said. "The developers don't care. They all have homes in northern Florida and the islands."

His eyes went back to the water.

"What's good about the ocean is there's no condominiums on that side of the line. There's plenty of wide open space right there. All the technology, all the beepers and pagers and e-mails and gadgets, but the ocean stays the same. Tide comes in, tide goes out. Stability. When it's windy, we surf. When it's calm, we dive."

Erik turned to me, plucked his tortoiseshell sunglasses from his face, and grinned. "Found these diving this morning. Pretty nice, huh? I find all kinds of things out there."

He put the glasses back on and turned back to the water.

"Meet me after work. I'm cleaning a boat tonight. Then you can come home and stay with us."

※

THOUGH HE HAD LEFT the Baptist church, Erik, it turned out, still ministered at every turn. When I met him at the beach after work, a kid was standing by Erik's truck. He was blond and shirtless and looked to be about sixteen. He wore cut-off army fatigues. Their ends drooped baggily below his knees. When I introduced myself, he reluctantly shook my outstretched hand. He didn't smile and said nothing.

When Erik and I walked around to the other side of the truck, Erik whispered to me, "He can't find his way in the world. Just like me. Matt doesn't have a father. I'm trying to help him. Give him confidence, teach him to believe in himself."

Tonight self-esteem was going to be gained by scraping barnacles from beneath the Lighthouse Point yacht that Erik had been working on for far too long.

"Got to finish this boat, the owners are getting anxious," said Erik. "But it's hard for me. I don't have much free time."

The three of us squeezed into the front of Erik's truck and drove toward Lighthouse Point. Matt sat mutely in the middle, staring straight ahead. He kept his legs pressed together, studiously avoiding touching either one of us.

Erik was in high spirits. He chatted merrily. "It's gonna turn dark on us. We'll just try to clean the propellers tonight. Now there's worms in the barnacles. I'll usually put cotton in my ears, but if one gets in you and wiggles around, don't panic. We'll just get a little alcohol in your ear, and it will fall on its keister and we'll get it out."

Not unlike Spring Break, I thought.

Matt stared straight ahead.

"Most people aren't that desperate to clean at night," said Erik. "I just keep running out of time."

We bumped up onto the flagstone driveway of the yacht's home. Erik was out of the truck and lugging the air compressor around the back before the truck's engine stopped ticking.

Matt and I stood next to each other in the driveway. "I don't want no worms in my ears," said Matt.

We dragged the gear—masks, snorkels, scuba tank, paint scrapers, torn garden gloves—to the dock around back. Above the water the *Princess Victoria* was as white and shiny as ivory.

Erik kept talking as he readied the gear. He'd already stuffed cotton balls in his ears. He wasn't quite shouting, but almost.

"You won't believe how beautiful it is under there! It's a form of escape, another world. I like to treat each boat like it's my own. I get to pat it. I'm grateful for that."

He leaped spryly aboard the yacht and banged on the sliding-glass door at the stern. Cocking his head, he listened for a moment, then hopped back down to the dock.

"Just to make sure no one's there," he said, grinning maniacally. "What I don't want is somebody to start up the engines!"

I wasn't entirely reassured. Matt might have forgotten that Erik had cotton in his ears. "Did you hear anything?" I said softly as Erik stepped past me.

He continued on without a word. "We're going to go under and do it by feel," he said to Matt. "I'll keep an eye on you. Ken, you watch the compressor and make sure it doesn't shut off."

The sun was down, its last light purpling the cumulus mounds on the horizon. Dark water slurped under the transom.

Erik yanked on a wetsuit, then pulled spattered brown painter's overalls over it. "Don't want the barnacles slicing up the wetsuit!"

He looped a string around Matt's waist. Then he took the long coil of air hose from the compressor and ran it under this makeshift belt, up and over Matt's shoulder, to his mouth. Matt had become a mannequin. He stared at the dark water.

Erik handed Matt the regulator. "Now if you run out of air, remember which way you went in so you can get out quick," he said. "It'll be pretty much pitch black down there."

Matt jumped into the water and clung to the boat's transom. Eric watched him intently. Matt dipped his face mask into the black water several times but made no move to go under the boat.

Erik turned to me, and I knew where I was headed. He handed me his scuba tank. He would use the compressor. I strapped on the tank, put on my own set of gloves and overalls, and slid beneath the boat. The last thing I heard was Erik boisterously assuring Matt that things would go better for him in the daylight.

Erik was right, it was spooky under the yacht, but it was eerily beautiful, too. The cotton in my ears removed most sound. It was velvet black. When I chipped at the propellers, which I located in Braille-reading fashion, tiny phosphorescent sparks exploded from the edge of my scraper and wobbled down through the water like drunken shooting stars. When I turned over on my back to scrape the boat's bottom, my bubbles spiraled upward, sparking like ashes from a rising fire.

Time oozed away. The water's warm press was hypnotically comforting. At one point I heard a deep basso sound, like Boris Karloff playing the organ. I was nearly giddy with joy bordering alarmingly close to delirium. Perhaps someone had started up the engines. In the pitch black it was impossible to tell if I still had all my limbs or not.

Occasionally I surfaced to reacquaint myself with the world. Night had fallen, and the stars were out. Treading water, I could see cheerful light pouring from the tony homes lining the water. Behind vast glass windows people moved about, cooking dinner, making phone calls. Inside the closest house I saw a little boy bouncing a ball.

We worked for about two hours. I'm not sure how long it was exactly. Scraping away in a twilight zone of silent phosphorescence,

I lost track of time. When I bobbed to the surface at the yacht's stern, Erik was standing on the transom beaming down at me. "Did you hear me singing? 'Bringing in the Sheaves.'"

I was happier than I had been in a long time, and breathing fast. "What was that beautiful phosphorescent glow?"

"Those were the worms," said Erik. "Hope you didn't get any in your ears."

No, but I suddenly realized I was tired, and why—in a life filled with fresh air, paddling, rowing, and scraping—Erik had the body fat of bamboo.

Erik smiled down at me. "In heaven there won't be any barnacles," he said.

We packed up and drove back to Erik's place. He needed to wash down the gear, so I drove Matt home in my van. Before Matt got out of the van and walked into the sort of nondescript apartment building that pocks much of South Florida, he turned to me.

"He's amazing," he said. I silently agreed.

We hadn't eaten dinner. On the way back to Erik's house, I picked up the milkshake he had requested. Erik loves ice cream.

We sat down on stools at the counter in his kitchen. Erik's wife, Sharon, had gone to bed.

"Scraping is hard work," I said, believing it with my mind and my forearms.

Erik's face drooped nearly into his shake. He looked as tired as I felt. He looked old, too, his eyes red from the salt, the skin under his eyes puffy and sagging. "What else can I do?" he said.

"Do you ever wish you were on the yacht and not under it?"

He brightened. "Never. I get to go down to the ocean before work, surfing a few waves, grabbing a few lobsters, paddling a kayak. That's all the yacht I need. Just be thankful. That's the secret. Fifty-four years old, and I can still do this. I know plenty of people my age with heart bypasses and diabetes."

I said nothing. My heart echoed every word.

The silence was filled with the soft hum of central air.

Erik shook his head.

"Man, I'm tired. Four hours last night. I have a hard time sleeping at night. I'm so excited about work, I keep waking up."

❧

ERIK'S LIFE IS NOT, by any means, all about Erik. He is no longer officially a minister, at least not one attached to any particular church, but official titles don't mean much to him. On Sunday afternoon Erik and I drove to Independence Hall. Independence Hall is a nursing home.

Erik was late.

"It's been a few months since I've been here," he said as we ducked through a side door.

We followed the joyous ringing of a piano and singing. When Erik entered the room, everything stopped. A dozen seniors were seated at round tables in a common room. In front of them a woman sat at the piano. Five singers, four men and a woman, stood behind her, suddenly silent.

Erik beamed. "Hey!" he boomed.

An old man in a jaunty beret and tweed jacket stood up suddenly as if called to attention. He had a jowly face and the expectant look of a happy beagle.

Erik strode over and pumped his hand. "Hey. How ya doin', Joseph?!" He turned to the room. "Hey, everybody! How ya doin'? I'm back from the sea!"

"Drifting in the sea!" piped up a woman.

"I'll bet," said Joseph.

"Oh boy, have I been drifting," said Erik. "Hey, let's get back to singing."

Erik joined the singers. He has a beautiful bass. I knew this already. Erik breaks into song often, usually hymns, under and above the water.

For thirty minutes the choir sang hymns. Ghosts and goblins, remnants from Halloween, hung from the ceiling, wafting in the air conditioner's currents. The seniors all had hymnbooks. Before each hymn someone in the choir would shout out the hymn number, the raised voice both joyous and practical, though sometimes not raised enough. Now and again Joseph would lean forward.

"What num-bah??"

Some of the seniors read along quietly. Some sang staring straight ahead without looking at the book. When a particular hymn struck Joseph's fancy, he sang boisterously, three words ahead of everyone else.

Erik may have been absent, but he had not forgotten.

"Mrs. Atkinson? Didn't you like the song 'Cleanse Me?' That was one of your favorites."

Erik sang with gusto, "Gloryland Way," "Abide with Me," "Where the Roses Never Fade," and "The Master of the Storm": " 'Out on the ocean of life we sail / Battered by many a raging gale, / Yet we are sure that we will prevail, / No storm can His Ship o'erwhelm . . .' "

When the last song ended, Erik walked around the room kissing the ladies.

A woman in a red-polka-dot dress had come in during the last hymn and taken a seat next to me. Our table was out of kissing range. "Guy going around kissing everybody," she said huffily. She looked more disappointed than affronted. At the other tables, all the other women puckered up happily.

Not everyone had the energy to kiss. After the singing Erik walked across the parking lot to Manor Pines. "The more infirm rest here," he explained. "Last stop before heaven."

Manor Pines is the uncomfortable place most of us know. In the halls old people in hospital gowns sat in wheelchairs, sleeping, staring straight ahead, or talking to nobody. In their rooms they did the same. The place was hung with the smell of disappointment and rubbing alcohol.

As we walked down the hall, Erik beamed at everyone we passed. "How ya doin'? My, don't you look nice today! Nice to see ya!"

We stopped outside a room. Erik peered at the name tag beside the door. "This is the one," he said, stepping inside.

A woman lay in one of the beds. Beneath the sheet that was

pulled up to her neck, her thin body gave only a hint of form. Her face was mottled and sagging, the collagen meltdown of old age. But the lift of her cheeks and her thick gray hair told of a former heart-stopping beauty.

"How are you feeling, Margaret?"

Margaret stared at us. If she knew Erik, I couldn't tell. "Not too good," she said.

"Are you having any pain?"

"Yes."

"When we get to heaven, we get new minds and bodies, you know."

Margaret's face remained blank. "That's good," she said.

"I just wanted to let you know that. My name is Erik. Erik the old lifeguard. Let's pray. For both of us. I'm still out there getting in trouble. I'm a bit of a rascal."

Erik prayed. Margaret shut her eyes. Her lips formed a slight smile.

Erik finished praying. Margaret's eyes remained shut. He bent and kissed her forehead. She didn't open her eyes.

"I'm going to see you again. You have a beautiful face. You know that song?" he said, crooning softly. " 'You muuuuust have been a beautiful baby, you must have been a bea-youuuuu-teee-fuullll girl . . .' "

He continued briskly down the hall. Orderlies smiled and hugged him. "I used to know everybody in here," he said to me. "I've been coming here for fourteen years. People just need a moment so they can talk. Very few people want to minister in a place like this. Nobody wants to face their own mortality."

When we finally stepped outside, I was depressed, and embar-rassed to feel relief. I looked at the flood of passing cars, their driv-ers going where they wanted when they wanted, with newfound appreciation. The "golden years" are a cruel joke.

I was drained and tired. "Does all of this ever wear you out?" I asked.

Erik's face registered genuine surprise. "No," he said. "You know what would tire me? Stupid staff meetings."

We joined the Sunday traffic.

"We were put here to love one another," said Erik. "To touch each other."

※

ERIK'S FAVORITE TIME is the morning. Before work he goes to the beach. He rows, paddles, runs, or does all three. If there are waves, he surfs. In season he free-dives for lobster. Sometimes Sharon comes with him, which is sweet and also something their counselor recommended to bring them closer. They have been married fifteen years, and not all of them have been easy. Sharon loves her husband, but at times Erik frustrates and puzzles her. Erik says it is not easy being married to Erik.

"I have arrested development," he will say.

Maybe. But he knows a special place when he sees it. Early mornings on the beach it's as if everything has been given a fresh chance. The night breeze has carried away yesterday's troubles. Man gets a clean start. This is not just philosophical. One morning as we drove along A1A, bulldozers groomed the beach and workers bent to pick up trash.

We drove to North 7, a lifeguard tower at the northern end of Lauderdale's strip. We passed closed tiki bars and T-shirt shops. On the beach tai chi exercisers raised their arms to the rising sun.

We parked across the street. Erik hopped out and immediately began extricating fins, snorkels, masks, lobster snares, and nets from the jumbled recesses of his truck. "We need to check out this spot for lobster," he said. "I haven't seen it in about four days. It could be good."

The morning was still cool, but the Atlantic was bathwater warm; slipping into it was like pulling on a blanket. Finning out, I watched the bottom slope away. In the shallows the waves had carved a marching line of thick ripples, sensuous, metronomic curves in a sandy sheet. Erik's lobster hideaway, two small rocks a hundred yards offshore, was clearly visible on the sandy bottom in about thirty feet of water. We descended to them. As I watched, he made a slow, methodical circle, pausing to peer into crevices for lobster. My own lungs pinched.

When Erik finally rose, a stream of silvery bubbles, fat as softballs, raced him to the surface, and the sunlight flared off his mask. There were no lobsters, but there was nothing else, either. We bobbed on the surface, the wind erasing the sound of A1A's traffic from our ears. We both faced the empty horizon. The world was nothing but sea.

Erik chuckled softly. "I like this place," he said.

That night I picked Erik up after work. He slumped, shirtless and sun-burnished, in the front seat. "I'm going to do this until I can't do it anymore," he said. "Then I'll probably go back to the ministry full time. This is ministry for me right now."

He pulled out a harmonica. As we crossed the Las Olas Bridge, he played "Amazing Grace."

2

THE LAST OF HUCK FINN'S
FLORIDA

FLORIDA HAS GROWN like kudzu with a thyroid problem. The underlying cause is simple: air-conditioning
and mosquito control have tamed the place. At the Covenant
Retirement Home a stately woman named Grace told me about her
parents' honeymoon in Fort Lauderdale.

"Mom and Daddy honeymooned in Lauderdale in 1912," she
said. "Just at dusk, and the Negroes were singing in the distance,
and all of the sudden this cloud of mosquitoes appeared, and they
ran for their lives."

Florida's first census, taken roughly 175 years ago, found 317
people living south of St. Augustine, a number not entirely accurate
since no one counted the native Indians. Until nearly 1900 anyone
who needed to get from Palm Beach to Miami was forced to walk
sixty-six miles of beaches. Sage travelers parted with five dollars to
walk with the postman, sharing his stowed skiffs to cross myriad
streams.

When you hear about Florida's past now, it sounds quaint and
improbable, a fairy tale with a concrete ending. In one book I read
that now 4,400 newcomers arrive in Florida each week.

No one changed Florida more than Henry Morrison Flagler. A
native of upstate New York, partner and founder of Standard Oil
with John D. Rockefeller, Flagler was sent to Florida by his doctor
to recover from a liver ailment. He spent the winter of 1883–84 in
St. Augustine and quickly reached a conclusion.

"It occurred to me very strongly," Flagler opined, "that someone with sufficient means ought to provide accommodations for that class of people who are not sick, but who come here to enjoy the climate, have plenty of money, but could find no satisfactory way of spending it."

Flagler dedicated the rest of his life to the cause. In 1886 he bought the Jacksonville, St. Augustine, and Halifax River Railroad and never looked back. Buying up surrounding railways, he assembled them into the Florida East Coast Railway and eked down the coast to Palm Beach (1894) and Miami (1896). Finally, an astonishing accomplishment in any day, he built track spanning 106 miles of water and coral islands to a terminus in a sun-torched outpost called Key West. The first train to cross an ocean did so on January 22, 1912. Flagler built lavish hotels at appropriate stops and saw to it that Miami Harbor was dredged to allow for cruise ship traffic to Nassau, where—no surprise—visitors found more lavish hotels waiting.

Flagler wasn't the only one putting his stamp on Florida. Ohioan Mathias Day founded Daytona in 1871. Ormond, just to the north, was founded in 1873 by Connecticut's Corbin Lock Company. Flagler's business partner, John D. Rockefeller, died in Ormond at age ninety-seven. To the end he walked around town handing out dimes to passersby to encourage thrift.

Northerners all, they are still coming, though there is nothing left for them to found. Young or old, their reasons for fleeing to Florida are not complex.

"Have you ever been to Buffalo in the winter?" said a man I met in the parking lot at the Ormond Beach Mall.

He looked to be eighty and wore plaid shorts, blue socks, and brown penny loafers. His face was nut brown, but his legs looked like they still lived in Buffalo.

"You can't dress like this in October in Buffalo!" he crowed.

All across Florida developers have heard this cry, and they are erecting their solutions at an astonishing clip. The first stage of development is the billboard. Traversing Florida's major thruways—and its small ones, too—I saw hundreds of them, splashed with enormous cheery people swinging golf clubs, dancing, or frolicking on the beach. Often their hair is gray, as if the pace of development has given them a fright. These enclaves-to-be have pithy, dreamlike names (points must be made quickly when your readership is moving seventy-five miles an hour). *Ocean Fantasies. Sanctuary II. Paradise Found: Why Live Anywhere Else?* A good question, until the next billboard roars up. Florida has more coastline than California, Oregon, and Washington strung together. Paving it over takes time, but the process is well under way.

Still, old Florida is not lost. It is tucked away, fighting for its life. Its foes are powerful: bright sunshine, warm water, big money, the Mouse.

"Rat Land" is what Don George calls Disney World.

Don George has a number of reasons to dislike the world's most famous mouse. Some are conventional. Mickey draws big attention and big crowds to Don's state. Plenty of other lifelong Floridians would like to see the Mouse on a skewer.

Don also has a scientific reason to dislike Disney World: lights. Don is a biologist and environmental planner for the U.S. Air Force. He oversees 16,000 acres of federal and military real estate, probably the largest block of undeveloped coastline in Florida.

"You're looking at about forty miles of coastline that's owned by the federal government, the air force, and NASA," he told me shortly after we met on a sunny midmorning at Grill's Seafood Deck, a local eatery and watering hole at Cape Canaveral. "If any one of those things disappears, it will be wall-to-wall condos in no time flat. That's prime-ass real estate."

Along the beaches of that coastline turtles—mostly loggerheads and greens, though now and then a huge leatherback—come to lay their eggs. When the young ones hatch and fling away the last covering of sand with their tiny flippers, they head for the light. Before man came to Florida, that light, on these beaches and others, was the reflective light coming off the breaking waves, which, happily, was where baby turtles are supposed to go. Now there are lights everywhere, beckoning the turtles away from the sea, where their already horrific odds of survival—it's estimated that one in a thousand hatchlings reaches adulthood—are further reduced.

In 1984 Don started a sea turtle light-management program, in essence a one-man effort to change every government light fixture he could. Every light on the Cape Canaveral Air Force station that could be replaced, be it a traffic light or a front porch light, had a low-pressure sodium light substituted instead: studies have shown that beaches illuminated with traditional artificial lights—which emanate ultraviolet, blue, and green wavelengths—disorient nesting turtles and hatchlings. The low-pressure sodium lights emit red, yellow, and orange wavelengths and don't seem to disorient the turtles. Some lights, like those above the gantries on the missiles, are left alone. Low-pressure sodium lights make it difficult to distinguish colors, presenting possibly dangerous conditions for working with missiles.

"You need color differentiation," explained Don. "You don't want the guy to put the green wire on the blue wire, so the lights on the missiles have to be bright."

But Don can't change everything. Orlando, for example. Its lights mimic the sunrise, and the instinctual hatchlings bumble happily toward it—where they meet their less-than-Disney end.

Don sees many problems simply: "Too many fucking people in the world."

It's not easy to find old-time Floridians like Don, largely because they don't want to be found. Don aches for recognition the same way Bill Clinton ached for celibacy.

Don lives just off Route 1 in Sharpes. You won't find Sharpes on many maps. It's what the locals call the place. The mailing address is Cocoa. Don owns a nondescript ranch-style house. He also bought the lot next door. It remains a jungled mass.

"Don doesn't want any Yankees moving in next door," Harvey Newton told me.

I met Don only because Harvey and Don are friends, and Harvey is a friend of mine. Harvey is a longtime Floridian, too. Both men came to Florida when they were just out of diapers and are now in their fifties. Both are Vietnam vets, both love the water, and both are bachelors. Other than that, they are the odd couple. Harvey moves through life meticulously, measuring his actions and his words. He is polite but direct, Felix Unger with competence. Harvey eats steamed vegetables and looks like he could still qualify for the U.S. Olympic weightlifting team he once coached. Don follows his own fitness regimen: "Drink beer, eat fried food, ride your bike, and live forever." When an acquaintance died of a heart attack while riding his bike, Don was forced to reconsider part of that equation.

"Bummer, I thought cycling was supposed to prevent that kind of thing. Guess I'll have to go back to fucking."

Burly with a thick mustache and prone to belching, Don operates within the military bureaucracy on his own terms. He answers to authority, but if a starched young officer stymies him, he knows what cards to play. "If they really get pissy about things, I bring up the fact I was in Vietnam," he told me. "That shuts them up real quick."

Don has led a varied life. Busing tables at the Mousetrap on the Cocoa Beach pier, he met the original seven Mercury astronauts—Glenn, Shepard, Cooper, Schirra, Grissom, Slayton, Carpenter—and got their autographs on a cocktail napkin. The Mousetrap, and the cocktail napkin, are now long gone, but Don did see John Glenn, or more to the point, John Glenn's back, just a few years back, when they walked together briefly at a Cape Canaveral dedication.

"God damn, that man walks quick."

Don's mom worked at the Sharpes post office. She told her son when his draft number came up. He came back from Vietnam and got a graduate degree in marine invertebrate zoology. In the early 1970s he worked on a commercial fishing boat out of Cocoa, where he met a man who very much impressed him.

"Foxy," Don said. "I don't know what his real name was. Just Foxy. This guy had lived in every Salvation Army from Seattle to Miami. Before we'd go out to fish for a week, Foxy would have me get him some gin. He'd finish the gin the first day. After that he'd buy my beers for two dollars a bottle. When we were fishing for snapper, he'd lean on the rail of the boat, and you could hear him say, 'C'mon, Red baby. Foxy's gonna let you watch TV.' "

There is some Foxy in Don. Before Don and I met, Harvey told me, "He's not apt to open up to you."

When Harvey and I walked into Grill's Seafood Deck, Don looked up from the beer he was drinking long enough to give us the finger. Thirty minutes later he invited me to spend the night at his house.

Don's story, and his memories, parallel those of many Florida crackers. The word *crackers* derives from Florida's cuss-tough cattle drivers, who made a cracking sound with their long whips. These days it's not a label bestowed lightly. It reflects residency, often generational. It also reflects attitude.

Don has seen many changes. When he was a child, the Army Corps of Engineers hewed out the Intracoastal Waterway through Cocoa, just inland from the Atlantic Ocean, creating islands with the dredged spoil. Don and the other kids made rafts with the sides of refrigerator crates, floating them with inner tubes, and paddling them out to the islands to fish, swim, and cast nets all day. The Indian River seethed with turtles. Splashing about on their rafts, they'd hook a fishing lure into the shell of a passing turtle. Then it was off on Mr. Toad's wild ride.

"I've been in this river ever since I was a kid," said Don, as we made the short walk down to the river from his house. "We were little Huck Finns."

It was a balmy October evening. The air, weighted with moisture, pressed against the skin with a mother's warm touch. In Buffalo it was twenty-three degrees. Don wore shorts, slaps, and a pink T-shirt with a turtle dead center. He carried a fishing pole and a serious leisurely attitude.

We walked beside the river along River Drive, a quiet two-lane road that slices through a tunnel of trees hung with Spanish moss. River Drive is lined with a mix of old clapboard homes with listing front porches and new faceless mansions with their blinds pulled shut. As we walked down the middle of the road, a man came out of the driveway of one of the new homes. He hurried out to his mailbox and rummaged through it, his head down.

Harvey hailed him in neighborly fashion. "No bills today?" he asked.

The man looked up. "Are you looking for somebody?" There was no trace of helpfulness in his voice.

"Nah," said Don. "We're just goin' fishin'."

Everywhere you turn in Florida, you see the subtle and not-so-subtle clash of old and new.

A few minutes later we walked onto a rickety wooden dock that poked out into the river. The wind whipped briskly across from the east. Just off the dock a patch of water seethed, as if a tiny rainstorm had just erupted above it, and a small fish jumped.

"Something's feeding on those mullet," said Don. "Mullet are herbivores. You open up the fish you catch here in the river, and the insides are black because the water is so polluted. You get mullet from the ocean, it's clean, white, and sweet as can be. Back in the old days when the river was really clean, there was nothing sweeter than mullet." There was no nostalgia or bitterness in Don's voice—just the biological facts.

"How is the water quality now?" I asked.

"It's slowly getting better. But there's a lot of work that needs to be done. They still discharge effluent into the rivers in some areas."

Don cast a line and fished for a bit. Far out on the river a sleek yacht headed south, throwing up a white flume trail. "The Intracoastal Waterway is so all the damn Yankees can come down here in their fancy canoes," said Don. "They would lose their cobs if they came down in the ocean. They built this canal so they won't spill their martinis." In truth, construction of the Intracoastal Waterway, a 3,000-mile calm water causeway that snakes along much of the East and Gulf Coasts, was authorized by Congress in 1919 largely to ensure the safety of commercial vessels ferrying everything from food to petroleum. But recreational boaters recognized the benefit, too—the opportunity to travel from Boston to Key West with marginal seamanship skills.

A man with a shaved head walked out on the dock.

As Don spoke to him, he kept his eyes on his line. "How you doin', Mr. Brewer?"

"I recognized you by your cast," said the man in an unhurried drawl. "You can recognize folks by their cast." He regarded Don and screwed up his face. "You know, the serious fishermen bring a landing net."

"If I have to, you know I'll jump in," said Don.

Mr. Brewer turned to me, extending a hand and a warm smile. "Gray. Gray Brewer. Just like the color of the sky."

His jaw sported grizzled gray stubble. The back of his neck bore thick creases. With his bald head, he resembled a turtle. He was wearing long khaki pants that looked as if they had spent most of the day crawling through the marsh. His faded yellow shirt was similarly splotched.

"I'm raisin' oysters in that greenhouse," he said, nodding back down the dock.

Across River Drive, in a tangle of brush, I saw the greenhouse.

"It's Gray's dock," said Don.

Gray didn't dwell on his proprietorship. "How come you haven't caught anything?"

"Ain't no fish in this brook," said Don. "There's too much damn vegetation in the water. *Vegetarian* is an Indian word for 'poor hunter.' Or in this case, 'poor fisherman.'"

Far out over the ocean stacks of white clouds mushroomed into the sky, edged with the orange light of the setting sun.

"Sure is beautiful," I said.

Gray nodded. "This is why people move to Florida," he said. "Yesterday we had a twelve-foot gator swim right under the dock."

At first I thought this was a non sequitur. Then I wondered if it was a comment aimed at keeping one more visitor from settling here.

"Strange about that gator," Gray continued. "Gators are very territorial. I was wondering what put him on the move. Nothing chases a twelve-foot gator but people. Encroachment. We used to hunt the gators. Then they were protected. Now there's so many gators, we have to hunt them again." He scratched the back of his neck with black-rimmed fingernails, considering the nonsensical cycle. "If we got rid of some people, we wouldn't have to get rid of the gators."

Indeed, the two clash. Up the road in Ormond Beach at Seabridge Riverfront Park, I had seen a sign advising parkgoers to "Be Gator Safe." Among the safety tips: "Don't approach an alligator's nest," "Don't feed them," and—my favorite—"Don't try to catch one." It occurred to me that anyone requiring such instruction might be better off removed from the gene pool.

Apparently the warning signs weren't posted everywhere. A few days earlier a headline in the *Daytona Beach News-Journal* had caught my eye: "Gator Bite Victim Mends." The article went on to say that forty-year-old David Coleman of New Smyrna Beach was in good condition, recovering from surgery to his left foot after stepping on a gator in twelve inches of water while wade fishing with friends at Merritt Island National Wildlife Refuge.

"They tend to bite first and ask questions later," said an unsympathetic Fish and Wildlife official, who apparently felt much like Gray.

Though local sympathies sided with the gators, the locals weren't averse to biting back. Earlier in the day I had found an interesting package in the refrigerated-goods section of a Canaveral store. Salted, brown-sugared, natural-fruitwood-smoked, and shrink-wrapped, those alligator legs were done running.

Don had wandered over to admire the contents. "Tell you what," he said. "Right off the smoker, those boys are damn good."

While Gray discussed the need to thin the human population, two teenage boys with fishing poles walked out to the end of the dock. One, wearing an Orioles cap, hooked into something as soon as he dropped his line. His pole bent severely. He bent with it. The creature on the end of his line marched him back down along the dock.

As he passed us, Gray said, "Where's your landing net?"

"Ain't got one," said the boy, shuffling past.

Gray smiled at me. "Nobody came down here to catch fish. They just came down to go fishing." He turned and walked back to his oysters.

Don watched him go. "He's a crazy son of a bitch," he said. "He was shaving his head before it was in vogue."

The sun had gone low, shading the water deep blue in the falling light. The smell of fish came off the river on the beating wind. The low-slung homes along River Drive were mostly hidden among the mossy trees. Along the river's edge palms bent over the water, and simple wooden docks jutted from the shore.

No grand artifacts of man's hand were visible, other than, in the far distance, the 528 causeway arcing over the river, heading for Orlando.

The setting sun flared off something white, high in the sky near the foot of the causeway. Don and I recognized it at the same time.

"A crane," said Don. "They're building another goddamn condo."

THE WALLS of Don's house are covered with paintings. His closets are stacked with them, too. The paintings are oils. With the exception of a few imaginative twists, they all depict one of three basic scenes: waves breaking on the beach, a Florida swamp out of which rises a stately mossy tree, or a riverbank. The scenes are idyllic: sunrises, sunsets, empty beaches, frothing breakers, wind-whipped palms, and quiet swamps.

Sage collectors like Don are well versed in the work of the Highwaymen, a loose association of twenty-five black men and one black woman who, in the late 1950s, painted images of a very real Florida dream, slung the still-wet paintings into the backs of their cars, and traveled the Florida coast peddling the paintings to restaurants, offices, motels, and banks. Curtis Arnett, Al "Blood" Black, Mary Ann Carroll, Alfred Hair, Harold Newton, and Livingston "Castro" Roberts were not finicky artisans. They painted fast and sold hard to avoid picking oranges for two dollars a day. They painted on Upson board, a product familiar to roofers, and framed the paintings with crown molding, a product familiar to anyone who has ever looked up at a ceiling. They painted so fast, they may have forgotten precisely what they were painting. Don has one Highwayman painting that he aptly describes as the "ocean breaking in a swamp scene."

The Highwaymen didn't even know they were the Highwaymen until 1994, when an art aficionado named Jim Fitch gave them the name, and they were rediscovered as American folk artists. It's estimated that anywhere from 50,000 to 200,000 Highwaymen paintings currently exist, and as you read this, more are in the offing, as some Highwaymen astutely recognize their new role as icons and continue to churn paintings out.

The concept of value in art, as anyone who has ever seen a lacquered tree stump priced at six figures knows, is subjective. One thing, however, is certain: the bank managers who sent the Highwaymen scurrying in the 1950s would burst into tears if they peered into Don's closets now. "On eBay these things are going for eight hundred dollars." Don peered absently into the closet. "Crazy stuff."

Don is an inveterate collector of many things, all of which he has gotten for cheap. He flipped through the paintings propped in the closet like a fat deck of cards, stopping to regard a swamp scene. "Hell, I wouldn't pay eighty dollars for that." He grinned. "I probably paid twenty for it."

In many of the paintings three small white birds drift somewhere in the scene. It seemed too coincidental, so I asked.

"Oh, the birds are there for a reason," said Don. "Supposedly they represent the Father, Son, and Holy Ghost." Not that the painters all followed the Word. "Al Black is serving time in a correctional institution for drugs, but he's still painting and selling." Don closed the closet door, plunging many thousands of dollars' worth of art back into the dark. "He's lined up fine when he gets out."

Don flopped into the kitchen for a beer. When he returned, we wandered through the house looking at the paintings that had actually made it up onto his walls. For the art-impaired, and I count myself among them, wandering through a collection can be a painful experience. *Ah yes, certainly the abstract vision of the artist suggests an inner turmoil that perhaps led to the cutting off of an ear.*

Don belched. "I like them because they're nice beach scenes," he said.

He doesn't care much for their value, either, though it gooses him when he buys a Highwayman at a garage sale and breaks a twenty to do it. He treasures the Highwaymen he has, some sixty-five in all, for a simple reason.

He considered a painting of a breaking wave, a frothy, emerald thing preparing to throw itself on wet sand glistening with rainbow colors. "When I'm riding down the beach in the morning checking the turtle nests, I get to see that," he said quietly.

The Highwaymen's scenes exuded a tranquillity I found consoling. Many of my own favorite memories had unfolded on similar beaches, in front of the timeless waves the Highwaymen had frozen for eternity. Someone from Des Moines could dismiss their work as cheap motel art, but anyone whose life has been piled with salt-swept memories can't help but be transported by the scenes. Standing in Don's living room was like being surrounded by familiar and comforting things.

It occurred to me that the paintings made a direct connection to a simpler time, a time when a small boy and his friends shrieked and shook the spray from their faces as a sea turtle dragged them along the river, a time before dewy-eyed turtles headed over the dunes and into the road toward a Disney-cast glow.

It's dangerous, though, to pretend to plumb a man like Don.

Over dinner, as he enthusiastically forked up various fried seafood matter, I asked Don if he was attached to the sea turtles. He sported a turtle earring, he wore a turtle T-shirt, and the license plate on his truck read TDL MON. He drove the beaches at dawn, searching for new turtle nests, meticulously monitoring the ones he had already found. He was the single line of defense for prehistoric creatures making their timeless way up the beach oblivious to man's space and defense efforts.

"Nope," he said. "Ever eaten turtle?"

"No."

"When I was commercial fishing, we'd catch turtle, and Foxy would cut it up into medallions, toss in flour with egg and cream, and pan-fry them. Bites of turtle meat. It's killer."

Sometimes, presented with things that don't seem to make sense, we simply repeat ourselves. "Why did you eat them?" I asked, though Don had just explained precisely that.

He turned back to his plate.

"Then they weren't endangered," he said.

※

LATE THAT NIGHT Don sprawled on the couch, half-watching Jay Leno, half-talking and dozing. This may be cheap psychology, but when people are tired, I believe they are more like themselves.

Don talked about turtles, the four to five thousand that crawled ashore on the beaches of the Kennedy Space Center, the several thousand that came ashore at Patrick Air Force Base, the roughly two thousand that landed at Cape Canaveral. He talked about the dawn beach runs he made on his ATV, the beach empty until meditative walkers began showing up and giving him snotty looks for driving an ATV on the beach.

Then Don started talking about the kindergarten and first-graders he used to read to once a week on his lunch break, the stories he'd read about happy octopi, starfish, and bluefish, and Henrietta Horseshoe Crab, and how important it is to keep the water clean. When he came into the school, the kids would see him in the hallway and shriek, "Mr. Don! Mr. Don!"

"The kids ate that up," he said quietly.

Mr. Don stared through Jay Leno. "I've always felt like if you're going to make any difference, you've got to teach people something they didn't know."

Tiny new Floridians hanging on Mr. Don's words.

"Shaping young minds of the future," he said. "Shit, that's a frightening thought."

※

TO GET TO KEY WEST, I drove on I-95 through Miami, a depressing strip of traffic lights, liquor stores, McDonald's, and Home Depots that keeps repeating itself so that you begin to wonder if a straight line can take you in circles. The only people I pitied more than the Chamber of Commerce folks consigned to promote this concrete jumble were the hapless pedestrians stranded on the traffic islands. They stood there, as lonely as Robinson Crusoe, looking vainly for a break in the torrent of tinted windows hurtling past.

But the cars must have turned off somewhere, maybe for a Happy Meal or a plumbing fixtures special, because just south of Florida City the road pinched to two lanes, and the traffic dissipated to a sparse flow. Before I could relax completely, a large yellow sign warned, "Thirteen fatalities this year. Drive carefully." It was followed by a succession of single-word signs you pass one at a time— "patience pays only 3 minutes to passing zone"—apparently aimed at Keys-bound tourists in a hurry to begin working on their third-degree sunburns.

I watched the license plates. Most were Florida tags, though now and again a New York or New Jersey tag appeared. I had been told that the snowbirds, folks from up north with winter homes in the Keys, didn't start their serious influx until after Thanksgiving. It was only the end of October.

In the small beach towns of northern Florida, places like Ormond and Flagler Beach, the months between Labor Day and Memorial Day still offer a quiet season when the visitors leave and the towns sink into relaxed torpor. Several days earlier, at the Flagler Beach pier, I had peered through a dusty window in the deserted lifeguard office at lost keys and missing-lens sunglasses resting on a ledge, the detritus of summer waiting against hope, like the land of the misfit toys. Signs on boarded-up businesses read, "See Ya in March," and at the stores that were still open, everyone looked up when I walked in.

In Miami and Fort Lauderdale there is no longer a quiet season. You can walk into a restaurant in October wearing nothing but water wings, and no one will pay you any mind. Here the snowbirds have come to stay. They are everywhere, easily distinguished by their accents, walking their dogs in sun-splashed parks, browsing the pharmacy shelves, walking back and forth across the Intracoastal bridges (the only hills in town), and complaining about the heat, the traffic, and the scarcity of good bagels.

In a Lauderdale coffee shop a woman with shellacked hair

scowled into her cup and, in a voice meant to be heard, said, "The coffee down here is terrible!"

Her husband spoke quietly. "You put too much cream in it."

The transplants I met talked incessantly about the North, simultaneously basking in their decision to leave the place and missing it at the same time. It seemed to me that, hot sunshine and lovely beaches excepted, in South Florida people move about as they do in any big city, in an antic and uncaring bustle.

In the Keys a sense of seasonality and tranquillity still remains. At the very end of October, with the snowbirds yet to descend, Route 1 arced over the sparkling Florida Bay into Key Largo, and my heart arced with it; the traffic fell away, and suddenly the world was sky and water. I felt like a Star-bellied Sneetch, tumbled round in South Florida's ringer, then spat out into a blissful world of blue.

Not that the Keys were untouched. Driving south—Key Largo, Plantation Key, Windley Key, Fiesta Key, Bahia Honda Key—I passed Boater's World, Diver's World, and offers to swim with dolphins, take crocodile tours, and hire fishing guides out of Robbie's, Max's Marine, Bud N' Mary's, and Cap'n Hooks marinas. There was lots of Big Stuff, too—Volkswagen-size swans, and shark-jaw doorways, and two-story snorkels—vying for attention.

But in the Keys—possibly because some of the islands are little wider than a good spit—it's easy to see past man's handprint. As I passed over the low bridges separating them, I saw herons as white as snow, and small skiffs with no one in them, dive flags bobbing in the water nearby, and everywhere water, an eye-popping expanse of cerulean blue splashed with sunshine.

I DROVE ALL THE WAY to Key West because my journey called for a south-to-north quest along the entire East Coast, and, short of a boat trip to the islands of the Dry Tortugas, Key West is as far south as you can go.

I also drove to Key West because I wanted to visit Craig and DeeVon Quirolo. When I walked into Reef Relief's office on the dock at the end of William Street, another famous Key West sunset was streaking the sky with slashes of red. Not that DeeVon noticed. Her desk was piled with fat folders of paperwork, and she was clicking out e-mails on a glowing computer screen. Tonight might have offered up a lover's sunset, but tomorrow meant a morning managerial workshop and an afternoon hobnobbing at the Key West Trade Show, and next week there would be a meeting with folks from Disney about a cruise ship education program. These efforts, and a potpourri of others throughout the year, are aimed at a single cause—saving coral reefs from man's good, bad, and indifferent attentions.

Husband and wife, Craig and DeeVon founded Reef Relief in Key West in 1987. Their reason was simple: Key West's reefs were in horrible shape, mirroring thousands of reefs around the globe. Initially, though, their only concern was their home waters. Craig had come to Key West from San Francisco in 1975. For a time he ran a charter business ferrying snorkelers and divers out to the reefs. Business was never all that great. In the mid-1970s almost every visitor to the Keys came there to sport-fish. The huge explosion of snorkeling and diving that has since turned the reefs off the Keys into the most dived place on the globe (the Keys receive ten times as many divers as the number-two destination, Australia's Great Barrier Reef) was unforeseen. Then *Jaws* came out and put another dent in the business. Craig and DeeVon went back to San Francisco, where he taught sailing and did glass etching.

But neither one of them could shake the Keys. During a sailing cruise off Mexico in 1985 they looked at each other and kept on sailing, right back to Key West. On returning, Craig made a beeline for his beloved reefs. It wasn't the homecoming he had expected. They had been destroyed, in large part by anchors. Craig was furious. He called Billy Causey, then manager of the Looe Key National Marine Sanctuary, home to the Keys' only protected reefs at the time. We want buoys on the reef down here, said Craig. Fine, said Billy, overseeing an understaffed, underfunded protective effort of his own. Go ahead and do it.

At this point many would have seriously reconsidered. Craig and DeeVon didn't hesitate. They got a $60,000 grant from the state and began installing and maintaining a series of mooring buoys above Key West reefs that would eventually number more than a hundred.

In the ensuing years they've done much more than keep reefs from being bludgeoned by indiscriminately tossed anchors, earning themselves plaques of recognition as well as heartfelt animosity. Reef Relief has spearheaded a campaign to improve water quality in the Florida Keys, working, among other things, to upgrade Key West's sewage treatment system—once mostly leaky septic tanks—to the highest level available. They helped ban offshore oil development in the Keys. They battled Big Sugar and other agricultural concerns that were dumping harmful chemicals in waters to the north. They drafted legislation designating local waters a no-discharge zone for boat sewage and helped ban commercial shark feeding in Florida waters. Since 1987 Craig has meticulously monitored local reef growth and health, diving local reefs and taking more telling photographs than a tabloid paparazzo, pictures that documented disease, polluting runoff, and, most important, still salvageable waters. Now they've extended their work to reefs in Jamaica, Puerto Rico, Cuba, Mexico, and the Bahamas.

Reef Relief's offices are no bigger than a few desks, a claustrophobic classroom—a podium set up in front of a crunched assemblage of some twenty métal folding chairs—and an attic crammed with boxes of videos, financial records, brochures, and leftover paint.

When I appeared at her door, DeeVon gave me a whirlwind office tour, said we'd get together with Craig for dinner—he'd spent the day diving and photographing out on the reef—and then plunged back into her paperwork.

Left to myself, I poked around some more. The walls were covered with paintings of sea life frolicking in sun-dappled crystalline waters and plaques of recognition, while bulging filing cabinets sported a merry hodgepodge of stickers (in DeeVon's office, a sticker screamed out "All Great Women Flaunt Convention"). An aluminum barracuda, made from beer cans found on the beach, perched with a bucket filled with several upturned sets of human legs in its mouth. The sculpture had been dubbed *Barracuda's Revenge* by its creator, Wally McGregor. McGregor drew inspiration for his sculpture from watching sportfishing charter boats engage in the unscrupulous practice of helping their clients catch hapless barracuda when the real prizes, like marlin and sailfish, had escaped them. The clients then had their picture taken at the dock with a big fish, and when they left the crew stuffed the inedible barracudas in the marina's garbage cans. Underneath McGregor's aluminum fish were the words, "What if the tables were turned and people were the disposable lives."

For a lot of people, reefs are esoteric things to grasp, clumps of seemingly invincible rock in colors and shapes that no hallucinogenic drug could match, lovely to look at but impossibly distant from our own lives. But a cure for cancer could arise from the toxins secreted by a reef sponge as likely as anywhere else. Yet oil spilled in a driveway in Iowa eventually makes its way into the Mississippi River and heads south, floating across the Gulf of Mexico to the Keys and killing those reefs.

Outside the door to DeeVon's office I saw a poster showing how long various innocuous items survive at sea. Paper towel, two to four weeks. Tin can, fifty years. Styrofoam cup, ditto. Plastic bottle, 450 years. Glass bottle, undetermined.

I picked up a small booklet titled "Tips for Divers and Snorkelers." Later Craig would tell me that many folks, in the throes of discovering the glories of coral firsthand, are so moved that they promptly surface and, on the shallower reefs, stand on the coral and holler to their friends. The booklet was intended for charter boat captains and provided an assortment of handy phrases for English-speaking captains who must explain the rules to passengers who speak only Italian, Japanese, German, Spanish, or French. Coral dies if you touch it: *les corailles mourraient si vous les touchez* ("Lay core-eye mooray see voo lay too shay"). No collecting: *Sammeln ist verboten* ("Sammeln ist ferb-boh-ten"). In a wholehearted fight, few stones can be left unturned. Victory requires singular focus on every small detail.

I noticed something else. Through Reef Relief's glass doors, the only thing visible in the dark was a grinning candle-lit pumpkin on a docked catamaran.

"Do you have any plans for Halloween?" I asked DeeVon.

She looked up from scribbling a note. "No, not really." She peered up over her glasses at me. "When is Halloween?" Then in recognition a soft smile came over her face. "It's tonight. I'm sorry. I've just been going too fast."

I walked out on the dock and stared at the pumpkin. It leered back at me from the bow of the catamaran, and my heart pinched. It was still midafternoon in California, but I knew that three thousand miles away two small boys were taut with excitement. Every Halloween our ritual is the same. Several friends come over. The mothers stay at our house passing out candy while the fathers walk the kids around our neighborhood. Actually it's more of a fast trot. We stand on the sidewalk while our kids run to the door, and the neighbors who know them peer at Cullen and Graham as they hold out their bags; they cock their heads and scratch their chins and say, "My, who is this lion and cow?" And then, once the costumed mass receives what it came for, it bounds off that porch, not bothering with the steps, and past us to the next door stoop, giddily going through the whole process again.

Halloween is one of my favorite holidays. You can't help but become seven again. The joy and excitement are contagious. I noticed the name of the catamaran was *Dream Finder*.

I called home that night. It was nine o'clock in the Keys, six in California. I was staying at Boyd's Campground ("The Southern-most Campground in the United States!"), rolling out my sleeping bag in the back of the van, parked on a finger of land that poked out into the water. I sat on a picnic table listening to the cell phone ring.

When my wife Kathy answered, it sounded like she was standing on the floor of the Stock Exchange. "Everybody's here, and they're just getting ready to go out the door," she said. "Hold on, I'll get the boys."

Graham came on the phone, breathless. "Hi, Dad! I'm Harry Potter! Can we call you later? Do you want to talk to Cullen?"

He didn't wait for an answer. I heard banging and laughing, and an adult voice shushing.

Cullen came on, two years older and a degree less frenetic. "Hi, Dad! I'm an injured soccer player. I've got a bruise on my head, and I'm all messed up. Sorry I can't be with you."

"It's okay," I said.

There was a pause. I could see him standing there in our living room watching the other kids clustered at the door, tiny rodeo broncs quivering to be set loose.

"Listen, Cullen, you'd better get going, or there won't be any candy left."

"Right, Dad! Here's Mom! Love you!"

Kathy came on. "It's pretty busy here," she said kindly. "Are you safe? We love you."

"You're a great mom," I said, because I couldn't think of anything else to say, and the lump in my throat didn't make it any less true. "I'll call tomorrow."

In the sudden silence I heard palm fronds clicking in the warm breeze. The stars glittered prettily overhead. From across the water came the schuss of passing cars, heading about their private business on Route 1.

🌿

CRAIG PICKED ME UP at the campground at eight the next morning. Craig and DeeVon are a perfect pair, both professionally and personally. She is petite and diplomatic, with a head for figures, names, and meetings. He is tall, with a predilection for sailing and photographing reefs, and a phobia for meetings. ("I actually get sick. From the time I walk in until the time I leave, I feel like I'm going to pass out.") Craig has a bohemian air about him that isn't misleading. For a while, living on a boat in San Francisco in the early 1970s, he spent time in the company of artist Jean Varda and the folks who stopped by Varda's boat, including Kurt Vonnegut and Henry Miller.

Craig and Deevon met in Key West. They arranged to have their wedding on a boat, but when they arrived at the vessel that morning, they could see fat rolls of bills in the captain's pockets and Cubans filling the boat. Craig and DeeVon wished him the best playing his part in the Mariel boat lift, the 1980 mass exodus of Cubans fleeing Fidel Castro's oppressive regime, then crouched on the dock and spray-painted a message saying the wedding had been moved to their house. This adaptability has served them well in their careers with Reef Relief.

On this particular morning Craig was headed up to Key Largo to consult with friend and colleague Harold Hudson on a project. In the world of marine sciences Hudson is internationally renowned, a brilliant man who has probably helped save more coral reefs than anyone on the planet.

The drive from Key West to Key Largo takes about two hours. On this clear morning it was a glittering commute, though for Craig, who rarely leaves Key West by road, it was filled with surprises.

Fifteen minutes into our drive we passed through a mess of road-widening construction. "Wow," said Craig, looking around. "All this shit's brand new."

He took a sip of coffee, nodding to a worker as we slid past.

"It's not the same here as it used to be, but no place is. There are more absentee owners of property. It's real common to live in Maine in the summer and down here in the winter. Everything is being upgraded. The whole town is going through a continuous gentrification. When I came here in the seventies, a dog could lie in the street all day and not move. We all rode bikes. I would drive from Key West to Miami and pass three cars the whole trip. We'd drive up for boat parts and race up the whole way, ninety miles an hour." He grinned. "We were bad."

We clacked across the Seven Mile Bridge, as pretty a span as you'll ever cross. The sun, still low in the cloudless sky, spread a sea of glittering diamonds across the water.

I reached for my sunglasses. "Is there much resentment among locals about the growth?" I asked.

"Most of the local people moved to Ocala."

Ocala is in central Florida.

"Isn't that a strange place for an islander to move to?" I asked.

"They could sell their house in the Keys for $600,000 and move to Ocala and get a mansion for $250,000," said Craig. "There's hundreds of Key Westers in Ocala. Every year they throw a big conch reunion up there. I don't know how much they really miss Key West."

It's true, Key West's commercial streets are lined with touristy bric-a-brac, shell shops, dive shops, Denny's, and Ramada Inns. But turn off those streets, and you descend into neighborhoods that still possess tropical charm. The night before I had followed DeeVon home from work; she rode her bike, and I followed slowly in the van. The narrow streets were dark and pressed in with thick foliage. Many of the houses were old wooden structures, with porches on the ground floor and balconies up above, all crowded with furniture, wicker rockers, and duct-taped overstuffed chairs, leading me to conclude that there was no air-conditioning within. The homes had a jumbled unpretentiousness, and the thick jungle surrounding them lent the neighborhoods a pleasant sense of hidden, cloistered comfort. At one point another car came down the street toward me. I stopped. I was certain we wouldn't be able to pass each other, but the man behind the wheel waved for me to come on. As we passed, our left-side mirrors locked. Mine is on a hinge, it bent back, then snapped forward again as we passed. I assumed my fellow driver possessed the same inventive mechanism because he proceeded on without a tap of his brake lights.

I told Craig that story now.

He smiled. "If you look around town, you see a lot of left-hand mirrors broken. That's mostly from the garbage truck coming down the street."

As we drove north, Craig talked about the reefs. Most of the reading I had done about coral reefs—in the Keys and elsewhere—was all gloom and doom. Pollution, overfishing, disease, ship groundings, and warming waters—a likely consequence of global warming, claims a National Parks Conservation Association brochure—have already killed at least 11 percent of the world's coral reefs. Another 40 percent will be lost in two to ten years if current trends continue. But Craig believes some of the reefs in the Keys are actually recovering, albeit slowly. Part of his optimism is a result of direct observation, diving the reefs regularly for the past fifteen years. He also believes because he has to.

"I think we have to take a positive outlook," he said. "All these people saying that the reefs will be dead in fifty years. If we believe that, what are we all working so hard for? We had hundred-foot visibility down here all summer. Corals are coming back. Sharks are chasing us out of the water. It's good news. It's important to keep a happy face on this."

He paused.

"Sure there are problems and diseases, but they're not always man's fault. Yesterday I was on the reef at Rock Key. I took photos of a white 'disease' that's been appearing on the corals. Nobody knows what's causing it. My nonscientific opinion is it's caused by fish shit."

We drove past a man squatting beside the road. His cardboard sign read "Why Lie? I Need Beer." This sort of honesty wasn't unusual. It might be a by-product of tropical torpor and lassitude, as if living in a dream meant it didn't really matter what you said or did. Whatever the reason, I found people bluntly casual in deed and word. One morning I passed a man standing in front of his house in his boxers, casually arranging a pile of personal detritus. A sign taped to the pile indicated it was for the Salvation Army. Perhaps in a fit of Good Samaritanism, I thought, he'd given away his pants.

One afternoon I walked into a corner deli for a drink. There were two people in the store, a man behind the register and a man sitting on a stool beside the drink cooler. The man on the stool looked up from his reading.

"How are you doing this afternoon?" I asked.

"I'm looking at naked girls in this magazine," he said, and returned to his study.

Craig Quirolo was equally honest. I have spent enough time around tireless environmental activists to know that they are supremely devoted and, well, tireless. I also knew, from talking to others, that Craig and DeeVon put in eighty-hour work weeks that paid just to the black side of nothing.

Now I asked Craig if he ever felt like leaving it all up to someone else, then waited for his ask-not-what-your-country-can-do-for-you reply.

"Shit," he said. "I say 'screw it' all the time. I'm always quitting. To get things done, you have to be on people's asses all the time, because frankly most people aren't that interested. I don't know why other people aren't doing what we're doing. I guess I'm not a good capitalist."

He thought for a minute.

"It irritates me a little bit," he said. "I'm at the age all my friends are retiring with more than Social Security. There's no gold watch at the end of my road. But it's a toss-up. I spent yesterday diving the reef. People retire to do what I do."

Here's something the plaques of recognition on Reef Relief's walls don't tell you: Craig and DeeVon spend a lot of time pissing people off—lobbyists for big agriculture interests, divers who want shark feedings, local boaters who want to flush their toilets wherever they damn please. The rosters of friends and foes, however, aren't carved in stone: if need be, the Quirolos will piss off an ally. "We don't follow the leader like people expect us to." Craig shrugged. "We're supposed to be the environmental voice, and we do what we have to do. People don't understand that."

Most people, I've found, strive their entire lives to be liked. Craig had a different take on this: "If you're not offending people, then you're not doing anything."

At ten A.M. we wheeled into the dirt parking lot in front of the offices of the Florida Keys National Marine Sanctuary, a nondescript two-story concrete block, partially hidden from the road by foliage. Craig reckons the building is nondescript and hidden away because plenty of folks in the Keys don't like the government meddling in their affairs, either above or below the water.

Harold Hudson is a restoration biologist for the National Marine Sanctuary. Craig's current project, and the reason for today's visit with Harold, a longtime friend, is Craig's proposal to build an

underwater park—the Key West Marine Park—off a stretch of local
resort beach. The park would work simply: three areas of water, just
off several of Key West's biggest tourist beaches, would be marked
off with buoys and closed to Jet Skis and boat traffic so that snorkelers could swim without the fear of being diced to chum. No boat
ride would be required to get there, just a stroll into the water and
a brief fin away from the beach. The marine park would protect the
coral and sea life already present, including grunts, yellowtail snap-
pers, queen angelfish, trunkfish, aptly named needlefish, and the
occasional young tarpon.

"It would be the first municipal underwater marine park that I
know of," said Craig as we marched with Harold around to the back
of the building. "The city commission is behind it, even though it
got me in trouble with the locals. It's controlling local use, and the
locals don't like any more control."

The gravel lot behind the building was littered with boat trailers,
sun-bleached zodiacs, and boat engines in various stages of disman-
tlement. We walked through sunshine and stopped in front of what
looked like three enormous cement droppings, perhaps from a
supremely constipated elephant, resting in the welcome shade of
some trees.

Earlier Craig had told me that Harold was a genius, "the
Michelangelo of the underwater world." A slim man with rounded
ears and a latticework of wrinkles around his eyes from squinting at
one hell of a lot of water, Harold spoke with a banjo twang and
flashed a twelve-year-old's grin.

"Welcome to Harold's world," Craig said, running a loving hand
over one of the droppings.

The three enormous hunks of rock—oolite, out of quarries in
Miami—sat on concrete bases. Bending to peer inside, I saw they
were rife with nooks and crannies. If all went according to plan,
Harold and Craig would plunk these man-made habitats into the
water: insta-condos for sea life to colonize.

"Look at the complexity in these suckers," Harold said to Craig.
"Let me tell you, the critters will love it. They're built to last, and
they're built for the critters. It'll be just awesome."

Craig straightened and grinned. "Harold, they're perfect."

"Well, I had a feeling you'd take a shine to them. Most of all, they're free and ready to go. Copying Mother Nature, you can't go wrong."

While the two men discussed particulars, not least of which was how to get the bulky habitats into the ocean, I took a closer look. They were indeed exquisitely intricate, with hollowed-out innards that ran off in different directions like some underground cave system. I noticed that Nature had already made Harold's creations home. Just off the end of my nose, a tidy line of ants carried the head of a cricket into a crevice.

In the shade of the tree it was still, and the heat was only slightly less stifling than it was out in the sunshine. Neither Harold nor Craig seemed to notice. "Think about what this is going to mean to future generations coming to Key West," said Harold, beaming. "When we're gone, future generations won't even know it's an artificial reef. It's the gift that keeps on giving."

There would still be hurdles. The waters of their proposed marine park fell under the jurisdiction of the federal government's Florida Keys National Marine Sanctuary.

Harold turned to me. "Politics are the only problem," he said. "We have met the enemy, and he is us." Then he clapped his hands together. He had worked for the government for most of his life, but all the hoop jumping and required stamps of approval hadn't pushed belief out of his life. "I'm the perennial optimist." His smile was infectious. "I really believe in Santa Claus and the Boy Scouts. This reef will go in."

Before we left, Harold put a hand on Craig's shoulder and spoke to me. "Craig and DeeVon don't get nearly the credit they deserve. I call them evangelists. They are emotional. They are vocal. They are dedicated, and this is their religion."

Heading back to Key West, we drove in silence for a time, Craig with his thoughts, me unabashedly grateful for the truck's functioning air conditioning.

Finally Craig spoke. "I hate being called an evangelist. I hate those people." He thought for a minute. "What we're doing is virtual reality. We are making a reef that would take thousands of years to develop. People say, 'Well, that's tampering with Nature.' Well, maybe in the twenty-first century that's what we need to do."

The air conditioning hummed. Hurtling along at sixty-five miles an hour kept the mosquitoes at bay.

"We've screwed things up so badly in this last century, and everything was gloom and doom," said Craig. "But now that we're at the beginning of a new century, I think we have to go rebuild and look to see the positive side."

※

THAT EVENING I went for a paddle. I had been on the road for less than two weeks, but the kayak had already proved its worth. It was bulky and took up lots of space in the van, and when I slept in the van, I had to yank it out and rearrange everything to make room for my sleeping bag. Once already it had slid from the top of the strongbox in the middle of the night, mashing my chest and glancing off my face. It scared the hell out of me—and likely did the same to the unfortunate late-night Wal-Mart shopper who, at that precise moment, walked past a darkened van suddenly rent with commotion and expletives. But I shouldered these minor inconveniences happily, because the kayak offered freedom, a chance to decompress, and, frankly, time to be alone. I enjoy the company of my fellows, but there are times when I yearn to escape them, and there is no better route than water.

I dropped my kayak into the waters edging my campground hotel and paddled away.

Much of the water surrounding the Keys is very shallow: depending on the tide, it can be as little as a foot deep a long way from shore. The sun beats down on this water. The result is a great tepid bath and a very pleasant place to paddle.

A brisk wind was blowing across Boca Chica Channel, but it carried no chill. With two hours until sunset I paddled west, passing under the bridge that connects Key West to Boca Chica Key and out into a vast spread of waters that marked the eastern edge of the Gulf of Mexico. Paddling has a pleasant, hypnotic effect. After twenty minutes or so of steady stroking I drifted into a trancelike world in which heart, lungs, muscle, water, and the metronomic beat of my stroke were all that existed.

Out on the water you realize what a fragile place the Keys are. On several occasions they have been nearly wiped from the face of the earth by hurricanes—no surprise, given that the Keys' high points are often but a footstep above the water. Far from shore the islands appear as they truly are, delicate scrims of sand all but lost in a vast sprawl of emerald and blue.

I paddled west longer than I planned. By the time I woke from my reverie and turned around, the sun was already low on the horizon. By the time I discovered Uncle Sam's home, it was very nearly dark.

I call him Uncle Sam because I never got his name. He didn't volunteer it, and I didn't ask.

I had paddled back under the bridge. I was skirting the mangroves that line the shore within sight of my camp, just a slight dip below the macadam of Route 1, when I noticed a break in the wall of fingerlike roots and leafy foliage. It was round, like the entrance to a small cavern, and so was begging to be discovered.

Inside, the dusk was darker still, so that it was very nearly night. I noticed the squatting form just before it barked at me, "Hey! What the hell you think you're doing?"

Startled and embarrassed, I couldn't think of anything but the obvious. "Paddling," I said.

I was relieved to see that the figure remained squatting. At this point only ten feet separated us.

"You got the whole damn ocean out there. What the hell are you doing paddling in here?"

There was still appreciable anger in his voice. He remained motionless. In the dimness I couldn't even tell if he was looking at me.

"I'm really sorry," I said. "I just saw the break in the trees and paddled over to look."

My eyes had begun to adjust. The man was squatting on a cement block. He was thin and shirtless. A grayish bedroll lay beside him. A few yards away, nearly hidden, a bicycle lay on its side. A small American flag, the kind they pass out to children at Fourth of July parades, was stuck neatly in a notch between two mangrove branches.

"I don't appreciate you being here," he said, shifting on his heels and pulling the bedroll closer.

"I'm really sorry," I said, and meant it.

"Can you back that thing up?" This time his tone seemed a bit softer.

"Sure," I said, and started to do so.

"Do you like my flag?" he said quickly.

I stopped my stroke. "I sure do."

We both regarded the flag in the last light. I dipped a blade and began to back out.

"I'm an American," he said. "It's my country, too."

Behind him the leaves of the roadside bushes bucked and rustled as America rushed past.

*

WHAT I NEEDED after all this adult seriousness was a kid fix. I got it in the form of Dora DeMaria. Dora is nine. She lives in a jungle-shrouded, shell-filled house in Summerland Key, down a side road off the ubiquitous Route 1. There are actually hundreds of roads like Dora's in the Keys, neighborhoods where families raise kids, drive to soccer and Girl Scouts, shop at the grocery store, work, fight, make love, and get up the next morning and do basically the same thing.

One of the underlying premises of my travels—more a profound hope, actually—was that there are people and communities along the shore that have yet to be swallowed up by the bland homogeneity that has overcome much of America. As a man in Fort Lauderdale aptly put it, "You could fall asleep at a traffic light in most places in this country, and when you woke up, you wouldn't know where the hell you were."

I hoped to find places where I could fall asleep at the traffic light and sleep for twenty minutes until the next car showed up. Places where porch rockers were worn from use and stores had owners you called friends, and stools to sit on and jaw with them when you came in. Places where bigger and faster weren't better. Places that felt like home.

Well, I can tell you resolutely that the charm of individuality, and a breath of the not-quite-past, still holds sway in the Keys, and I got my first glimpse of it through a little girl's eyes. Not that we bonded. Dora was cautious. I was a complete stranger who came to her door, though I did know her parents.

Dora's parents are Don and Karen DeMaria. Don has lived in the Keys since 1978. He arrived from Jacksonville, a commercial fisherman looking for a warm climate to fish. He had actually planned to keep on going right down into Central America or the South Pacific, but gringo fishermen weren't warmly welcomed in those places, so he settled in the Keys. Don fished hard, lived on his boat in Key West, and saved money. He bought the house that Dora now casually accepts as home. It is paid for.

"Don didn't go out and party like so many other fishermen," Karen told me. "He knew what he wanted, and he saved for it."

Karen is forty, eleven years her husband's junior. She grew up in Toms River, New Jersey, catching crawdads in the river and blue crabs in the bay, peering curiously at the glistening creatures that were trying to pinch her deft hands. She still catches critters, only now she does it for a living, primarily as a biologist for the state, conducting life history studies of local fish so Florida can figure out how best to manage a dwindling resource. Fish are deposited on her doorstep. At her office—several mightily scarred worktables under a ceiling of fat-leafed foliage—she lays them on a table and thoroughly dissects them, making painstaking observation of many variables. Among other things, she delicately removes the otolith, a small bone in the skull behind the brain, sections it, and counts the rings (like the rings in a tree) to determine the fish's age. Ring structures vary from fish to fish—some species lay them down more quickly than others. When I arrived, she was doing a lot of counting.

"Right now I'm the Angelfish Queen," she laughed. "Angelfish have thousands of rings. You're like, 'Oh my God.' What I do helps the state decide when people can catch a species and when they can't. And when people start yelling and screaming about unfair size limits, we have the data to back our decisions up."

Karen also does work for various private research institutes, collecting invertebrates for cancer research. Don helps her collect specimens, too, while diving in different parts of the country. He does a small amount of commercial fishing, but most of the local reefs have been fished out. Don saw this coming, but instead of turning his back on the problem, he began working with local preservationists to put the brakes on breakneck fishing—sport and commercial—an effort that hasn't made him popular with many of his former commercial fishing cohorts. Scientists hire him as a consultant for local research projects because he knows the area. He also sells live rock—"basically putting rocks in the water and letting things grow on them"—to the aquarium trade.

There is not much nine-to-five banker-doctor-lawyer simplicity in the Keys. Many people work several jobs to make ends meet. It gets confusing. Don's business card reads "Commercial Fishing & Diving, Fishery Research, Underwater Photography"—and it's probably easiest to leave it at that.

Don and Karen's liveliest collaboration is Dora, a forthright, long-legged little girl with her daddy's observant blue eyes and her mother's fair hair and complexion. When I arrived at the DeMarias early on a Sunday morning, Dora answered the door, gave me a child's appraising once-over, and then went off to find someone more interesting, in this case her friend Torey, who had slept over.

Don and Karen had helped me several years before when I had come to town to write an article about reef preservation. In the time I spent with them, I had been impressed with their encyclopedic knowledge of their home waters—and the simple life they had made for themselves.

Sunday is a day of rest for many, but not for Karen and Don. When I arrived at their house at a little past nine in the morning, Karen was at the dining room table with paperwork splayed out in front of her. Don, said Karen, was planning on going diving.

"To collect fish for dissecting?" I asked.

"Actually, he's hoping to get dinner," said Karen.

Don could have told me this himself. He was standing beside me. But Karen often talks for him. This isn't a matter of talking over her husband, as it is in some marriages. She does it to make things easier for him.

Don is a quiet man. He has piercing blue eyes that miss nothing and sun-bleached hair that is now mostly gone on top. He will answer questions that are directed his way. He listens politely and laughs softly, but if the conversation isn't aimed at him, he will drift from the room to go about his business, whether it's shuffling through diving equipment or getting into trouble with Dora.

"I have two children," Karen told me happily. "One's fifty-one and the other's nine."

At noon Karen was taking Dora and Torey and a half-dozen other squeaking little girls to a religious medal class for Girl Scouts. Karen oversees all Girl Scout activity for the Lower Keys. "We're not religious," Karen explained. "I'm a scientist. But we want them to know about God and Jesus. It's nice to have the moral backing and the standards."

Right now, though, the girls and Karen had other plans. We all piled into Don's truck and drove over the bridge spanning Niles Channel to Ramrod Key.

Just across the bridge Don turned off the road. There was a locked gate and a weathered wood sign on which the words "Beware Bad Dogs" were barely legible.

Dora hopped from the truck, unlocked the gate, and swung it open.

"No bad dogs?" I said.

"Naaaaw," said Don. "But I keep my boat here, and it cuts down on unwanted traffic."

We jounced along a rutted road, passed a windowless shell of a house with trash spilling from every available opening, and pulled up at Don's dock. As we clambered out, the smell of new lumber mixed with the silence.

The girls made a beeline for the dock. Don's boat, the forty-three-foot long *Misteriosa Torres,* rested in a quiet finger of water edged with dry brush and buttonwood trees. Dora and Torey hopped on board.

"Just moved my boat here last Saturday," said Don. "Used to have my boat in Key West, but it's gotten to the point where I couldn't leave anything on it without it getting stolen."

The girls then made for a nearby rope swing. The rope looped up and over the branch of a tree at the water's edge. At the swinging end was an orange buoy, the kind you see novice boaters frantically throwing over the side before they slam into the dock.

One at a time the girls straddled the ball. Karen gave one or the other a healthy push. Don held the opposite end of the rope. The girl swung out, once, twice, maybe three times over the sparkling water. When stoic buoy and squealing girl were far out over the water, Don let the rope slide through his hands. The victim, eyes wide, nose pinched, plunged into the water with a shriek and a splash.

After ten minutes of dunking Don decided to up the ante by repositioning the rope so it swung out farther. Making this change required climbing into the tree. Don and I crunched through the dry grass to the tree's base.

"I was bitten by a snake here building the dock," said Don matter-of-factly. "The leg swelled up and turned black and blue. I'm guessing it was a rattlesnake. Two little marks on the shin. I've been bitten by spiders, and they just rot your skin. There's actually a lot of rattlesnakes on this property. You wouldn't think of rattlesnakes in the Keys."

I was now. "Weren't you worried at all?" I asked.

"Well, I was going to go to the doctor, but then it didn't get any worse. It obviously didn't inject much poison."

That the rattler might still be in this grass, aching for a second chance, didn't seem to bother Don much. He tromped about briskly, then climbed up into the tree.

When he came back down, the rope was positioned for some serious swinging. Dora and Torey looped far out over the water, and they were braver now, too. Reaching the swing's apex, they let go, throwing their arms wide and occasionally—forward motion being what it is—nearly landing flat on their face. Undaunted, they struggled back up onto the muddy bank as fast as they could. Waiting their turn on the bank, they issued resounding belches.

The morning was hot and bright. The water sparkled happily. The smell of mud rose from the bank, set loose by the girls' squirmings as they wormed their way back up the slick bank. Again and again they flew free, arms spread to the sun.

I remembered my own childhood in Virginia and a rope swing that took us far out above the Potomac River, the thrill of release, the heartbeat pause before gravity took effect, the joyous plunge into sudden cool darkness. I ached to swing again, but it was not my turn. It was enough to be happy for Dora and Torey.

Karen stood next to me, her pink top soaked from hefting the girls up onto the buoy.

"This is a great place for kids," she said. "It's safe. You can keep them fairly naïve down here. Far longer than you would in a big city."

Dora windmilled and shrieked.

Karen shook her head and smiled.

"With all the modern toys and games, a simple little rope swing," she said.

⁂

AT NOON the girls went off to visit with God, and Don and I went spearfishing for dinner, but in the end I believe we all ended up doing the same thing.

Don pointed his Carolina skiff west into the mangroves, then gunned the motor. As the wind whopped in our ears, everything but the sky and water fell away. I sat in the bow. Even with the wind it was like pressing my face into a warm sponge. Cumulus clouds erupted into the sky like cotton-candy towers. I jounced atop a wood-topped cooler and watched the bottom flash past, a liquid blur of sand and sea grass. Don directed the boat on a mildly sinuous path, gauging what, I don't know. The skiff drew roughly eight inches of water for a reason: at their deepest the flats over which we flew reached two feet. It was like skipping across the face of a great turquoise marble.

The distant shorelines of Summerland Key and Ramrod Key unwound alongside us, away from Route 1 until they were nothing but a blurred green of tangled vegetation. Out in the channel, islands of mangrove hammock rose from the emerald green.

After about twenty minutes Don eased back on the throttle, and we slid in near one of the tiny islands. Ospreys and cormorants registered our approach, rose from the branches in a sea of slowly beating wings, and swung away.

Don eased the skiff toward a small opening in the tangle of branches and shut off the motor. "This is a good spot," he said, surveying the water. "Lots of snapper here. Goddamn lemon sharks are a pain in the ass, though. You can only spear so many snapper, and then they come in and you've got to get out of the water. Had one cut a fish in half right in my hand."

Before I could digest this information, we heard an odd slurping sound. We both stood up and turned around. A dorsal fin was moving away from us. It was small, brownish in color, and floppier than I would have expected. "Awww geez," said Don. "The fuckers are here already."

Suddenly there came a much larger slurp, from somewhere inside the mangroves. Even Don looked interested. "That's bigger, isn't it?" he said, peering into the mangroves.

He moved to the bow, pulled up the anchor, and used a wooden paddle to move the skiff slowly in the direction of the larger shark. I could see the fin of the smaller lemon moving out away from the mangrove, then turning to vector back in toward us, as if playing some kind of now-you-see-me-now-you-don't game. The shark moved with a fluid ease that was beautiful to behold.

Don was thinking dinner. He dropped the anchor again. We hadn't moved more than ten yards, but the smaller shark had covered that distance in two winks.

Don was sitting on the bow. First he put on what looked like a neoprene skullcap. Then he slipped on his mask and fins. The remainder of his diving gear consisted of gym shorts, a T-shirt, and the spear gun, fitted with a three-pronged spear that looked effective.

The droopy fin had disappeared. We heard no slurping, either.

"How dangerous are they?" I asked, trying to sound nonchalant.

"They'll take your hand off," Don said distractedly. "They're not scared of anything, these little ones. You wouldn't think they'd come back into the mangroves, but they do." He snapped his last fin in place. "Well, we'll look at least. Spear something and see if they want it."

We've all heard the tired story that one's chances of getting hit by lightning, or even getting killed by a pig, outweigh the odds of experiencing a shark attack. Now, though, those odds seemed slightly higher. The sky was clear blue, and there was nary a pig in sight, but if one had been present I would have happily tossed it to the sharks.

I am at home in the water. I have been scuba diving with sharks. While surfing in Indonesia, I watched their fins patrol the edge of a reef not twenty-five yards away, cruising for snacks. Still, I felt I needed some minor direction. "If they come after you, is there anything you can do?" I asked.

"Not much," said Don, and slid over the side.

It was hot in the boat. The deck radiated heat, the water threw off heat. Now that we had stopped moving, there was no breeze. The effect was like bending to pull dinner from the oven, an analogy that, given our surroundings, seemed ominously apropos.

Don had already finned quietly into the mangroves. I couldn't see him anymore amid all the brambles, but I didn't hear any thrashing and shrieking, either.

It has been my experience that experienced water folk are not risk-takers—they leave that up to pea-head adrenal freaks on Shark Week. But sharks, as a rule, really aren't much interested in man. We're big and unpalatable, to boot. If Don was in, I was in. I slipped on my own mask and fins, listened a moment for slurps, and slid overboard.

The world went sooty gold. The water was only about two feet deep. I finned slowly around the outside of the mangroves, staying close in case one of the lemon sharks came in from the open flats. Then I noticed the fish right in front of me. Mangroves serve as a juvenile nursery for many fish, kind of a protected romper room before they move out into sea where the food chain operates at mercilessly full speed. Schools of juvenile barracuda morphed out of the haze, hovering motionless, same needle shape, same outsize jaw, perfect replicas of adult barracuda but only four inches long. Other fish-tots moved casually past the end of my nose, again wholly formed but no bigger than a thumbnail. It was beautiful and bewitching to see, these perfect miniature works drifting through a golden world. The water was still and church quiet—none of the incessant crackling you hear while diving reefs at sea—salty-buoyant and warm. After a sleepless bout of mosquito swatting at Boyd's the night before, I might have easily drifted off to sleep had part of my mind not been occupied with the lemon sharks in the foggy periphery.

We circled the mangrove for about twenty minutes. By the time I hauled myself up out of the water, Don, fishless, was already pulling up the anchor.

"The sharks must have disappeared," I said.

His bushy eyebrows went up slightly. "Didn't you see them?" he said. "They were right there." He started up the engine. We motored a short distance to another opening in another stand of mangroves.

As we drifted into a dappled opening, a tart, pungent smell, made heavier by the heat, surrounded us. The leaves of the mangroves looked as if they had been splattered with white spray paint. "Bird shit all over the trees," said Don. "Pretty little spot in here."

We both crouched on the bow to avoid being pronged by the branches or smeared with bird-shit leaves.

"See the boat?"

I looked into the water directly in front of us. The mossy green outline of a small boat, its bench seats covered in algae, morphed before my eyes.

"Lot of wrecks out here from hurricanes," said Don.

There were no sharks here, but there was mangrove snapper.

Under water I was occupied with crawling over mangrove roots—their bowed, mossy branches like skeleton fingers—when a gape-mouthed snapper suddenly appeared in front of my mask, affixed to Don's spear, proof positive of dinner tonight.

Don hung his snapper on a branch above the water and went looking again. He speared a second snapper, and we were finished.

Crawling out of the mangrove, a branch gave me a healthy scratch across the top of my head. "That's why I wear this funny cap thing," Don said as we pulled our gear off in the boat.

My head was stinging, but that didn't detract from my joy. I felt exhilarated, as if I had been handed a rare sooty gold gift and a glimpse into Nature's private workings. "It's beautiful out here," I said.

Don is not prone to fits of emotion. This time, though, he smiled softly at me. "Not a lot of people dive these mangroves," he said. "They all want to dive the pretty reefs. I almost never see people out here."

༜

WHEN WE RETURNED home, Dora was back from her Girl Scout outing. Don disappeared to clean the fish. Karen returned to her paperwork.

I walked into their backyard, which was more of a small clearing bordered by jungle. Dora was standing there, warming up. Earlier she had shown me her two hamsters, Vanilla and Midnight. Her father had taken me fishing. Her mother had given me a tour of their yard, pointing out wild dilly, umbrella trees, royal poinciana, Washingtonian palms, and wild broccoli and spinach—the latter two deposited from someone else's yard courtesy of a hurricane storm surge that had filled their house with a foot of water. During the yard tour Dora had skipped ahead of us, climbing into trees and dangling from their branches.

I had entered into the outskirts of the circle of trust. Still, Dora regarded me warily.

Once again a pungent smell hung in the air, this one fleshy and unidentifiable, at least to me. Eight strands of what looked to be hair in sore need of conditioner dangled from an awning, turning slowly in the breeze.

"What are those?" I asked.

Dora regarded me with her father's clear blue eyes. Children don't bother with masks. She was dumbstruck by my ignorance. "They're pigs' tails," she said, enunciating each word as if she were teaching English.

Good morning. My name is Ken. I would like some pigs' tails.

She offered up another bit of information to help me grasp the obvious. "My dad went pig hunting. He just got back in time for Halloween."

The pigs' tails didn't give Dora a moment's pause, but other things she couldn't stomach. Don came around the corner with the post-filleted remains of the snapper. He grabbed a pickax, moved some earth, dropped in the head and bones, and covered them over.

Dora drew herself up. "I'm not walking over *there* anymore," she said.

Don smiled good-naturedly at his daughter, then turned and whispered to me, "All kinds of stuff buried in this backyard."

That night, though Dora would have preferred boiled eggs, Don cooked us mangrove snapper with stewed tomatoes. He made it up to her by wrestling on the couch while Vanilla rolled in and out of various rooms inside a hamster ball, clacking across the hardwood floor in a happy scramble.

Dora laughed at Vanilla and her dad.

This was a little girl who could identify fish gonads and had a backyard that George of the Jungle would envy. A girl who fished in hidden canals and spent hours picking through sea grass at the tide line, finding prizes like pipefish, crabs, brittle stars, and seahorses. A girl who had seen dolphins swimming in the mangrove flats, and probably sharks, too. A girl whose dad supplied dinner without his wallet. A girl whose mom had recently turned down a high-paying job in Atlanta because she couldn't imagine not being near the water. A girl who flew through the air, pinched her nose, and plunged into warm green water.

Like most children, Dora won't realize how happy she is now until later.

But Karen is no longer a little girl. She had told me about the job offer—environmental consulting work for a firm in Atlanta that paid twice what she made now.

"My first thought was, 'But there's no ocean there,' " said Karen, the two of us standing alone in the backyard. "If it was about the money, I wouldn't be here. I already quit a good government job for a part-time consulting job so I could live like I do."

She thought for a minute.

"It's weird about dreams," she said. "I always dreamed I wanted to live on an island. I'm on an island now. When I married Don, the first real gift he gave me was a mask, fins, and snorkel. We live comfortably. We're very comfortable, very moderate."

She stood in the jungled quiet.

"He basically gave me my dreams."

꒰✾꒱

SOUTH FLORIDA BEACHES in winter are little different from the beaches we all know in summer—the water is lazy-warm, the sun beats down, and salt dries on your back and your lips. Here in the Keys in November, the big difference is that the beaches, for the moment, are fairly empty. At the campground I had already run into a first trickle of happy escapees from the North—John from Pittsburgh, anxiously awaiting the arrival of two strippers; a family from New York who informed me that their hometown had seen its first snowfall; and one morning while I was shaving, a cheery fellow multitasking in his stall. "Man, I had to give you a call. I'm just doin' great. I'm so relaxed . . ."

The real deluge was yet to come, said Karen. The older snowbirds, retirees with a second home in the Keys, would begin to arrive in early November. The main tourist season would begin around Thanksgiving, hitting full stride just after Christmas. "The joke is, you know if the tourists are here when you have to turn right to go left," she said.

At the moment, what mostly traveled down the simmering strip Route 1 through Summerland Key were rusted pickup trucks and the occasional bark of a dog. Dogs may not be able to lie in the street without interruption, but in the Keys a sense of escape and hammock ease still permeates the proper nooks and crannies.

Paddling one evening, the sky purpling blue, I passed a ram-shackle white houseboat, more a square of floating wood than a boat. Two equally weathered skiffs were lashed alongside, and two rusted bikes leaned against the houseboat's wooden railing. A man and a woman sat on that railing, their faces turned to the last of the sun. At dawn the next morning I paddled again. When I passed the houseboat, nothing had changed, except now the man and the woman had turned to watch the sun rise.

Still, the North loomed in my mind, scaring me—news reports of unusually heavy snowfall in Boston and frigid temperatures in New York—but also beckoning me. Winter was already fomenting, massing like some great dark Tolkienesque army, and winter was what I sought. The nastiness that would sweep the fickle snowbirds south would also leave behind those who chose to—or had to—stay. Whether they reveled in or hated their lot in life, I couldn't say. I hadn't been there yet. But it was their lives, their communities, and their frosty seascapes that I needed to see.

Still, it is not easy leaving a place as pleasant as the Keys. Plenty of people had politely tried to reacquaint me with basic meterology, and when that didn't work, they might mention how their aunt's cat had been found on her Maine porch, stiffer than British aristocracy, after the cat door had frozen shut.

When I told a Key West fisherman about my plan, he had cocked his head and squinted hard, as if he had just hauled up an octopus with twelve arms and an artichoke for a head. "Hmmmm, south to north," he said, when he was finally finished scanning my face. "Makes a whole lot of fucking sense to me."

But north was where I was heading. I spent the night on the DeMarias' couch. When I left early the next morning, the Weather Channel called for a high of eighty-eight degrees in the Keys.

Karen screwed up her face. "I don't want hot," she said. "I want fall. I want winter. Well, our version of winter."

On the north side of the Seven Mile Bridge I stopped at the 7 Mile Grill for a cup of coffee. Locals bellied up to the long counter, having breakfast. Behind the counter a sign on the wall read "Of all the things I've lost, I miss my mind most." And I thought, *I know exactly what I'm doing.*

3

OH BLACK WATER

I SUSPECT I WAS subconsciously dawdling. Florida was warm and cheery, its powdery beaches hung in fall with the perpetual under-the-sheets warmth that is both the state's siren song and its doom. Much of South Florida is terminally overrun. But bereft of tourists the small beach towns to the north, places like Flagler and the poetically named Summer Haven, had descended into syrupy ease. Kids rode skateboards down the middle of the street without a backward glance, and fishermen cast nets from solitary sand spits. At night I walked alone by the ocean's edge, while on the horizon heat lightning flicked towering billows of cloud from gray to white-bright, a cosmic light switch with attention deficit disorder.

Florida is also big—another reason it took me nearly a month to leave the state. But I finally did, crossing the St. Johns River under a blackened pot sky that pitched slashing rain and split-fingered lightning. In the North winter was already rumbling, its first strokes—moderate snowfalls in New York, Philadelphia, and Boston—merely glancing blows from a petulant child, the first signs of what would morph into a winter to remember.

The South didn't want to be left out. As I drove into Georgia, weather forecasters broke in on the radio describing a series of deadly tornadoes walloping much of the South and Midwest. A tornado had descended on Van Wert, Ohio, winds of over 200 miles an hour tossing cars and homes like children's blocks. Tornadoes, roughly seventy in all, were raking Tennessee, Alabama, Kentucky, Louisiana, Mississippi, and central Georgia.

I had provisions for traveling into winter's teeth, including a down comforter to keep me warm on nights when I slept in the van, a dozen cans of chunky soup, and a dollar-fifty ice scraper I would buy later that also expunged a clear fluid that smelled worse than formaldehyde, a handy extra that might help keep me alert should I begin to freeze to death. In my preparations I had not considered tornadoes. I scanned the black ceiling of clouds for funnels and wondered if I should have packed extra soup to keep the van planted firmly to the road.

Fortunately in southern Georgia drumming rain, not wind, was the featured element. Americans being who they are, those away from the carnage lent an ear of interest to the tornadoes before quickly returning to more pertinent matters. When the weatherman signed off, the two deejays resumed debating who had the hairiest butt.

In terms of coastline, Georgia is the eastern seaboard's unsung state. There is a reason for this: if you are looking for beach in Georgia, you have come to the wrong place. About a third of Georgia's coast is salt marsh. For those seeking out traditional coastal respite, a marsh is not a pleasant place to lay out a towel. Georgians, however, are proud of their marshes, so much so that estimates of the amount of Peach State coastline occupied by marsh vary wildly, from a generally accepted one-third to the figure given me by a gas-pumping Brunswick resident: "Hell, son, the whole damn coast is soupy marsh! We're wallowin' in the glorious stuff!"

The blue-collar port of Brunswick—ships the size of small states move through its deep-water harbor—sits just west of St. Simons Island. Mainland and island are separated by, yes, a vast spread of salt marsh and are linked by the F. J. Torras Causeway. St. Simons is one in a chain of nine major barrier islands off Georgia's coast—including Little St. Simons Island, Sea Island, and Jekyll Island—dubbed the Golden Isles.

I called George Baker from the Brunswick gas station. George lives on St. Simons Island. A friend had given me his name and this recommendation: "Few know the Georgia marsh like George Baker, and I know no one like George Baker."

It was the first time George had ever heard of me, but like everyone else I had imposed on so far, he was happy to make time.

"Well, yes sir, I'd be pleased to meet with you," he drawled, his words ambling leisurely to my ear. "Meet me at Frederica's Café tomorrow morning for breakfast at nine." And then he added, "We've been havin' some bad weather. You drive real careful."

This last comment, which I initially took for amiable kindness, may in retrospect have been George's attempt to save himself some extra work. Driving toward St. Simons Island in the last light of day, I had difficulty telling if the sheets of water were drumming down from the sky or rising up out of the vast tracts of dark marsh. Now and again a sudden spewing of rainfall completely obliterated my view, and I could only hope the road didn't make a hairpin bend. It would have been a simple matter to bump off the asphalt and plunge into the bordering marsh, which, over a long, colorful, and often sad history, has swallowed plenty of things besides cars. George has had much experience with this phenomenon, one reason I wanted to meet him.

I spent the night in Brunswick. The next morning dawned bright and sunny. I took the causeway over the Back, Mackay, and Frederica Rivers, sun-spackled ribbons meandering through the marsh, to St. Simons. George Baker and Terri Collins were sitting on a bench in front of Frederica's Café waiting for me.

The café was a bright, cheery place with a black-and-white-checkerboard floor, and in the kitchen—visible behind a long counter—several cooks moved efficiently to produce a lovely smell of sizzling eggs. We sat at a table near the door so George could greet everyone he knew, which turned out to be everyone who came in.

George is in his mid-fifties, a solid man with thick shoulders and a drooping belly, like a football player gone to seed. He has stubby fingers and a working man's hands, profusely scarred and nicked. His small ears pinch in close to his broad head. His eyes smile often, though his mouth doesn't always follow suit because it is often chewing on a cigar. He moves slowly, as if many things pain him. A small radio rides on George's weathered black belt.

Terri proved to be a quiet woman. This was partly by choice ("You learn a lot more with your ears than you do with your mouth," she confided, after George ambled off to the men's room) but largely by necessity. As George cheerily put it, "I do like to talk. Sometimes I let my mouth outrun my heinie."

George and Terri's business is rescue and recovery, mostly in the marshes, though sometimes they are called to duty out to sea. Terri is a relative newcomer. She arrived on St. Simons in 1994. George has been plucking things from the marshes since 1967, which explains, in part, how he knows most everyone in Glynn County. His job falls, as far as I could figure it, under the auspices of the county's police department.

"Hell, the badge and the ID card don't mean nothin'," George said affably when it became obvious to him that I couldn't figure out his place in the local emergency services hierarchy. "It's who you're going to help when you get there."

Terri is George's dive tender and Glynn County's search and recovery chief, the first woman ever to hold that position. Quiet apparently does not mean incapable. According to George, she is more organized than a pipe-fitters' union and just as tough.

George's business card reads "Blackwater Recovery." It is not a term chosen by happenstance. "Most times you don't see anything down there at all," said George, forking up a great pile of eggs. "It's a natural phenomenon of the upwelling of the marshes here. What I specialize in doing is finding things lost in the mud and helping folks out. We're kind of like volunteer firemen, only a bit different."

The more common calls involve things like shrimp boats and tugs whose props have sucked up an old crab trap or their own net, or flotsam from sunken boats, ropes, and steel cables. "Prop gets fouled, the boat's stuck, and they can't budge," said George. "It's called a rope in the wheel, kind of the flat tire of the ocean. Only with the average shrimp boat the prop alone weighs about as much as half an automobile, and them engines are powerful. When something goes in the propeller, it's in there."

George descends with the appropriate finely tuned equipment—a sledgehammer, a chisel, a king-size Fleco cable-cutter—his mind working in the blackness, envisioning lines and angles, working out how whatever is jammed in the rudder or the prop can be freed with the least amount of damage to the boat, and to himself. A severed steel cable comes loose like a cobra, the only warning a metallic banshee shriek before it lashes the water looking for something to dismember. As an added plus, the cutting and hammering to free it often take place in surging waters. Rescue calls rarely come in post-card conditions. "It's almost a law, like a doctor delivering babies." George grinned. "The calls only come at three A.M. in lousy weather."

Whatever he dredges up in this silent, midnight-black world varies. It might be a stolen car. Might be jewelry. Might be a body, or a body part. "I've gone in after false teeth," he said.

This struck me as funny. "All that trouble for false teeth?"

George poked up some egg. "You priced a pair of false teeth recently?"

Like many folks I had met in the South, George possesses healthy dollops of patience and life-smarts. He has gotten plenty of frantic calls from Yankees who have lost a precious item in the marsh. He rushes when it is called for and waits when it serves him, though when he returns the prize, he doesn't always tell the client which approach he applied. The marshes around St. Simons ebb and flow with impressive tidal fluxes; the difference between low and high tide might be six to ten feet.

"Had one gentleman lose a gold and diamond Rolex watch in the water. Boy, he was excited," said George. " 'Bout three o'clock that morning when the tide had gone out, I sobered up, got my metal detector and my rake . . ."

Not everything in Georgia's marshes is dead and decaying.

"Gators can be a concern," George opined. "I always carry an old .44 Magnum. I don't like to shoot gators. If you poke 'em in the nose, they aren't used to that kind of treatment, and they usually go away. Sometimes I'll swat 'em with a piece of electrical conduit."

The American alligator, *Alligator mississippiensis,* which occasionally troubles George, is an impressive predator. Hatchlings eat insects and small invertebrates, but once they grow to twenty feet, they require something more. Its heavy head helps a gator catch prey by smashing through intervening vegetation. In the dead of winter gators can be found, alive and well, frozen solid in the marsh with just their nostrils protruding. A territorial male may issue a loud warning bellow to ward off intruders or may remain stone quiet. Alligators have played a timeless and storied role in the marshes. Slaves, brought from Africa and elsewhere, were put ashore on sandbars and left there to recuperate from their time in the ship's hold. The reptiles served as deterrents, preventing them from swimming off. Later, they were rewarded: slaves who did not recuperate were thrown into the river.

Gators sometimes factor into the search for missing bodies. "If we don't find the body and a gator's got it, then we got to go find it, more than likely tucked up in a gator hole under a bank," said George. "You don't really want to be in that gator hole at the same time as the gator. Sometimes we'll pour out a fifty-pound bag of lime along the banks. If the gator swims in that, it burns his nose, and he comes out of there. Hopefully. If I'm not sure, that's when I send the new guy in."

George scratched the back of his neck.

"They can get pretty damn big. Here in the saltwater environment, nothing constrains their growth. But you really don't want to shoot 'em. It took God a hundred years to make 'em."

There are times, though, when God tosses aside the solemnity of his position and has some fun. Once, George was working under a dock when something whacked him hard. "Shot off my bang stick quick as I could. I got me a double-ply Michelin tire that time." He shrugged. "There's some exciting times. But most of it is just long, boring, cold hours."

After breakfast we left Terri. George was running errands, so we both hopped into his Chevy Bonaventure van. He has a real fondness for Chevy vans, though that interest doesn't extend to their upkeep. Faded gray, chipped and peeling, George's van looks like it might have been recovered from the swamp. "No sense worrying about the finish when you're always around salt water." He shrugged, settling into the driver's seat. "This is a brand-new truck underneath an old beat-up body."

A powerful engine is required to haul George's gear. Behind the two front bucket seats, every inch of space is filled. Shirts hang on hangers or lie where they have fallen. Dive tanks stand tucked upright in homemade wooden shelves, wrinkled towels are crushed into corners, tools rest here and there. Think Jacques Cousteau, moonlighting as a carpenter. It wasn't in the back now, but George also has a seventy-pound magnet—a long metal bar with yellow floats across the top—for hauling cars up to the surface. He thought up the device himself and is proud of it, though Terri informed me of at least one drawback: "Try breaking it loose."

We drove along two-lane roads under a clear blue sky. St. Simons is a lovely island. The parts that aren't developed flip-flop back and forth between expanses of open marsh and thick stands of trees: red bays, marsh elders, and massive, ancient oaks that explode out of humus-rich soil eight feet deep. The oaks are liberally hung with weepy strands of Spanish moss. In many places the great trees form a canopy over the road. Plunging from a bright, open marsh into a shadowed tree-tunnel produces an involuntary intake of breath.

George plucked a chewed cigar from the dash and popped it into his mouth. The brown stub rolled between his teeth, seeking unattainable balance. The smell of warm mud drifted through the van's open window. He nodded out the window at an innocuous stretch of marsh. "This is the famous Dunbar Creek," he said. "There were six or seven plantations on the island. The local landowners imported slaves to work them. A plantation owner had arranged for the delivery of slaves, part of the Ibo tribe from West Africa. They were being unloaded here, and depending on the version you believe, they decided they would rather commit suicide than be slaves. Walked into the water and drowned themselves. Legend is they went into the water saying, 'The water brought us here, and it will take us home.' "

We shot into a corridor of trees.

"I'm not making judgments," said George. "Those were different times."

Different, and unimaginably difficult. As one author writes, "Plantation life was hard and mean, working from 'til to can't." During the antebellum years cotton fields blanketed St. Simons. The island specialized in sea island cotton, a particularly buxom strain that sold in Europe for twice the price of traditional cotton. But planting, tending, and harvesting the crop was only part of plantation work—something we forget in times when everything comes to us on neatly arrayed shelves. On plantations chores were endless. Cotton fiber had to be spun into thread and woven into cloth to make clothes. Wood had to be cut, cows milked, butter churned, fish, shrimp, and crabs caught, oysters gathered, and their shells burned to make lime. Pillows had to be stuffed with feathers plucked from geese and chickens (for the plantation owners and their families) or corn shucks and dried Spanish moss (for the slaves). Making soap required effort and ingredients that are foreign to today's mind: people boiled water, then tossed in old lard or fat, pieces of scrap meat left over from hog killing, and homemade lye.

Also dim to many memories today were the horrors endured by the slaves in their voyage to this new land, horrors driven home in "Ibo Landing" by Ihsan Bracy, the haunting tale of Dunbar Creek. To read this story is to experience a rush of emotions: shame, repulsion, sadness at man's inhumanity to man, and perhaps most of all a profound, albeit heartrending, reaffirmation of the strength of the human spirit.

Bracy tells the story of Ibo Landing in terse, poetic passages, with not a word out of place. The story plunges the reader into a world so unfathomable, it is mesmerizing. Reading, you descend into a ship's hold filled with slaves from many tribes: men, women, and children, unknown to one another before they were massed together in pens, unable to move without communal shifting, lying atop one another for weeks, breathing, defecating, dying, the dead thrown to the sharks that were always in the ship's wake. You hear, in the darkness, the commanding voice of a young Ibo warrior calling the name of his people; his idea spreads quietly through the pens and is ruminated on in the interminable hours of darkness and stench as the slave ship plies west. On the day of the vessel's arrival the human cargo stumbles above to the deck and is ushered ashore in the painfully bright dawn, for a communal washing in preparation for the auction later in the day. I read, my heart weighted with sadness, yet at the same time soaring, as the Ibo, thirty or more, turn and stride silently into the water, the guards stunned, then cursing, then transfixed. Knee deep, waist deep, chest deep, gone.

"As they reached the place of the waves, each would reach to grab the hand of the one before . . . stepping over wave after wave, they strode confidently, unhurriedly, past the ship lying in the sunrise," writes Bracy. "Nearly everyone in the vicinity of Ibo Landing that day came to see, before the silent band was lost from sight."

I read this account later, in a library in Beaufort, South Carolina. When I went to the small library at St. Simons and asked about the Ibo and Dunbar Creek, the librarian looked at me closely, then firmly shook her head. "No," she said. "I don't think we have anything on that."

Today St. Simons is an odd mix of golf and history, in that order of importance. Georgia seceded from the Union in January 1861, but in the end it did no good. The Union has returned in a swarm, an army of silver-haired retirees whacking small balls with sticks. As George told me moments after we met, "I want to caution you. Golf here is revered slightly above the church. While you're here, you should realize that you *will* listen reverentially while people describe their golf game."

Occasionally golf and history walk the same green. George told me of the Retreat Golf Course on Sea Island, which has an old cemetery, and how now and again they shut the course down so folks can bury their dead.

George has seen plenty of change on St. Simons since his arrival by train, at age ten, in 1957. "There were three thousand people on St. Simons when I came. If we didn't know you, you were a tourist. Most of the roads were shell and gravel. Nowadays, this is about a hundred percent a resort community. It's awful hard to find the home boys here anymore. Now there's probably thirty thousand people in summer. Chamber of Commerce can tell you. But I'll tell you a secret"—he winked—"whatever they tell you, half again."

St. Simons remains spellbinding, though the roads are no longer shell and gravel, and the plantations of old—Retreat, Cannon's Point, Hampton, Orange Grove—are now gated communities. But the setting sun still torches the marsh grass plains gold, and when a storm approaches, masses of white herons perch in the protective foliage of cedar trees, like slender white fruit defying the laws of gravity. Nonetheless most of the home boys have left town, said George, with fat wads of cash in their pockets. "Pretty hard to resist when you spent your whole life livin' on twenty thousand a year and somebody shows up and offers you two million for your land. The waterfront beaches are premium property. So in come the developers, and in the end you end up spoiling the thing you like the most."

Some still refuse to be bought. Driving around the island, here and there we passed hand-painted signs nailed to trees: "Don't Ask Won't Sell." But just off the island we also drove past a billboard trumpeting "Trupp Hudnett's Listings on the Real Estate Show— Channel 64/65— . . . 24 Hours a Day 7 Days a Week."

Much of St. Simons is no different from any other resort town. Mallery Street, the island's tourist center, is lined with bistros, cafés, pizza joints, and vintage clothing stores. One store offers shark jaws—"25 percent off the regular price!"—that smell of decaying fish.

But even in the civilized places, I felt the press of the marsh. St. Simons is not a big island. Roughly twelve miles long and four miles wide at its widest point, it's about the size of Manhattan. Many people view Manhattan as the epicenter of civilization and, as such, a place of great importance. On St. Simons I was struck by the thought that these simple marshes would outlast Manhattan and the rest of civilization, as well. On St. Simons the future and the past still tussle for predominance.

George drove us toward St. Simons' Atlantic shore and Gould's Inlet. The cigar was now lit. He blew a cloud of thick smoke, and as its gray tendrils wandered slowly out the window, he regarded me with poker-faced sobriety.

"Over on Little St. Simons we had a little tragedy a few months back," he said somberly. "See, there's this horse stable, keeps ten to fifteen horses, you know, so the tourists can ride them. Well, the other night they left one of the horses out, and four or five of the mosquitoes dragged the horse off and devoured it." He dispensed another cloud of smoke. "We know it was only four or five mosquitoes because the bones were left."

He grinned.

"We tell that story to the tourists. They come back a few days later and say, 'You know, you're right.' Hell, if it wasn't for the sand flies, the gnats, and the mosquitoes, this place would be ruined by tourists."

We pulled up at Gould's Inlet, just short of noon. The sun was bright, though I noticed its brightness did not have the squinty intensity of Florida's sun. Here, a bit farther north, it had been scrubbed down a notch, like silver a few weeks after a polishing.

Water strained through the inlet in oozy circles on the outgoing tide. Across the inlet we could see the tip of Sea Island, home to exclusive resorts like the Lodge and the Cloister, named as if no other lodges or cloisters existed. Thankfully, from where we stood all we could see were trees and an empty sand spit looping out to sea. Apparently resort builders had understood enough about the ocean to leave the sandy tendril undeveloped.

It was a calm day on the water, no swell and little wind. Yet from where we stood it seemed as if tiny waves were breaking all the way to France. "It's dirt flat around here, out to sea, and in back behind us," George said. "At high tide you can get out of your car and smell salt water forty miles inland. At low tide you could probably be six miles out in the ocean and spit sand."

Before us the sandbars meandered enticingly, each looping its own path out to sea. I made a mental note to myself, and George read it.

"I wouldn't go out on these sandbars if I were you. Say you go out walking and you lose yourself in the scenery. Now you turn around and the tide's going out, and there's three feet of water behind you. So you start wading back. When you get back to this cut"—he gestured to the water near the inlet's mouth—"what was three feet deep is now six to eight feet deep and hauling ass."

He pointed toward a patch of water and sand roughly two hundred yards from where we stood. I couldn't tell exactly where he was pointing, because the spot was indistinguishable from the rest of the surrounding sea and sand. "Right there's an eighty-foot, hundred-plus-ton shrimp boat buried in the sand," he said. "There's a lot of sand and water moving around real quick."

That something so large could vanish from sight is both astonishing and, for those who believe in man's ability to control his world, disconcerting. Those who live on the water have a clearer view of man's control and Nature's capriciousness. As George boats through the marshes, sometimes his mind walks the bottom, his keel and his memory passing over the murky darkness that has swallowed Spanish galleons and conquistadors' dreams and the broken planes and plans of dope smugglers. Saints and sinners, beer bottles and gold sovereigns, the remains of brash men, brave women, and frightened children—the marsh cradles all to its bosom with equal fervor, jumbling them by whim of tide and mud so that occasionally a fishing trawler scoops up a dinner plate with the pope's personal seal from the 1600s or spills British gold sovereigns on the deck.

George knows where some of these treasures are hidden, but he doesn't care to resurrect them. He has learned from the past and places his priorities and perspective in proper order. Stung by jellyfish, accompanied by water moccasins, he has, with pit bull tenacity, painstakingly searched murky wreckage and wormed into dark gator holes, a graveyard of bones wavering in the beam of his light.

"I'm not much interested in treasure. All gold has blood on it," he said quietly. "But I do feel a personal commitment to the family of a drowned person. My expertise is finding victims for their family's sake and, later, their peace of mind."

I stood quietly, thinking about my own family and our supreme fortune in avoiding the random slings of fate.

On this white-bright day, George was reluctant to dwell on death and dark gator holes. "I like to call it the unspeakable treasure," he said, smiling wide. "The real treasure is what I've discovered about myself through this job. I love to help people." He clapped me on the back with a meaty paw. "Hell, all this philosophizing is making me hungry. Let's get something to eat."

We drove into Brunswick for lunch. Heading down Norwich Street, we passed a distinguished-looking gray-haired man standing in front of a line of sparkling Mercedeses. George waved, and the man waved back.

"Well, I see Mr. Brazwell is out there hustling Mercedeses to all the rich people," said George. His face screwed up. "Hm. Is it Brazwell or Bracewell? Hell, I've only known him for forty years. Nice guy."

In the time I spent with George, he waved to almost everyone in eyeshot and pumped hands with those within arm's reach, though he couldn't always remember exactly whom he was acknowledging. "I feel plumb ashamed," he said to me, after one hearty, though nameless, greeting. "People come up and greet me like a long-lost friend, but I don't know their name. Been so many people, I've been blessed. The author John D. Macdonald had a theory that there were ten thousand people in the South, and if you knew one of them, you knew them all. I just wish my memory was as good as my mouth."

George did remember everyone at Captain Roy's Diner. We took a seat at a long horseshoe-shaped counter. George ordered from the eraser board. Captain Roy's has no menu. The most expensive item was $7.99. As Kelley, our waitress, explained, "Our menu changes depending on what they're catching, so a printed menu makes no sense. Whatever we have fresh is what we serve. Whiting, shrimp, scallops. Oysters twice a week from Apalachicola."

After she left to put in our order, George leaned toward me. "I'm so damn proud of that girl. Like she was my own," he whispered, offering no further explanation.

Terri had quietly joined us for lunch. Two other people sat at the long horseshoe counter, as well. A gray-haired gentleman sat at the horseshoe's apex. Directly across from us, June, the other waitress, sat folding silverware into paper napkins.

Though we were scattered about the restaurant, an amiable con-

versation ensued. Our food arrived. A steaming platter of fried oysters—far heavier on the oyster than the fry—arrived, and it was
some of the best seafood I had ever tasted. I said so.

"I'd stand this seafood against anybody, anyplace, anytime,"
smiled June.

"Food can't be too good if the cook's so thin," said the gray-haired
man.

The cook, a rail-thin black man, had come out of the kitchen to
make a phone call. On the wall beside him an enormous sign proclaimed, "Come Lord Jesus Be Our Guest, Let This Food to Us Be
Blessed. Amen."

"He eats nothing but toast," said June. "He might eat thirty
pieces of toast a day. He loves toast."

The cook made no comment. Whether he was listening to someone on the other end of the line or simply thought his diet made perfect sense was anybody's guess.

"Eatin' that much toast ain't right," opined the gray-haired man.

"It seems to suit him fine." George smiled. "Leaves more oysters
for us."

Later, in overgrown Hilton Head, South Carolina, and Ocean
City, Maryland, I would see people studiously ignore one another or,
if forced by proximity or actual spoken word, address one another
rotely and without heart, anxious to be done and away. But again
and again in the small coastal towns I visited, I watched people
engage in conversation in this easy informal way, as if they had just
seated themselves at the family table, picking up the conversation
from the last meal.

George hadn't let me pay for breakfast. I tried to hand him a
twenty for lunch. He pushed it back. "Can't take it," he said. "Hell,
that wouldn't be southern hospitality."

Driving back to St. Simons, George regarded the marsh. "People
here never seem to give up on the past," he said, a comment seemingly apropos of nothing, yet connected to almost everything we had
talked about. "It all ties back to the water because around here,
that's where the past all came from."

I could see why the locals took pride in their marshes. To the cursory glance, they appear as a plain of vast, soothing sameness, run through with glimmering, veiny waterways. But they are not sameness at all. They are one of the most biologically active cultures on earth, a fecund explosion of spartina, glasswort, saltwort, salt grass, and, above the high marsh, needle rush, yellow-flowered sea oxeye, and stands of pine.

Names tag, but they don't touch the soul. So we turn to the poet:

Somehow my soul seems suddenly free
From the weighing of fate and sad discussion of sin,
By the length and the breadth and the sweep of the marshes of
*   Glynn.*
Ye marshes, how candid and simple and nothing-withholding and
*   free*
Ye publish yourself to the sky and offer yourselves to the sea!
Tolerant plains, that suffer the sea and the rains and the sun,
Ye spread and span like the catholic man who hath mightily won.

Sidney Lanier's poem "The Marshes of Glynn" is beautiful and his words apt, but they are not entirely true. The marshes don't so much suffer outside elements as absorb them: false teeth, bodies, and finally memory itself.

When I asked George if the sadness of his job ever got to him—by his estimate, he had recovered well over a hundred bodies in thirty-five years—he nodded thoughtfully. "It is depressing. We'll often search so long that we have to bring in dogs for sniffing bone fragments the raccoons and other predators have scattered around the marsh. Folks never give up hoping. It's a sad thing, that waiting."

In the end, though, George preferred to take the optimistic tack. As I watched the sun set, the marsh sea, gold in the softening light, ran into the fuzzy distance, a soggy Serengeti, wafting mud and out-waiting time.

I remembered George's parting words.

"The marsh is the mother of all life," he had said, and the cigar butt in his mouth danced appreciatively.

4

VALONA, GEORGIA

A Shrimper's Last Cast

VALONA, GEORGIA, is twenty miles north of St. Simons Island and fifty years behind. To get there, I drove up U.S. Highway 17, past egrets lifting from ribboned creeks and dented trailer homes with clothesline-strung undergarments proudly drying in the sun. It was November 15.

Not everyone believed Valona was a pleasant step back to a simpler time.

My last afternoon on St. Simons I walked the waterfront at the island's southern tip. It was hot—even in late November Georgia can still radiate summer heat. Shrimp boats moved through the channel between St. Simons and Jekyll Islands headed for the hazy Atlantic, their nets hanging from arms on either side of the vessel, making them look like insects readying to spread their wings.

Near the St. Simons Island Pier a woman lay on her stomach in a lounge chair, tanning. I had never seen a darker, more leathery personage. She resembled a mummy, only mummies are rarely found in bikinis. She appeared to be in her fifties, though she might have been five hundred.

I was busy waving away a swarm of gnats when she suddenly sat up, reached into an Armani handbag, and produced a bottle of baby oil. She was liberally applying the oil, which disappeared into her pores with uncommon swiftness, when she spied me. Her cold gaze ran over me, trying to decide whether I was a purse-snatcher or, worse, a dermatologist.

I nodded and smiled. "Don't the gnats bother you?" I was trying to be sociable.

"No," she said brusquely, nudging the handbag closer to her chair with a mummified foot. "They bother me when they get bad. But they aren't bad now." Her tone implied a certain weakness on my part.

The gnats did seem to circle her at quite a discreet distance.

I continued to swat and weave like a boxer, only boxers connect with their opponents. George's voice echoed in my head: *Hell, if it wasn't for the sand flies, the gnats, and the mosquitoes, this place would be ruined by tourists.* I wondered how the gnats distinguished between residents and tourists.

Possibly by attention span.

"These gnats aren't bad at all," the woman said again.

I wanted to say, "They couldn't get to your nerve endings without a jackhammer." But instead I said, "Well, I guess I'm just not used to this."

She fixed me with a scowl. "You're not from here, are you?"

This was one of only two times on my entire trip that this question was voiced aloud, and the only time it was voiced as a challenge. Almost to a fault, people made me feel as if I belonged, even when I obviously didn't. But this woman was having none of that. She regarded me like a bouncer who has already made up his mind.

"I'm passing up the coast, heading for Valona," I said.

Her eyebrows arched, and though it didn't seem possible, a few additional creases crinkled her forehead. "Valona? I'd be careful up there. That's hardscrabble country. McIntosh County is one of the poorest counties in the South. They depend on shrimping and tourism, and these days neither one is much help."

Her voice had an ominous tone, as if those folks in Valona who weren't trawling for shrimp were trading in tourist pelts. "Yes," she said, turning back onto her stomach. "Valona, that's real hardscrabble country."

Instead, the first person I met when I crossed the Altamaha River was open and friendly, though he was a little piqued. Crossing the river, Highway 17 dips you promptly into the county seat,

Darien, eleven miles south of Valona. Where it was visible, the architecture of St. Simons had been a chic potpourri of Nouveau Spanish and Antebellum South, banks and boutiques of smooth adobe with Spanish tile roofs, and colonnaded homes with wrap-around porches large enough to serve as a landing strip. In contrast, downtown Darien's buildings were square blocks of brick, stone, and wood—except for the churches, which spiked proudly into the baby-blue morning sky. Darien was settled in 1736 by Scottish Highlanders. The Scottish verve for frugality and simplicity appeared to live on in the town's architecture.

I love towns like Darien, places that don't pretend to be anything other than what they are. There is no cute, gussied-up tourist facade fronting the town. Rusted pickups pull into the local gas station for coffee. A woman, her hair in curlers, pushed a torn stroller. Every fifteen yards or so she had to bend and flip up a shred of dragging cloth to keep it from getting caught under the wheels.

I parked the van behind City Hall, which was just coming to life at nine A.M. On the hour church bells pealed "God Bless America," the clear chimes hanging in the air for an extra moment as if reluctant to leave. I strolled the outskirts of Vernon Square, a lovely green sward pocked with thick, silent oaks, the chuk-chuk-chukking morning sprinklers sending up transient misty rainbows.

Beside the Darien United Methodist Church I read a plaque proclaiming that the church was twice set afire by Union troops in 1863 but did not burn. To remind those with a short attention span, a plaque beside City Hall informed the reader that on June 11, 1863, Darien was vandalized and burned by Union forces, even though the town was of little consequence to the Union cause and was almost deserted, to boot, most of Darien's five hundred residents having fled inland before the troops arrived.

In some quarters, forgiveness for this slight is still to come. I struck up a conversation with that piqued man fishing beside the river. When I commented on the plaques, he nodded. "I'll drop my drawers so each and every one of those soldiers can kiss my Confederate ass," he said.

There was no obvious rejoinder, so I remained quiet. The last tendrils of morning mist rose off the river. Invisible creatures set off concentric ripples on the Altamaha's mirror surface.

"I know that sounds bitter," said the fisherman eventually. "But that punishment makes as much sense as burning Darien did."

We watched the muddy river as it slowly ferried sticks toward the sea. Darien was once a port of great consequence. Huge mills sawed forests into a seemingly endless supply of lumber, which was taken downriver to the Atlantic by timber schooners. On Darien's waterfront wharves workers loaded equally heaping supplies of plantation rice and sea island cotton, their shouts and beehive clamor ringing across the river.

Today the morning was hung with absolute silence; the world was passing Darien by as surely as its impassive river was. The plantations are gone, done in by emancipation; the great mills disappeared in the early 1900s with the depletion of the forests. Yet man, the worker bee, still hews out a life for himself—breeding, building, dreaming, fighting, burning—as the water passes quietly, caring nothing for the next scene. A stone's throw downriver three shrimp boats rested against the river bank. The name of the nearest boat— *Blessed Assurance*—was visible across the stern.

Life, of course, is anything but assured. Yet in the very face of this bleak thought, I felt the surge of optimism and hope that I feel every time I look on water. Ocean, lake, or river, its prairie spread always leaves me feeling both inconsequential and reassured. Towns, cultures, individual lives and fortunes will flare and fall, but the waters remain, their backdrop of comforting sameness trumpeting continuity and, with that continuity, hope. Like children, we need something to believe in, a face that will always be there, an anchor we can always return to, and when we can't return, our children can, and their children, too.

I must have drifted. The fisherman was looking at me with mild concern.

"You doin' okay?" he said.

"Never better," I said, and meant it.

"Good," he said. "Thought I might have offended you with that talk of ass-kissin'."

"I thought it sounded fair enough, though I was thinking all the puckering might leave you a little chafed."

He grinned. "Well hell, we've all got to shoulder a little discomfort to stand up for what we believe in."

His line strained for the sea as he robbed my thoughts.

"Plenty of days I feel like I could stand down here forever," he said.

⚜

I DROVE TO VALONA, a few miles down State Highway 99, to meet Hunter Forsyth, a shrimper. George knew Hunter and praised him highly.

"Hunter, he's a hardcase old-time southern fisherman," George had said. "He's been everywhere you can drive a shrimp boat, twice. The man fears neither man nor animal, though he does snap to his wife."

I was interested in how the local shrimpers were faring. Driving up the coast, I had seen their trawlers throbbing out to sea and moored alongside various docks. Having shrimped for forty-one of his fifty-nine years, Hunter would have more perspective than most, I expected.

It was easier to find Hunter now than it might have been in the past. The dirt road turnoff to his home was clearly marked with a street sign that read "Hunter Place."

"They put that sign up about two years ago, mostly for the EMS," Hunter later told me. "Before that, somebody got sick, they didn't know where the hell you were."

Hunter's home sits at the end of Hunter Place, on a peaceful spread at the edge of the marsh: a carport, a swimming pool, and a simple brick rancher shadowed by enormous, regal oaks, some of them, by Hunter's estimate, three hundred years old. Everyone should have something in their yard that is older than they are, placing life, and themselves, in proper context.

Hunter is a bit oaklike himself, a stolid man with pale blue eyes, thick forearms, and an easy drawl that rumbles up from his chest attached to a bit of a rasp likely brought on by the pile of Camel butts always somewhere in his vicinity. You don't find many fishermen who are health nuts, and Hunter is not one of them.

He has driven shrimp boats since he was eighteen, except for time off during the Vietnam War to pilot boats ferrying classified messages and important personages through foreign-sounding but familiar-looking waters. "The Vietnam coast is a lot like coastal Georgia," he said, as the two of us sat at a table just off his kitchen, drinking coffee. "They got about a seven-foot tide, and when the tide goes out, there's a lot of mud. Because of the similarity, it was a little easier for me to navigate the rivers than someone from Kansas."

Shrimping proved to have other wartime applications. Once in Danang Harbor, Hunter had to deliver a group of officers from his 36-foot gig to a 400-foot cruiser for a big brass meeting. A heaving swell made climbing a ladder between ships too dangerous, so Hunter rigged a cargo net. "Up they went, feet and arms stickin' through. They looked like pure hell going up. Eased 'em right down like a big clump of rice bags. It was a very undignified way for a superior officer to get on the ship. I don't think they wanted to send home a picture to their wives. They wasn't much different than pullin' shrimp nets."

Like most fishermen with a marginal budget and plenty more expenses, Hunter is supremely capable. He can fix almost anything, and on the ocean he has gotten himself and his crews out of some serious jams. He moves with placid assurance. Aboard his trawler and elsewhere, he doesn't issue commands; he makes simple statements that others act on out of respect and habit. But plenty remains outside his control.

Two dogs lolled near the table. Fiddler was recovering from knee surgery. Now and again Striker, a black lab with a loyal, graying face, issued a guttural cough. Striker would not recover from lung cancer. The cancer was a surprise, and originally so were the dogs. "I told Suzanne before we got married, no dogs," Hunter said. "We hadn't been married for a few weeks, and we had dogs."

When something surprises Hunter, it doesn't spell out on his face. He simply shakes his head slowly. Forty-one years on the water have bled overreaction from him. Once, trawling in the Gulf of Mexico, a freak twenty-five-foot wave broke on Hunter's boat. The wave blasted out the windows. The water had to go somewhere, so it tore all the doors off the pilothouse, too. The wave nearly killed one of Hunter's crew, "slammed his damn head through the bulkhead. If there had been something solid behind that bulkhead, it would have killed him. That wave damn nearly did us all in."

Through unplanned dogs, weather, economics, and shrimp falloffs, Hunter has had to roll with the churning seas. I'll give a pound of sweet, fat Georgia brown shrimp to anyone who can name a profession that demands more patience in the face of more obstacles than commercial fishing. It's no surprise Jesus was a fisherman.

Here's how shrimping is these days, at least for the shrimper who goes out and catches the shrimp God made. Shrimp farming—in places like Thailand, Vietnam, Brazil, India, and Ecuador—has served a bitter blow to the trawlers, as pond-raised shrimp undersell the shrimpers' catch.

Shrimp farming is a heated topic, and before you choose to discuss it along Georgia's backwaters, it is wise to recall that this is not the realm of *Face the Nation*. "College types comin' down telling us how seafood farms is gonna save the day," snarled a shrimper on St. Simons. "They're all full of bullshit, and if they go on too long, they all bleed the same."

Hunter sees the shrimp farm debate as a matter not of pugilism but of simple economics. "The Chinese can actually raise their shrimp in a pond, box 'em up, freeze 'em, and ship 'em over here for way cheaper than we can go out and catch the wild shrimp. Imports started in the early eighties, and they've been hurtin' us bad ever since."

Still, Hunter and his two-man crew set out, because fishing is about optimism and the lucky strike. If the shrimping is good and the weather cooperates, they may stay out for as long as a week. Hunter used to stay out longer, trawling in waters as distant as the Gulf of Mexico, but he's had enough encounters with foul weather and rogue waves far from home. On a typical day he and crew will make four to five drags, trawling the funnel-shaped nets along the bottom for three hours before hauling them aboard and separating the shrimp from the seething mass of whiting, silver eels, squid, butterfish, silver perch, weakfish, tonguefish, and who knows what. Some of the larger fish stay, to be cooked or eaten aboard, or carried home for the crew's families. The rest is shoveled overboard, and the nets are lowered again. It takes about half an hour to get the nets overboard, and the same amount of time to haul them on board properly. If the nets aren't straight, they won't catch anything. The day begins at dawn and generally ends at nightfall, conditions permitting.

What they need to do, ledger-wise, is simple: catch enough shrimp to cover their expenses with money left over. Nowadays there are plenty of times when Hunter simply turns the boat around and heads home early, knowing the math is woefully stacked against him.

He usually has three men on standby so he can count on two being ready to go. "It's not easy getting crew anymore," he lamented. "A lot of 'em have gone to working on dredges and land jobs because shrimping isn't dependable anymore. They got families—you can't blame 'em. They would rather shrimp, but it's a matter of simple arithmetic. If you can't make enough money to pay your bills, you better hunt something else up." Hunter pays for what the crew eats on the boat and buys them cigarettes. "There's no way they can go out on a boat and owe more money than they made when they come back in."

Unfortunately that rule doesn't apply to the captain. In a bad year Hunter might lose $10,000. In a good year he has cleared $50,000 to $100,000. He has not had a good year in a long time. The price of shrimp peaked in 1979—at $6.50 to $7 for a pound of jumbo shrimp—but these days it's usually well below that. Operating expenses, of course, have not remained stationary.

Hunter was ashore on the day I visited because it didn't pay to be anywhere else. "They ain't catchin' anything at the moment, and it just ain't practical to drag for less than a thousand dollars a day." But he isn't much for complaining. He stubbed out another Camel and reached for a replacement in his shirt pocket.

"Compared to people in this area, it's been a fairly good living. If you're driving a car and you got central heat and air-conditioning and you have a meal on the table tonight, what damn difference does it make if you're making $30,000 or $300 million? People dwell on too much about what they don't have instead of being thankful for what they do have."

I thought of the peevish woman on St. Simons. Wealth is a relative term. "When will you be able to retire?" I asked.

Hunter smiled slowly. "I think semi-retirement is as good as I'll ever do until they plant my ass."

Striker coughed. Hunter's voice had a similar rasp.

"Hell," said Hunter. "I don't mind."

⁂

HUNTER'S SHRIMP OPERATION runs out of a small dock a few minutes from his house. We drove there in his burgundy Lincoln, jouncing softly down a dirt road. The road ended at a white wooden shed that looked as if it might, at any moment, heave a final sigh and settle into the marsh. A refrigerator truck sat out front, alongside a few rusted cars. Behind the shack was a short dock and three shrimp boats, each with an American flag lofting in the light breeze.

"Ain't nothing glorified about this." Hunter stepped out of the car and chuckled. "It's called a shrimp factory. You expect this damn huge thing with smokestacks."

Inside the shed coolness rose from the concrete floor. The wooden ceiling barely cleared my head. There were several long steel tables, upon which engines sat in various stages of repair. At the marsh-facing end of the shack there was a hundred-pound scale. "This is where the shrimp are weighed, iced, and packed off to the distributor," Hunter explained.

Two men, out on the docks when we arrived, stepped inside. David Poppell is the captain of the *Three Cees,* docked outside with a shrimp etched on the bow. David looks like a younger version of Hunter—same thick forearms, same capable gaze—only the ocean and economics haven't yet scared his black hair gray. Fred Braddy is part of David's crew. He is slender and was silent, probably because he was eighteen. Both men nodded to me but otherwise remained quiet. David carried a bucket of shrimp, which he dumped onto the scale. They were fat, wet, and pink.

"That's fresh shrimp," said Hunter, eyeing the scale. "They're for my nephew in Beaufort. He loves fresh shrimp." He raised his eyebrows in mock surprise. "I don't know why, my family wants shrimp, they all think they can come right here. Hell, they can get it anywhere."

Having weighed out the gift shrimp, Hunter made for the dock. Before he could get there, he was headed off by a woman, who spoke quickly. Hunter listened, and then we all followed her down along the marsh.

Fifty yards down there was a house. About a half-dozen folks stood at the edge of the yard where it dropped into the marsh, watching a pelican. The bird stood stoically in the muck of low tide, its backside to them. "He has something in his foot," Marianna said to me.

Marianna, who had fetched Hunter, is Hunter's wife's sister. Though I never figured out the exact limbs of the family tree, I'm pretty sure the rest of the assembled group had either a direct or an indirect familial connection to Hunter.

Hunter appraised the scene, then turned smiling to young Fred. "You got to go get him."

Fred walked slowly down a boat ramp. He was wearing white rubber boots, but he still stepped gingerly out onto a piece of wood that was bogged in the muck.

Pelicans are large birds with impressive beaks. They are not docile creatures when cornered. This one was injured. I was struck by the bird's prehistoric look. A picture suddenly popped into my mind, a drawing from one of my boys' dinosaur books, a pterodactyl winging nestward with a nearly-diced lizard clasped in its jagged maw.

The pelican kept its back to Fred but, via subtle shifting, indicated it was fully aware of his presence.

Hunter grinned and whispered to me, "That thing will beat hell out of Fred."

Fred made no move. The pelican mirrored him.

"Wassamatter, Fred?" said Hunter. "You got to go get him."

"Hell," said Fred, "I don't want to get sunk."

"Fred, it ain't got any teeth," said David. "He ain't gonna bite you."

Fred's eyes didn't leave the bird. "You want to borrow my boots?" he said.

Between Fred's reluctance and the pelican's nonchalance, it was apparent this standoff might last a long time. It was time for a decision, and the alpha male quietly made it. "We'll get a cast net," said Hunter. "I see the bird done scared Fred off."

Someone produced a cast net, and Fred quietly returned to the marsh bank. Hunter carried the net down the boat ramp, but not before whispering to a wide-eyed little girl resting in another man's arms, "We're gonna save him. Don't you worry."

Hunter stood at the edge of the boat ramp, separated from the pelican by ten yards of muck. The pelican kept its back turned. Our world went still, the moment of reckoning at hand.

David turned to me and grinned. "Hunter can't throw a cast net." Before the last word was out, the net was filled with lively pelican. David didn't bat an eye. "First cast, huh?" he said.

Two treble hooks were stuck in the pelican, ugly barbs, one protruding through at the base of its wing, the other one in its foot. Keeping the bird firmly in place with the net, Hunter expertly cut each barb off at the end with a pair of needle-nose pliers, then slowly pulled out each hook.

Fishermen are often painted as indiscriminate killers, but I have found this is rarely true. Sure they kill to make a living, and some of their fishing methods produce frightful waste. I once read a report stating that U.S. shrimpers throw nearly a billion pounds of bycatch overboard each year. But for the fisherman this is not waste. It's just part of doing business, and he gives it no more thought than, say, a writer gives to paper provided by trees.

I am not going to argue rightness or wrongness here. But I will say that, taking a net and a sometimes-thrashing bird into consideration, Hunter's was a deft bit of surgery.

"You've done that before?" I asked, after Hunter pulled out the last hook.

"I've gotten maybe a hundred of them out of pelicans fishing down at the beach," he said.

When the net came off, the pelican wandered leisurely down the ramp with the relaxed air of a retiree strolling to the end of a dock to watch a sunset.

He shook his backside.

Hunter grinned at the little girl. "He wagged his tail. He's sayin', 'I'm gonna be all right.'"

⁂

HUNTER WILL CLOSE out his life as a fisherman, but his son Will won't. Not long ago Will, Suzanne, Hunter, and Will's new wife, Joanne, all signed up for a real estate course. Hunter lost interest, but his family didn't. In the last four months Will had sold close to a half-million dollars' worth of real estate, though Hunter suspects Suzanne funneled some business their son's way.

Real estate may prove to be the way to go. Folks on St. Simons are now casting an eye toward Valona.

"In the fifties and sixties St. Simons was like Valona is now," said Hunter. "Now it's crowded. People want to get away from the crowds. That's the reason people find Valona attractive. Lot of rich retirees are looking this way. Once you go south of St. Marys, Georgia, it's condominiums, hundreds of miles of them, all the way down to Miami. Here the only islands that are inhabited and ruined are St. Simons and Sea Island. Our barrier islands still look like they did when the Indians were here."

In the afternoon we drove down to Suzanne's real estate office in Darien, which, as it turned out, was just up the Altamaha River from where I had met my retribution-minded fisherman friend. The office was small and empty, except for Suzanne.

Suzanne was born just down the road from Hunter. They have been married thirty years, but they have known each other all their lives. Suzanne is as energetic as Hunter is placid, and she knows the marshes almost as well as her husband. She is as pleasant and welcoming as Hunter, but she talks three times as fast. She had to. Suzanne also ran the business end of Hunter's dock and, a stone's throw downmarsh, the dock she owned. At both docks Suzanne ordered the fuel, oil, and ice, driving the ice truck to the ice plant, and hauling eighty-pound blocks of ice, counting and dividing the shrimp by size. Seven boats operate out of Hunter's dock, some twenty out of Suzanne's. She also does natural history tours of Blackbeard and Sapelo Islands and takes bow hunters over to the barrier islands to hunt for deer. Not surprisingly, her family lineage meanders back to the tough Scots who settled the area.

Suzanne isn't a Realtor in her heart, and she was starting to discover this. She stared out the open door at the soft afternoon sunshine. Hunter sat in the chair behind her desk, quietly eating a hamburger.

"I don't know how much longer I'll be doing this," she said to me. "I'm a country mouse, I ain't a city mouse. This is a lot harder than I thought it would be. I love this place. People here stay put. In real estate school they told us people sell their houses every three to five years. I'm like, 'Whaaaat?' "

A car shushed past. A crow cawed in the ensuing silence.

"I still live in the town where I grew up," said Suzanne, smiling. "I used to be ashamed of that. At high school reunions I would hang my head and apologize for still living here. Now that I'm old, I'm proud to say I like it here. And now the people I knew in high school who moved away, they want to come back. The area is still untouched. If you go out to Blackbeard Island during the week, you won't see anyone."

It was a question that had to be asked, though I hated to ask it, since the Forsyths were so gracious: "Do you see a conflict between preserving Valona and selling real estate?"

Suzanne smiled. "We decided to try to do it with a sense of preservation. We're trying to make direct sales to historical preservationists, to keep things out of the hands of the developers. We want to try and base our business on that. Try to protect what's here."

Perhaps, I thought to myself, that's why business was so tough.

Historical preservationists don't come to town with fat checks in hand as often as developers do.

Hunter had stepped outside. Suzanne watched her husband through the open door as he waved to a passing car.

"We're just not movers," she said quietly. "Here we still are."

※

IT IS A MISTAKE to see a place like Valona as removed. The wind ruffles empty marsh and wood, and for those accustomed to modern society's clamor, the silence is so heavy it assumes a palpable press. But in Valona residents very much feel the pinch. Developers know the place. Government has established regulations for almost every move Hunter and his fellow shrimpers make. The stretch of marsh that borders Hunter and Suzanne's property—marshland Suzanne owns and once farmed for oysters—is now off-limits by government decree, to protect it from man's many hands.

As we drove back to town along an empty Highway 99, Hunter slowly shook his head. He never went to college, but you don't need a degree to see things clearly. "More and more automobiles, more and more boats, more and more airplanes, more and more pollution and problems. All that boils down to too many damn people. If we don't practice some damn birth control, I think there's gonna be some bad results."

Hunter has played the piano since he was eleven. Now and again, when it all gets to be too much—the skyrocketing operating costs, the shrimp falloffs, the government regulations, the aching toll on a body that has hauled nets for forty-one years—he goes to the piano and plays. The chords rise and drift out the screen door, dancing like church chimes, faintly, across the marsh.

There would be no piano playing tonight. Today was Hunter's birthday.

5
ROOT OF GOOD,
ROOT OF EVIL

ME MIND GOES all about frum de time de dew cum t dayclean.

Poetry of sorts, this is actually phonetic Gullah. Translated, it means, "I think about many things from early evening until daylight the next morning."

This happens during quiet moments on journeys of any kind, except perhaps for mindless ones. Not that there isn't joy in mindless travel. For one thing, it is easier to sleep.

On this particular evening I lay in bed puzzling through many intriguing possibilities. It was Merle Burge who had first alerted me to the Gullah culture and its spiritual-cum-voodoo offshoots. I met Merle in Bluffton, South Carolina, just inland from Hilton Head Island. I had explored Hilton Head before meeting Merle, and the most intriguing thing I found there was that the island no longer has any connection with the South, washed clean as it is by northern retirees.

But what Merle spoke of has roots as long as time, roots that bear down into soil, black and long-hidden. "You should go to St. Helena Island," she said. "They still practice a kind of voodoo there." She leaned forward, lowering her voice. "A neighbor of mine had someone cast a spell. The spell was cast on a girl who had eyes on her husband."

There was a pregnant pause.

"Did it work?" I asked.

"Oh, it worked."

"What happened?" I asked.

"Let's just say she had a very hard time after that," Merle said cryptically.

Though short on specifics, it was obvious Merle wouldn't be openly coveting anyone's husband anytime soon.

She glanced around, then lowered her voice another tic. "A lot of people don't believe in voodoo, but I do."

Even if it wasn't true, this voodoo avenue offered mystery and promise. At worst, I would find nothing, or perhaps end up with a pig's tail. Lying in bed, I made my decision: I would go to St. Helena Island.

※

GULLAH CULTURE arrived at North American shores from Africa on the manacled joints of slaves; how far back in time it meandered before then is a matter of academic debate. Like experts on any subject, those that delve into Gullah culture disagree on many things, though in my readings I found they universally adhere to one shared belief, namely, that they are right and everyone else is daft. The Gullah name originated in Angola, where the choice slaves came from, states one author. No, says another, Gullah derives from "Golas," the name of a group of Liberians who lived on the west coast of Africa between Sierra Leone and the Ivory Coast, and "Gwalla," a powerful tribe of Cammi or Comi Negroes in the French Congo. Consult the ancient maps, says a third, and there, between the Gold Coast and the Ivory Coast, you will find the forgotten Gullah coast.

Whatever their heritage, the ancestors of today's South Carolina Gullah came to this country unwillingly; slaves were shipped to Charleston and the surrounding areas in roughly 1670 to work indigo, rice, and cotton. The largest concentrations of today's Gullah live in the low country and sea islands off South Carolina, Georgia, and Florida, islands and hamlets with singsong names like Daufuskie and Frogmore, places hung with the smell of woodsmoke, marsh, and brine and the possibility of something dark and strange.

Gullah culture is steeped in herbalism, spiritualism, and—on

this many authors agree—black magic. Certain Gullah had practiced a brand of magic called "the root." The root was a charm.
Some roots were cloth sacks the size of a pecan. Some were liquids
in small vials. Some were actual roots—magnolia, sparkleberry, wild
azalea—tidily wrapped in a flannel strip and bound by white string
with intricate knots and crisscrossings. Some smelled. An evil root
might give off a slightly nauseous odor, courtesy of a dusting of
stinkweed. A love root was often heavily perfumed. Roots could be
carried, chewed, hidden, or buried.

Whatever their form or placement, roots were administered or
removed by root doctors, powerful men who could bring you money,
love, health, or a life worse than miserable. It was said that skilled
root doctors had spirits at their command, nasty things that might
settle upon you at night while you slept, sucking the air from your
lungs and the blood from your body. Some root doctors wore blue
sunglasses, which they tipped down slightly to give victims the evil
eye. Root doctors often took the name of an animal, so that, had
there been a phone book, you would have found what you needed
under Dr. Bug, Dr. Crow, Dr. Fly, or Dr. Snake. They worked their
spells quietly and without fanfare, sometimes from a great distance,
so that it was impossible to link them to the calamity itself. They left
no trail.

Stories of their power abounded. Few things please folks more
than a good scare suffered by someone else. I am no exception—I
devoured the Gullah stories. They run the gamut, touching on all of
humanity's sins, fears, and foibles. Root doctors helped clients pick
winning lottery numbers, cured them of tuberculosis, and helped
them enjoy proper vengeance. When a Beaufort man announced to
his wife that he was leaving her to marry another, the wife obtained
a white powder from a root doctor. Taking a pair of her husband's
briefs, she dusted them thoroughly. The man remarried, but he was
never able to perform. His new wife left him, and he shot himself in
the head with a revolver.

Other tales are even darker: of dust gathered at midnight from
the loamy graves of criminals, of spirits who appeared as a six-legged
calf or a headless hog, of murderers lured to their deaths in silent

dark waters by the victims themselves, of men who, with a glance, brought slow death.

Among the coastal marshes and islands the root doctors moved, imperious as kings, bestowing favors or punishment as they felt necessary, leaving lesson and legend in their wake. The tales are not all ancient: the Beaufort man's briefs were powder dusted, and impotence purportedly rendered, at about the time Neil Armstrong was setting foot on the moon.

Much of this root activity, the books say, centered on St. Helena Island, which was home to Dr. Buzzard (real name Stephaney Robinson), purportedly one of the most powerful root doctors who ever practiced. It is said that with merely a stare, Dr. Buzzard once caused a witness whom he wished to remain closemouthed "to shake, to groan, to beat himself all over like he was covered with stinging ants. He fell to the floor, thrashing and rolling, his eyes rolling back into his head, and frothing at the mouth." Today many lawyers behave in the same fashion. But the courts of yesterday were stymied by such behavior, and Buzzard's aura grew. Tall, slender, and dignified, Buzzard held sway on St. Helena for nearly forty years, from the early 1900s until he died of stomach cancer. Stomach cancer, at least, was the recorded cause of death. Powerful men have powerful enemies.

It wasn't all about voodoo. I find the Gullah culture fascinating, though now and again in the pages I read, its members spout a sadly militant diatribe. Shrieks one author, "We will not allow people to come in and excavate the seeds of our heritage and put them on display for money, awards, for the purpose of putting the excavator's name up in lights." I thought she ought to be true to herself, so I put her book aside and bought a different book instead.

In another book I found a list of Gullah phrases. To the outsider, some phrases are indecipherable (*Mout mek you backside lib high*— Don't sass, and keep your gossip to yourself, or somebody might give you a whipping). Some take some mild figuring (*Eber ting n de milk ain white*—Something crooked is going on), and some, given context, ring clear, like the one used by a woman bemoaning an insufficiency in her life: *"Me ol man n me ain ka-neck-up n de bed fa moos tu years now."*

Later I would discover similarly unique and wonderful dialects up the coast on Ocracoke (North Carolina) and Tangier (Virginia) Islands, further proof of the loveliness of islands and the priceless service of water. Islands are buffered, moat-ringed, and harder to storm. Given a personality, they are more open-minded and accepting than their stolid, land-locked geological counterparts. Islands have welcomed miniature mammoths (the now extinct pygmy mammoths of Santa Cruz Island) and tennis-ball-size birds (the Galápagos sharp-billed finch) that plop on the backs of bigger birds and drink their blood. Biologically, culturally, and—it can easily be argued—sociologically, islands are the last refuge of the strange, a place where untoward behavior and the outcasts who exhibit it are not wiped clean by the frowning homogeneous mass.

Ours is a culture that prides itself on individualism, but really we are a culture of absorption, gathering in the huddled masses, ironing out their annoying wrinkles, and then pressing them seamlessly into the tapestry of American life, so that they too wolf down cheeseburgers, shop at cavernous superstores, and devour the breaking romantic-financial-drug woes of the latest sacrificial icon. Along the coast, especially in the small communities, there is still happy evidence of resistance. People don't know if Michael Jackson sleeps with a teddy bear or with a llama, and they don't care. I don't know why this is. Maybe the elements make coastal folk tougher to iron. Maybe it's just a little harder for homogeny to make inroads where the roads are only dirt until they dissolve to sand, salt, and sea.

The Gullah and their culture still retain a foothold along the low country and its islands, but the foothold is slipping away. Developers have already bought up much Gullah land. Those who choose not to sell often lose their land when they can't afford skyrocketing property taxes after a once-quiet island becomes a desirable resort. Hilton Head Island, at one time, was largely Gullah. Now you can walk up to anyone you please and say *"Mout mek you backside lib high"* with impunity.

The other problem is equally Darwinian in its finale: the young have little interest in the past. Writes one Gullah historian, "Gullah culture is fast disappearing as the older folks who know it are dying, and children of each new generation are growing up with little or no knowledge of its existence."

I began asking almost everyone I met what they knew about the root. The question produced interestingly mixed results.

"I don't know of any root doctors," said Grace Morris Cordial, a resource librarian at the Beaufort County Library. "But bear in mind, when I heard about putting bay leaf in your wallet, I did."

"Why?"

"It makes you rich."

"Did it work?"

Grace smiled. "Well, I'm not broke." She paused.

"There are still people here who pass the youngest child over the dead person's casket to protect the child from the dead person's spirit. They might do it quietly, but they still do it."

John Hendrix, an Episcopal priest in Beaufort, told me he performed funerals for the area's poor. Now and again, he said, the coroner wasn't quite sure what to put on the line marked "cause of death." "I've seen people die of no apparent causes. It's strange, I know, but the power of suggestion is strong."

Another man was certain of the existence of dark evil and knew precisely where I would find it. "Shit," he said. "You just need to meet my ex-wife."

Then, in a book plucked from the stacks of the Beaufort County Library, I read this: "Dr. Buzzard's mantle passed to his son-in-law, who plied his trade at Oaks Plantation on St. Helena Island . . . until his death in 1997. . . . Though it is uncertain exactly who has taken over Buzzy's practice, someone most likely has."

※

SOUTH CAROLINA'S low country is aptly named. Along the coast, away from the cities, woods and waters reign and often meld. As I drove along raised roads, I peered into those woods. The fall leaves lay motionless on the black forest floor, while brackish water seeped up and pooled so stealthily it appeared hard as earth. It was, of course, an illusion. To walk through these woods meant splashing through knee-deep water. It was like watching the passage of time, as imperceptible as it was certain. Children become men and women, parents become children, invisibly, yet clear as leaves floating in a forest.

I had been gone from home for over a month.

When I called, Graham, our seven-year-old, answered. His voice was shaky. "When are you coming home, Dad?"

"Not for a while," I said, feeling as hollow and distant as I sounded.

"When you left, I started to cry," he said.

Our cell phones stuttered with broken reception, an added complication when your heart is already breaking.

Children are both honest and focused. "Wait a minute, Dad." His voice was now businesslike. I heard the sound of his footfalls moving to another room.

When his sweet voice floated happily back to me over the miles, it echoed clear as a bell.

"Hey, Dad! I'm sitting on the toilet, and I'm not doing anything!"

❧

THE NEXT DAY I drove to St. Helena. The island sits just to the north of Hilton Head and east of Beaufort across a string of waterways and bridges. Heading east, I eventually passed over Cowan Creek on a narrow bridge that barely cleared the marsh grass tips, then went on to St. Helena.

It was a squinty-bright fall day, two weeks short of Thanksgiving. The sun shone cheerily, sending flickering light onto the main road as it ducked into thick corridors of trees. The street signs were bright blue and appeared new, proudly describing dirt roads— J. Stevens Path, Donna Road—that forked off the main road and disappeared into the woods. Weathered clapboard churches and homes dotted the roadside. Hand-scrawled signs planted in front yards advertising hot boiled crab. Great mossy trees hung timeless and silent, and the air seemed to have been scoured to a pleasant freshness that tickled coolly when inhaled.

Some of the homes were splashed with bright colors—greens and reds and yellows—as if a child-giant had gone after them with markers. The window shutters and the trim around the windows and doors were all painted a lovely blue. Haint blue, to be precise. Haints are creatures of darkness, devil creatures that will not enter a blue opening of a house because blue is the color of heaven. The scent was getting stronger.

I stopped to buy shrimp from a man alongside the road. He was selling them out of the back of his station wagon for $3.99 a pound. The shrimp were fat and red and rested heavy and wet in my hand.

He chattered merrily as he bagged up the shrimp, but when I asked him if he knew anything about root doctors, his eyebrows did a quick bob and his eyes went dead.

"Well, there was root doctors," he said, giving great consideration to the shrimp he had just been ignoring. "It was real big in the forties and fifties, but now most of the older ones that used to be here, they died out. The last one died about twenty years ago. Mostly the older people had the skill, but the younger people ain't interested."

Other inquiries produced the same result. Folks were polite but noncommittal. Yes, root doctors had existed. No, they didn't know of any practicing now. But the faces were furtive.

Later I would find I was up against two obstacles. The first was one of wise circumspection. South Carolina has no laws against casting or removing hexes, but anyone who gives a client a salve, body oil, or any potion taken internally can be cited for practicing medicine without a license. I might have been an undercover agent, albeit a dim-witted one.

The second obstacle was one of skin tone.

"You're white," John Hendrix, the Episcopal priest, told me later. "They don't trust you."

After a few inquiries I stopped asking. It was pointless to continue, and frankly I like to draw a line between curious and nosy. If the residents of St. Helena didn't feel like giving up their root doctors, that was fine by me. Plus, if I didn't broach the subject of voodoo, people treated me kindly. They politely inquired about my business ("You about three months too late. Most tourists come in the summer.") and willingly volunteered details of their own lives and their island at length.

"Don't mind talkin' at all," said a straight-backed elderly gent named Robert. "It's enjoyable to look back where you came from, talk about the people you grew up with, the stories. It's good to look back."

Robert was in his late seventies. He had grown up on St. Helena in a different time. He spoke slowly, considering his thoughts before voicing them.

"Back then there weren't that many jobs here. Mostly farmin', fishin', and survival. Everybody was like family. You could go from one house to another freely. No one had locks on their doors like they do today. It was a community. Everybody had their own little farm. Whatever you made, you sold or you shared from one person to another. My father told me, 'If you have a roof over your head, a meal on the table, and Christ in your life, you're lucky.' "

He had left the island to fight in Korea, then lived in Philadelphia for a time before coming home. He had never doubted where he would come to rest. "I love this place more than I do anyplace else. We still don't have a whole lot here, but most everybody is happy. And something you don't have much in the world today is happiness."

We stood in the shadows of a grove of great oaks. It was still. A pleasant lassitude held sway, a lassitude that permeated the whole island. On the glassy waters even the ripples spread slowly.

"Yes," said Robert, "I love this place more than I do anyplace else."

When I left St. Helena, an enormous sun hung low, ladling the creeks and marshes a blood-orange hue. The island disappeared behind me, as stoic as time.

Apparently I hadn't been the first to experience this mute stonewalling. "Pot smugglers were more willing to talk than root doctors," Roger Pinckney once lamented in a magazine interview.

Pinckney is the author of *Blue Roots,* a book detailing the root in Beaufort County, where Pinckney was born and raised. His own roots didn't help him much. Apparently the black community was equally reticent to help its white own.

Still, Pinckney's book provided me with the link I needed. In *Blue Roots*—named after the dreaded blue root, known to cause wells and cows to dry up, and to bring on fearsome ailments and death—Pinckney documented the exploits of J. E. (Ed) McTeer, who was appointed Beaufort County sheriff in 1926 at age twenty-two and served the office fully and well until his retirement in 1962. He came to be famously known as the High Sheriff of the Low Country, his fame deriving in part from his purportedly powerful skills as a root doctor.

Over the years stories accumulated like Spanish moss, and McTeer's legend grew with them. Once, writes Pinckney, the sheriff entered a local beer joint to investigate a problem. The lights went out, and gunfire erupted. When silence settled, the sheriff stepped outside, suspect in hand. The suspect had emptied his gun of bullets; McTeer's gun had never left his holster. Word spread. Powerful magic had made the High Sheriff bulletproof. McTeer himself didn't discount this rumor. Later, shot at by a burglary suspect, McTeer refused to let the prosecutor add "attempted murder" to the charges. "There was no murder attempted, since he had no chance of hitting me," the sheriff reportedly explained.

McTeer battled bad roots where he could, most notably locking horns with the infamous Dr. Buzzard, the most powerful, and feared, root doctor of the time. McTeer was white and Buzzard was black, though skin color mattered little in this clash of clever wills. Those who believed in the power of the root didn't put any stock in skin color. They turned to the man who could save them from grievous harm.

It wasn't McTeer who eventually put Buzzard away, though not for lack of trying. The State of South Carolina eventually nailed Buzzard for practicing medicine without a license. But at one point during the McTeer/Buzzard battle of wills, Buzzard's son was killed in a car accident. Word wafted through wood and marsh. The accident was no accident. The High Sheriff had inflicted grievous harm on his foe.

Perhaps to underscore his invincibility—but more likely to live in a fine and pretty spot—McTeer moved his own family to the heart of root country and St. Helena, buying a plantation spread between sound and sea ironically named Coffin Point. The High Sheriff died in 1976, but a passage in Pinckney's book nailed itself to my eye.

"His youngest son," wrote Pinckney, "has begun to dabble in his father's work, and is one of the few—if not the only—white root-workers in Beaufort County."

Blue Roots was resting on Thomas McTeer's bookshelf when I visited him a few days after my foray onto St. Helena. The High Sheriff's son, now nearly sixty himself, lives with his wife and two grown children in a nondescript brick house on a suburban Beaufort street.

"That boy Roger Pinckney is my wife's first cousin," said Thomas, eyeing the book on the shelf. "I'm not all that crazy about his book. I don't think I ever finished it."

Ed McTeer's son has an open face, a friendly easy manner, and a throaty cough, the last vestiges, he said, of a respiratory problem known locally as the Beaufort Crud. "Man, it's killin' me. Comes around every year. I think I'm almost over it."

We sat out on his back porch, which commands a lovely view of the marsh and beyond it the Beaufort River. In the silence birds cried, and frequently we heard the distant rumble of jets taking off from the Marine Corps air station across the river.

Thomas answered my questions directly, with nary a sign of the squirming and hairsplitting I had seen in my other sources. No, he had never seriously practiced root doctoring himself. He'd made a root or two, but only as a joke. Yes, he believed root doctors still practiced their magic, though he also believed the art was fading. Yes, his father had practiced voodoo.

"He was what they referred to as a white witch doctor," said Thomas matter-of-factly. "Not white because he was white, but because he practiced white voodoo. He took bad roots off of people.

Over time he developed a reputation among the local population for having some sense of understanding voodoo, and the power to be able to implement it. People would come to him that were blind, or their legs had quit working. They had bad roots on them. He'd put a good root back on them and make sure the person understood that the good root had overpowered the evil one."

"You've seen it work?"

"I've seen 'em come in blind and go out seeing. I've seen 'em come in can't walk and go out dancing. I've seen 'em come in can't talk and go out saying the Lord's Prayer."

Thomas saw the look on my face. He chuckled and tapped his forehead.

"It's a psychology thing. Some people referred to my dad as the poor man's psychiatrist. That's kind of what it's all about really. It's all upstairs. The whole voodoo thing is all psychological. Everybody knows there is no person in the world who can cut the head off a chicken and hide it under your mattress and make you get a backache. It physically can't be done. But it can be done through the mind. It's a big mental thing, is all it is. My mom and my sisters would make the roots for him."

I had done enough reading to know that good roots could contain gunpowder, sulphur, salt, red or black candle wax, or dirt from the grave of a righteous Christian. Bad roots often contained animal parts—crow feathers, salamander feet, a black cat's left thigh bone—or dirt from a murderer's grave.

This stuff wasn't easy to come by.

"What was in the roots?" I asked.

"Awww, shit out of the yard probably. You can put anything in there you want. You can just make stuff up. Yeah, right. The left eye of a titmouse caught on Thursday."

We both laughed.

I asked Thomas about some of the stories. Had his father walked away from a shower of gunfire without ever pulling his own pistol? Possibly, said Thomas. But he never carried a pistol in a holster, though he did keep a .38 special under the seat of his car.

What did he think about the story of his father being responsible for Dr. Buzzard's son's car accident and death?

Oddly, Thomas answered in indirect fashion. "I never did come right out and ask my dad did that happen." He went quiet.

I liked Thomas. He had welcomed me into his home and treated me hospitably. Though we had known each other for only an hour, sitting on the back porch I felt we enjoyed a kind of friendly camaraderie.

But I had to ask. It seemed a ridiculous question, but I was curious what the answer would be: "Was your father capable of that sort of thing?"

"Of what?"

"Of making an accident happen?"

Thomas was polite enough not to call me an idiot. Then again, maybe he had seen enough oddities to cause him to question the standard line between fact and fantasy.

"Nobody can cause an event to happen," he said. "But you can take an event and make it seem to have happened a certain way. The real art form is to have other people do it for you; then you're not involved in the loop at all, so all the credibility is there. My dad didn't run around the streets going, 'I'm a voodoo doctor.' But he didn't discourage the stories, either. Might have happened kind of that way, might not have happened at all. But sometimes those kinds of little legends become fact after a while."

He laughed.

"There's a statute of limitations on what's fiction and what's fact."

The conversation idled away from voodoo. We talked for a time about black-white relations. When it came to blacks, said Thomas, Beaufort County had long been something of a liberal bastion. Penn School, the first trade and agricultural school for freedmen, had been founded in 1862 on St. Helena Island. Blacks, he said, had always received better treatment in Beaufort County than in other parts of the South. The High Sheriff of the Low Country had been a shining example. "My dad was known to be a very fair and equitable person to both white and black. For that reason black people tended to trust him, certainly more than they would a lot of white sheriffs of that era."

He paused and drew on his cigarette, then turned his blue eyes to the marsh. I watched a pair of squirrels chase each other around the trunk of an oak.

"They say Dr. Buzzard's grandson still practices on St. Helena," said Thomas. "But it's not like it used to be. Up through the sixties this area was as rural and backwater as any place in the country. Those old beliefs were sort of fermenting here and being passed around among the community. But society has changed. There's too much knowledge now. Information is everywhere. It undermines the real deep spiritual beliefs of people. They become more worldly and less inclined to believe in voodoo, or even religion and God. Kids today, things are concrete. You've got to be able to hold it in your hands or see it on TV."

A breeze carried a crow's strident cry in from the marsh. The tide was out, and the exposed mud, liquid and shiny, radiated the smell of decay.

Then Thomas said, "I got a bag full of bad roots my dad took off of people. He'd keep the roots."

A cloud seemed to pass over the sun.

"We found them in a box when we were cleaning up after he died. Nobody else in the family wanted them, so I took 'em."

I didn't ask the question, because Thomas answered it before I could. He had a half-smile on his face, but there was no humor in it.

"I don't bring them out. I keep 'em put away up in the attic. I'm leery about even handling them. They're bad roots. There's enough of that up here"—he tapped his forehead—"that could transpose into everyday life. I suppose I have a good deal of respect for that sort of thing."

Another jet rumble drifted across the marsh.

"My dad, he truly believed. The evidence was right in front of him. If you do certain things, it can have a certain effect on people. It happens through the mind, that's the only way it can work, but the mind is a powerful thing. We don't really understand what it's totally capable of."

Before I left, Thomas took me back inside and showed me a small plaque on the wall. It read, "To J. E. McTeer Sheriff Humanitarian Robert Smalls Sr. HI 1962."

"There's not much to it, but that plaque speaks more to me about my dad than any other thing he has," said Thomas. "Robert Smalls High School was a segregated black school in 1962. For a white sheriff in the late fifties and early sixties to get something like that from a group of black people was an incredible statement in itself."

And, I thought, perhaps the man was magic.

6
MURRELLS INLET
The Last Little Piece of Heaven

THE LAST LITTLE PIECE of heaven sits at a fork in the road. It is not heaven as most people think of it. For one thing there are no angels, at least not in the traditional sense. It is just over two acres of woods, except for a clearing with a fire ring, a horseshoe pit, and a trailer, white with brown trim and neatly lived in. Even in November when the trees are bare, they still press together closely enough to hide heaven from the road.

To reach Harry Strayer's trailer, you drive along Route 17, heading north from Georgetown, South Carolina. The road forks just before Harry's place, offering you a chance to continue along the main route or take the business bypass into Murrells Inlet. These days the main artery of Route 17 has a considerable flow of traffic year round, thanks to burgeoning growth in the area fueled by Myrtle Beach, seventeen miles to the north. But fork off onto business 17 and into Murrells Inlet in late November, and the road is largely leaves blowing in circles.

To reach Harry's, though, you stay on the main thoroughfare. Most everybody passes by Harry's trailer except for the folks who count, whipping past R N S Auto Sales ("Walk In—Drive Out Now!!") and the dirt driveway meandering into the woods. Without thought, you pass hundreds of thousands of turnoffs like this. Harry's mailing address is simply Route 17 Bypass. It is still a quiet place. Mickey Spillane, the mystery writer, lives around the corner.

On a brisk South Carolina morning, the sun just risen and not yet around to warming away the frost, Matt Lebherz and I bumped down Harry's drive. Matt is an old friend. This small slice of coastal Carolina has been his home now for twenty years. The place suits him. The pace is slow, and if you know where to look, people's hearts are big. Without Matt I never would have found Harry, Cotton, the H&C Fish House, or the Coffee Club. None of them hanker for attention.

The world today is filled with people who tout themselves as characters or yearn for recognition—usually both—and there is no shortage of media outlets hungry to acknowledge them. We have made great cultural advances. A generation ago sharing a bathroom with a TV crew while you flossed your teeth would have been cause for alarm; today it is opportunity for a book deal. I was interested in people who didn't particularly want to be found. They weren't hermits; they were simply comfortable leading their own lives, from birth to death, without ever needing an audience. A lot of these people have fled to the water's edge because this is as far away from today's silliness as they can run.

In Murrells Inlet I was told to look up a fisherman named Eddy Clark. Several years back Eddy's boat had been cleaved in two by a freighter. This sounded interesting. I found Eddy hurrying up from the dock.

"Come back Saturday afternoon," he said, giving me a toothy grin. "I got me a TV show and everything." That was enough for me. I saw no more of Eddy.

Harry and Cotton don't have their own TV show, though the TV in Harry's trailer is on pretty much constantly. Sometimes it provides backdrop in the form of country music videos. Sometimes it provides opportunity for commentary. Other times the Weather Channel is on and the sound is off with jazz playing, since weather pretty much explains itself.

When Matt and I pulled into the woods at just past seven, a pickup was already parked outside Harry's trailer. The woods were quiet and bathed in dusty morning light. When we knocked on the trailer's door, a voice boomed inside: "I'd get up, but that would be polite."

The inside of the trailer was dimly lit. Two men were seated on couches, a coffee table between them. The man closest to the front door was burly, with gold-wire glasses and a short gray beard, neatly trimmed. The other man was slight and in the half-light nearly invisible in a ball cap and baggy sweatshirt that read "Still Crazy Fishing Fleet." The big man who had issued our welcome was Harry Strayer. Harry looks a little like Burl Ives, only with a rougher edge. He was wearing a rumpled T-shirt, his meaty white legs stuck out of black gym shorts, and the hair that remained on his head poked out in various directions. He could have just rolled out of bed, and he might have, seeing as his bedroom was five steps away. The smaller man was Cotton.

Harry gestured toward the kitchen. "Help yourselves."

There was hot water on the stove, and a sugar bowl, a jar of Folger's instant coffee, and some mugs on the counter. The Coffee Club operates simply. Those with an open invitation, fishermen mostly, stop by Harry's in the morning before they start their day. The Coffee Club operates six days a week, except for Sunday mornings, which Harry likes to have to himself. It's a crowd in flux. If the boats are out, it isn't a crowd at all. If the boats are in, it's a full trailer. The men sprawl on Harry's couches, smoking and drinking coffee and making idle talk beneath the black marble eyes of a white tail and mule deer. Fine art lines the wood-paneled walls. "Beer," reads a poster in the hallway, "Helping Ugly People Have Sex Since 1862." There is a small aquarium, with tropical fish drifting in a bluish light. Cotton often arrives first at the Coffee Club. He picks Harry's paper up out of the dirt and reads it in the cab of his truck. By the time he's through with the first column, Harry is usually up and boiling water. It's nothing planned—everybody just comes by. Even when Harry is gone, they come over. Hot water's ready by seven. Generally everybody is gone by eight.

Not everyone is welcome. Harry keeps an eye on the clientele. Fishermen are a fast-living bunch. Harry doesn't object. He's a fisherman and has lived plenty fast himself. His son goes to the University of North Florida, but Harry can't drive there to see him because Harry lived in Florida long enough to run afoul of Florida's DUI laws. But Harry knows the difference between good and bad. There are fishermen who spend all their money on drugs. They aren't welcome in Harry's trailer, though he has quietly seen to it that there's Christmas money for their kids.

"Fishermen are mostly fine fellows," said Harry. "You won't meet anybody around my house that isn't. The sorry ones don't come around."

Today's crowd numbered three. The fishing boats were out. Harry was temporarily unemployed. Matt was painting. Cotton boxes fish at the H&C Fish House just around the corner, a job he has held longer than most people can remember, and longer than he likes. "It ain't no glamorous job messin' with fish all day," he grumbled.

"Cotton likes to bitch about his job," said Harry. "If he's not complainin', he's not happy."

Cotton smiled wryly. "I'm always happy."

In the days I spent with Cotton, I saw he is spare with words: the H&C Fish House is "the House." His sentences are equally concise. When the boats are in, the fish spill off the conveyor belt like a piscine monsoon, and Cotton's world narrows to ticking time. While boxing fish, he speaks only when he has to. If a fisherman begins some idle banter, Cotton often becomes annoyed. Words chip away at time. Even away from the job it is as if words still get in the way. His real name is Gary Collins, but plenty of the fishermen, many of whom have known him for years, don't know who the hell Gary Collins is. Cotton is Cotton. One word is better than two.

Cotton is Cotton because of his white hair, cinched curly and close to his head. He is as much a part of Murrells Inlet as the silent inlet itself. "Everybody knows him," a fisherman told me. "He's been here for ages. He's just Cotton."

The conversation in Harry's trailer unspooled casually, filled with comfortable gaps of silence. Coffee aroma commingled with smoke, the two scrolling up to the ceiling. It was like waking up slowly in your own home.

An infomercial unfolded on the TV. A half-dozen perfectly proportioned models stood around an exercise machine that none of them needed, murmuring appreciatively as one of their number pushed and pulled at the machine's bowed extensions. Everyone glistened as if they had been dipped in motor oil, though the lubricant had done nothing to loosen up their repartee.

"My!" said one of the models enthusiastically. *"You won't find this kind of workout anywhere!"*

"No!" said another. *"It's hard work, but it gets results in no time!"*

The models who hadn't gotten these plum speaking roles were focusing on holding their breath and flexing. They smiled warmly at one another, and we all secretly wondered who among them would be the first to explode.

Harry looked down at his ample belly. "Shit. I need to lose some weight. I was a lot thinner when I was fishing." He was off the water at the moment, courtesy of torn tendons in his right shoulder. "Hunting accident."

"He slipped and fell." Matt grinned.

"I heard a fish break in this creek and I walked over to check it out and I slipped." Harry shook his head slowly. "I don't fall very good anymore." He put his hand to his shoulder and rotated his arm. "Now the shoulder pops and grinds."

"Mine, too," said Matt.

"That's from jerking off," said Harry.

All three men have their share of pains. Cotton has shoulder problems. Matt, who also worked for a time boxing fish at H&C, has undergone a hip replacement—his genetically weak bone was weakened further by 130-pound boxes and concrete floors. He is now painting. Harry has an ugly scar on his right ankle. When he got up for more coffee, he limped into the kitchen. "I was finned." He poured more coffee. "Big gutted grouper lying on the deck. The boat listed, and its fins flared, and it stuck right into me. Stupid. I was wearing flip-flops." He settled back on the couch. "I have trouble with my ankles swelling up, too."

"Is that from the finning?" I asked.

"No. It's the constant motion on a boat for years and years. You're always having to counterbalance yourself wherever you go. It catches up with you after a while."

After about thirty minutes Cotton stubbed out his Marlboro Light and unfolded from the couch, with a final glance at the TV. "Waaaaall, I got to be going," he said.

I glanced at my watch. It was 7:40. After a few days I made a game of it. I doubt it was coincidence that Cotton unfolded from the couch each morning at precisely the same time.

Matt left, too. Harry and I listened as Cotton's pickup started up.

"Cotton's funny," Harry said. "You know when he talks, he sometimes mixes up his words and we make fun of him. You talk about numbers, though; he'll spit shit out that will blow your mind. The best I've ever seen."

I stayed and talked with Harry, who is smart and articulate. He wanted to go to college, but his timing was bad ("I just had too big a wild hare in my ass"), so he started fishing instead. Thirty years have come and gone. Now he is putting his own son through college. He will never have a degree, but he knows how the world turns and where his place is in it.

"My daddy was a fisherman and I was a fisherman," he said. "Fishing's been real good to me. I put two kids through college. Now I'm fifty years old and broke. So as soon as this shoulder's healed, it's back to fishing I go. It's not a bad thing. I know more of what I'm doin' when I'm out there than I do when I'm on the hill. Out there, there's nothing else to do except for what we're supposed to be doin'. It's a good, simple place."

Soliloquies like this lead many to romanticize fishing. Ah, the fisherman: astride the deck, awash in independence, answering to none but the salty sea.

Truth is, commercial fishing is a more complex business, and the salty sea weighs in on only part of it. Earlier that week I had read a newspaper article about the hazards of commercial fishing. According to the article, 152 of every 100,000 fishermen are killed on the job, the highest fatality rate of any profession, a notch higher than loggers and nine times the rate of firefighters and policemen. The article ran down the litany of possibilities. Boats capsize and sink in fierce storms, fires burn boats to the waterline, and freighters run them down. Fishermen ignore or can't afford safety equipment. Some simply slip and fall overboard on the calmest of nights.

These dangers are familiar to most of us, but there are others you might not consider. In the early 1970s Harry was fishing out of Jacksonville, Florida, with a friend who was a retired cop. The man woke Harry in the middle of the night, waving a pistol in his face, shouting about them being boarded.

"He was all kinds of excited," said Harry. "I'm going, 'Now chill out.' Back then I carried this sawed-off shotgun on board. I'd tell people it was for the sharks, but it had other uses. He's radioing the Coast Guard shouting to them about us being boarded and giving them our coordinates. I went out on the deck. I could see this other boat. All the lights were off but one, and I could see them lowering a boat off the stern. You could barely hear their motor. My friend is still radioing the Coast Guard, and I'm saying to him, 'Nobody's crossing this water in front of a sawed-off shotgun.' But looking back on it, it's a good thing he got on the radio because they didn't come across, and that may have been what scared them off."

I tried to piece this together, but it was easier to ask, "What were they doing?"

Harry took a sip of coffee. "Well, that night I was guessing it was one of two things. They were coming for help, or they were coming for my boat. Well, the Coast Guard caught 'em the next day. I walked into a mini-mart, and there's a picture on the front page of the newspaper of that same goddamn boat right there. The *Heidi*. I mean it stopped me dead in my tracks. And it was full of pot. Full."

"What would have happened to you?"

Harry stubbed out his cigarette. "They come on board, slit your stomach open, and throw you overboard, and you're fish food. They use your boat to run the drugs ashore, and then they sink it. Nobody ever knows what happened to you."

There are other instances where fishermen simply disappear. Collisions with freighters are not at all uncommon, and the end result is often fatal for the fishermen since commercial freighters are now the size of small countries and commercial fishing boats are not. A commercial freighter running down a fishing boat experiences much the same sensation you do when stepping on a beetle in thick grass. "Everybody has had close calls with ships late in the night," said Harry. "The ones that get run down, well, they're gone, and the freighter keeps right on truckin'."

Harry had had his own near miss. He was fishing off Cape Fear, North Carolina, that time. He knew he was in a shipping lane, but he had been fishing a sunken wreck and the fishing was good, and when he finally lay down at two in the morning, he was too tired to move off. Later that night he went up onto the deck to pee, groggily noting that it was a velvet-black night.

"I looked up for the stars and couldn't see anything. That ship passed about thirty feet from us. I could have thrown a rock and hit it. Easily. I guarantee you, they never saw me. I've only been scared a few times in my life, rubber-knee scared. That was one of those times. I was sleeping so hard, I didn't hear a thing. Usually when you're lying there with your head on the pillow, you can hear the prop thumping."

On TV a cowboy on a barstool was picking a guitar while women in tight jeans and T-shirts gyrated around him. The cowboy was nonchalant, but Harry was interested. "That boat was called the *Still Crazy I*," said Harry, idly watching the TV.

"Are there other *Still Crazys*?" I asked.

Harry smiled. "All the boats down there at the H&C are named the *Still Crazy.*"

"Is there a reason for that?"

"Absolutely," said Harry, though he paused a few ticks before thinking of the best one. "I guess it takes fishermen a long time to grow up. Too much fresh air or something."

Harry—fifty, broke, sore, low on Folger's, and lucky to be alive—certainly felt that way.

"I have really good friends," he said. "If something happened, I could pick up the phone and ask them for something, and they won't ask why. You'll find a lot of good people in fishing."

Cotton is one of them.

❧

THE NEXT MORNING when Cotton unfolded from the couch to drive to the H&C Fish House, I went out behind him. But I wanted to give him time to get situated before I started following him around asking inane questions, so I drove the length of Murrells Inlet first. This took five minutes. Going north, the two-lane road first passes a few simple ranch-style homes, their docks poking out into the sun-spackled inlet. At Morse Landing Park, a banner read "MI Xmas Tree LTN Dec. 1," and across the browning grass the inlet spreads perhaps a mile until it abuts the low slash and big summer homes of Garden City, the barrier island that separates Murrells Inlet from the Atlantic Ocean. Then there was a flurry of fisheries. Murrells Inlet claims to be the seafood capital of South Carolina, and I certainly won't argue the point, though not just because I sampled the local cuisine. Lining the road there was Murrells Inlet Shrimp & Fish, Nance's Restaurant, Admiral's Flagship, the Inlet Grille, Inlet Seafood Hut, Harrelson's Seafood Market, Dockside Restaurant, Drunken Jacks ("All u can eat crabs/crab legs"), Seafare Restaurant, the Captain's Restaurant, Fisherman's Market Restaurant, and Seven Seas Seafood Market. Finally came a small wood sign—"We Hope You Enjoyed Our Inlet. Please Visit Again!"—and then Murrells Inlet was gone; 3.6 miles total. The town was named for John Morrall, who did nothing other than buy 610 acres on the inlet in 1731. I liked that.

I drove back and parked in a dirt lot next door to the H&C Fish House. The fish house borders the business bypass, but you could easily miss it. It's nothing fancy, a squarish building, white on the bottom, wood up top, with a big opening out front where the trucks pull up and load the fish. It isn't a big place. H&C shares half the building with a scuba shop.

Today H&C sat under a blue sky and fleecy clouds, the picture of serenity. A sign on the front door read "Authorized Personnel Only," but I walked right in because I was with Cotton.

Some days when a load of boats is in, Cotton arrives at the fish house at eight in the morning and doesn't leave until ten at night, and he moves quickly most all that time. A boat with three thousand pounds of big fish—say, grouper or amberjack—might take ninety minutes to unload. A boat with a like amount of small fish might take two hours. Bring six boats in to the dock at the same time, and you have a full day.

No boats were in today. Two boats were expected in tomorrow and Cotton was ready for them, so aside from wiring together boxes, he had time to give me a tour. Still, I felt funny. Harry had told me that no one worked harder than Cotton, and he didn't like to be interrupted while he was at it.

"Sorry to make trouble for you," I said, and meant it. "I know tours aren't part of your normal work day."

Cotton waved away my guilt. "It ain't no trouble. Though I'm not as apt to be social on a busy day."

Like Murrells Inlet, the H&C is a model of simple efficiency. The first floor is dominated by a single large room, mostly open, with concrete floors and a few steel tables. One end opens to the dock and boat on the water, the other to the freezer trucks. The crews toss the fish onto a conveyor belt, which ferries the fish up to the warehouse. There Cotton, and whoever else might be working, sorts the fish by species and size, tossing them into their respective boxes, where they are sandwiched between ice. The wooden boxes have four sides and come as long slats. Cotton assembles them—a bottom, four sides, and no top—by cinching down their metal wiring with deft screwdriver twists. At the moment the wooden boxes ran up the walls, precisely stacked and waiting. Just inside the loading dock I counted twelve rows of boxes, six high. Most of the time Cotton has at least two hundred empty boxes ready.

Several rooms branched off the main area. Cotton swung open a heavy freezer door. The fish cooler was smoky cold and filled with boxes. Inside, boxes of glistening fish rested under ice. Some were spotted and dull brown. Others were cheerily colored and striped.

They came in a marvelous spectrum of shapes—from sleeker than torpedoes to nearly as round as dinner plates. Cotton moved from box to box, pushing aside ice with his hands.

"That's your yellowfin tunas. That's pompano. That's swordfish; I think they got those in Florida. This here's your scamp grouper, and these are triggerfish." He lifted a fish, easily recognizable by its pan-flat shape. "Flounder's local. Last week there were about 22,000 pounds of fish in here. We average about 60,000 pounds a month. We run through a pretty good number of fish. Probably pack more bottom fish than any fish house on the East Coast."

In another room a man named Joe was cleaning fish, expertly carving them up into squares, then sliding them into plastic bags and weighing them. Beside him a trash can was filled with fish guts, skin, and bone. He gave me a brief nod and went back to work.

Cotton peered into a wheelbarrow that contained a long, sleek decapitated fish. "This here is your dolphin," he said. "They call it mahimahi, because it sounds better than flipper."

The mahimahi, flown in from South America, would soon end up on a local restaurant table. But most of the rest of the H&C's fish go north to Baltimore, New York, Montreal, Ontario, and Quebec. But as far as those diners are concerned, they were caught in the kitchen, then cooked and prettily garnished, their long journey as invisible as this quiet man.

"Do you eat much fish?" I asked.

"I eat plenty of fish," said Cotton, "though I prefer shrimp and crab. I see more than enough fish in my day."

Upstairs there were some small offices. When Cotton took me up to use the bathroom, a man on the telephone turned at his desk and gave me a dull, unfriendly look. I hesitated, but Cotton ignored him.

"The sign on the door says 'Out of Order,' but that's bullshit," Cotton said loud enough for both of us to hear. "They just don't want anybody usin' it." He wasn't exactly sure what went on upstairs, but whatever it was, he wasn't sure it was necessary.

"How many people work here?" I asked, when we'd left the sourpuss upstairs.

"Three," said Cotton. "We had a guy who just left. There's a new guy upstairs now learnin' the ropes. I don't know what the hell he does. He's sellin' the fish. Fish sell itself. They're here every week. There's two owners, too, but they ain't around much."

"How many people are involved in the hands-on stuff?"

"Ninety percent's me."

Harry had told me the H&C's owners were both millionaires. I had seen Cotton's truck. It seemed a shame to do all the work, with so little stake in the profit.

"Do you ever wish you worked for yourself?" I asked.

In a small town you don't have to look far to see your mistakes. Cotton walked slowly to the front of the building where it looked out onto the empty street. There was no bitterness in his voice, just a simple accounting. "I should be packin' my own fish." He gazed across the street, then paused.

A cool breeze came in off the inlet, blowing through the innards of the H&C, snatching up the sharp and briny odor of fresh fish on its way.

"I used to have my own place, but I let my partner buy me out," said Cotton. "I messed up. See that fence over yonder? Well, there's a building over there. It's called Southbend Seafood now. It used to be called Sea and Sea. That was mine."

I didn't press him for more.

A weathered Ford truck pulled up. A man who looked to be in his sixties exited spryly and trotted up the stairs. There was no exchange of greetings.

"How ya' doin' with the quittin' smokin'?" asked Cotton.

"You got some?" said the man.

"I've got some Marlboros," said Cotton. "You helpin' me out by smokin' 'em."

The man took the offered cigarette, tapping it in his hand. "Today's the Great American Smokeout, I heard."

The two men smoked and considered this fact.

❧

THE NEXT MORNING I saw Cotton in action. When I pulled into the lot next to the H&C, a full moon was descending in the pale blue sky. Inside Cotton was already on the move. He glanced up and nod-ded to me. He kept it brief, but his manner was friendly.

"There's two boats in," he said. "First boat got about fourteen hundred pounds. Other one, maybe a hundred pounds. The one boat had to tow the other in. A busted trip."

Three empty boxes sat at the end of the conveyor belt, a shovel-ful of ice in the bottom of each one. The smaller fish would come off first. If the crew packed the smaller fish on the bottom out at sea they'd be crushed by the heavier fish bouncing around above them. The first lot up the belt would be vermilion snapper.

Several fishermen stood watching, including the captain of one of the boats. Cotton flicked a switch, and the conveyor droned to life. He stepped into a worn yellow slicker, hitched the shoulder straps over his gray H&C T-shirt, and pulled on a pair of rubber gloves and boots that looked as if they'd been plunged directly into the trash can of fish offal and wiped clean in the dark.

Cotton had two clipboards and one helper, Jo Jo, who looked to be in his mid-thirties. His dark hair was neatly combed, and an expensive-looking pair of sunglasses perched atop his head. He was wearing dress slacks under his slicker and trod about in rubber boots that were Suzy Chapstick white. Jo Jo was the biggest man in the room, but among Cotton and the lean, sun-burnished fisherman he looked soft and white, like a frat boy who had mistakenly crashed a party for Navy SEALs. Jo Jo had been at H&C for only about six weeks.

The snapper—lovely rose-hued fish—came up the conveyor and dropped into a box. Cotton plucked them up with nary a look, simultaneously assessed their weight by heft—three-quarters of a pound to a pound, one to two pounds, two to four pounds—and in the single same smooth motion laid them out neatly in their respec-tive boxes. Jo Jo resembles a blackjack dealer with Alzheimer's. He scooped the fish slowly, as if the air were thicker where he stood, and held them for a few ticks or more, now and again gazing intently at them as if they were an old forgotten friend. Rapid fire or no, the fish went into a box. When a box was ready, it was dragged over to the scale, weighed, and marked, and a shovelful of ice was thrown on top. Music boomed from a beat-up radio: Hendrix, Steppenwolf, the Doors.

I knew from the previous day's tour that each box should contain roughly fifty pounds of fish. The box had a weight of its own, plus the ice, so Cotton had to factor that in. When Cotton figured a box had reached its limit, he yanked it over to the scale.

"I shoot for fifty-one point one to fifty-two point six pounds, box and all, and I just round it off to fifty," he said.

A box was hefted on to the scale. One of the fisherman called off the weight: "Fifty-one point six."

I smiled, and Cotton grinned. "I get close every now and then," he said.

Cotton scratched figures on every box—"50," "1–2," and "II"—etchings that appeared runic until he explained them. " 'Fifty' is pounds, 'one to two' is the weight of the fish, and the 'II' is for fish that come off the *Still Crazy II.*" Cotton moved back to the conveyor. "That way if someone comes back and says that fish was weak or that fish was real pretty, I know what boat it came from. These fish'll be goin' to Montreal tomorrow."

After a time I saw that there were numbers everywhere. They spilled from the holds of the boats out into the sunshine, swam about in the cavern of the H&C, and affixed themselves to boxes and clipboards with the precision of perfectly thrown darts. The boxes weighed 6.4 pounds. A shovelful of ice, five pounds. Sixty thousand pounds of fish went through this routine each month, nearly every pound fixed and noted by Cotton's vigilant eye. Ounces were not set adrift. Ounces became pounds, and pounds were dollars.

The choreography, at least on Cotton's part, was equally precise. Not once did Cotton stop; nor did he look around for anything, unless someone else had misplaced it. Boxes stood at the ready, and clipboards hung on the wall. Everything was numbers and dance steps. Cotton knew them all. Rain Man meets Arthur Murray.

It was inspiring to watch. I told Cotton that Harry had said he was a genius with numbers, and that I believed Harry.

"I guess I can count," said Cotton.

He yanked a box up off the floor. Cotton hadn't been a particularly impressive physical specimen when slouched on Harry's couch. Now I noticed that his back was broad, and when he picked up a box, his forearms flared. I imagined the glistening infomercial models eyeing one another mutely in intensive care. *My! You won't find this kind of workout anywhere!*

Jo Jo was decidedly less focused than Cotton. He had been out at a bar last night. He'd had a time and was eager to talk, mostly about near conquests with various women. He plucked a fish from the conveyor, regarded it as if he'd never seen a fish before, then absently pitched it into an adjacent box. Now and again his cell phone rang, and he pulled it from under his bib and carried on a casual conversation. Cotton wouldn't have taken a call from God, unless God knew of a misplaced box of snapper.

Cotton turned to me. His tone wasn't malicious, just matter-of-fact. "See Jo Jo, he likes to shoot the shit a lot. He don't like to work. Wearin' those polo shirts and that Ralph Lauren shit. A rich kid come to work for his buddy."

Jo Jo was not the first miscast Man of the Sea, and he wouldn't be the last. Would-be Jack Londons show up on the Murrells Inlet docks regularly, hankering for a life at sea. Sometimes the boat captains take them because they are strong-backed and tough. These types leave the dock standing tall, brimming with the prospect of cash and adventure. They return to the dock oddly bent and lurching, and if they can drive, they promptly make a beeline for the Midwest, where they no doubt received a respectful berth, wearing, as they do, vacant-eyed looks and clothing that looks as if it has been used to mop up an explosion in a pizza factory. Puking won't kill you, though many have sorely wished it would. Jo Jo will eventually go. Cotton will remain.

I liked Jo Jo. I believed he was good-hearted, just misplaced. Later when the two of us were standing alone, he turned to me. "I got this girl flying in today," he said quietly. "She's real nice. I think she might be the one. I'd like to settle down."

The fish kept coming, and they got bigger—amberjack, grouper, and red snapper. They too went into their respective boxes. Still, the catch was lousy. The one boat had broken down. The other had had to cut short its trip to tow the crippled boat in.

"No matter how much you dislike people, out there there's no repair shops, so you got to help your fellow man," said Larry Smith.

Captain Larry is beanpole-built, with reddish hair going gray and a goatee doing the same. When he smiles, he displays teeth admirably crooked. Fishing doesn't come with a dental plan. I was never sure if Larry's was the boat that had been towed or done the towing. I didn't ask—I didn't want to rub his nose in sad circumstance—and he never did say.

Whatever the circumstance, Larry didn't seem upset by it. He ambled about, peering into boxes, though I noticed he stayed out of Cotton's way. He walked me over to a box and gestured at the grouper inside. The gape-mouthed fish had been neatly halved with a clean horseshoe bite. "See what that shark done," beamed Larry. "Probably a mako."

"What happens to that fish?" I asked.

Cotton walked past, whistling "L.A. Woman," and gave the box a dismissive glance. "Can't sell it."

Larry grinned. "I eat it."

※

By 9:45 it was all over, even the math. Captain Larry had gone back down to the dock, but he was back in time for Cotton's tally.

"There you go, Cap," said Cotton. "You got fifty pounds of grouper, twelve pounds of ling, twenty-eight trigger, and thirty-six caberra. All right, suh?"

It wasn't all right. It was a busted trip. Before he walked back to the dock, Captain Larry handed me a plastic bag with several thick slabs of neatly filleted grouper.

"There you go, friend," he said. "Fresh fish for dinner."

When I told Cotton about Larry's kindness, he nodded. "Fishermen are good sorts," he said. "They just fish, and drink, and drug."

I saw Larry's crooked grin and remembered Harry's words and eyes. "They seem happy," I said.

Cotton consulted his clipboard. "Well, they don't know if they're happy or not."

After the boats had been unloaded, I went for a walk. Being a weekday in November, most places were closed. But Perry's Bait & Tackle was open. I found that out when I stepped up to read a piece of yellow paper taped to the window. It was a notice that read, "Wal-Mart in Murrells Inlet? Get the facts, Pro and Con Wednesday November 20 6:30 P.M. Family Life Center Belin Memorial United Methodist Church. An Evening for Our Future."

It was November 21, but I was curious, so I stepped inside. Winston Perry was sitting in the back in an overstuffed and duct-taped barber chair, next to a great big cardboard box with an equally large tan dog somehow folded inside. Winston ambled slowly to the front of the store to meet me, and he wasn't particularly friendly until he figured out I hadn't come in to try to buy his store.

Here was the thing about Winston's place: it was anything but fancy. The wooden floor looked to be fifty years old, worn smooth and white by the shufflings of countless fishermen. Lures dangled from the racks, fishing rods leaned in a jumble against an equally worn wooden counter. Outside there were a few picnic tables. But from the back of the store I could see Winston's house, and behind that house was God's own view: sweet green grass falling away to marsh, the marsh in turn disappearing beneath the sparkling waters of Murrells Inlet.

"You wouldn't believe it," said Winston. "We've had people just beggin' for this place. I'm sixty-six years old. We've had this place since 1954. I'm at a time now, I don't want anybody to take my place where I'm livin'. I don't plan on living much longer. Money don't mean much to me. Three guys come in here asking if I'm selling. I told them it's not for sale, and they just smile and say, 'Everything's for sale,' and I said, 'No sir, you got that wrong.'"

Winston's voice was certain. His gaze followed mine.

"When I was first come in here, God, it was so lovely," he said. "It was like a dream. I felt like I'd died and gone to heaven. I picked oysters to build this place. I was out on the oyster beds every day. I'd pick anywhere from fifteen to twenty-five bushels a day. Nobody would believe it. I came here from a farm. I wasn't afraid to work."

We talked for twenty minutes. I liked Winston and his store. Both reeked of genteel and fair treatment, and transactions that unfolded slowly around long conversations. He insisted I sit in his barber chair—"It's an old-fashioned barber chair. Set down, go ahead and set down in it"—and when I did, it absorbed me like a mother's lap, and he beamed proudly.

Winston stood straight, and though he moved slowly, he seemed to be the picture of vitality. But during our conversation he made several veiled references to his health. After a time I began to think that maybe Winston really wasn't planning on living much longer. There was a ponytailed young man outside. When he came in, Winston introduced him as his son. Winston's son had many years left in him.

Before I left, Winston's eyes locked on to mine. "Folks have offered me a million dollars," he said. Suddenly he looked befuddled, and my heart sank. "What would you do?" His voice was plaintive. "I can't just walk out. We've been here for too long."

The next morning I saw in the paper where the residents of Murrells Inlet had said no to Wal-Mart. At the Coffee Club I mentioned this to Harry.

Harry smiled wanly. "That don't make no difference," he said. "Money talks, and bullshit walks on down the road. There's seven new banks within a quarter-mile of here. Why so many banks? Because they're fixin' to have a shitload of people move in here."

This last little piece of heaven, reckoned Harry, was worth a cool half-million.

7
NAKED NATURE

THE OCEAN'S EDGE sends mixed messages. For many, the beach is a stage for joy, inhaled thoughtlessly in the heat of the present, and then preserved in delicate detail—touch, sight, scent, thought, laughter—forever. It means seaside remembrances, carried through life and pulled out in dreamy moments, or when dreamy moments suffice better than the moment at hand. It means family vacations, as languid and simple as life should be. It means secret dune sharings, as brief as summer and equally sweet, coupled bodies bared to each other and the caress of sand, passion's flood and ebb etching a tumult of grainy waves, ably smoothed, in short time, by gravity and wind, Nature's chambermaids preparing the boudoir for the next pair of lovers. It means happiness taken alone, too: sunrises and sunsets absorbed in mindless and mindful repose; moonlit walks, bare feet washed by warm and foamy murmurings; pleasure as simple as drying salt lightly pinching the skin. Running before a light breeze on a fresh-born summer day, the sailor doesn't see the schooner's ribs below him, or the winter storm that drove it to the bottom.

Before I left Murrells Inlet, I went for a paddle. The morning papers trumpeted whopping winter storms to the north, great droppings of snow that had wrecked travel plans. Here in the south there was no snow, but the coast had taken on a brown and waiting look, and when I drove across to Garden City, ten minutes east of Murrells Inlet, and looked out at the Atlantic, the wind blew cold over the small waves.

I parked the van in a small sandy lot pressed between wood-stilted homes. Windows were shut, blinds were pulled, and rockers sat silent on not-quite-straight beachfront porches, nudged slightly askance by migrating dunes. The screen door of one of the homes had been flung wide by the wind. It sat hopefully ajar, waiting for the traffic of bare feet.

A short boardwalk led through the dunes, identified by a sign as the Laurice Rhem Walkover. The humble pathway stretched fifteen yards at most, much of it buried now by the unfettered winter sands. I would see these memorials everywhere on my journey: plaques on boardwalk railings and ocean-view benches. And though they spoke of death, they always made me smile. I could think of no greater tribute to Laurice than to guide new generations to a place she no doubt loved.

I saw dolphins off the beach. Earlier, to the south, I had seen dolphins in St. Augustine; they had often followed me as I paddled. This pod followed me now beneath a pewter afternoon sky, five of them, their slick, dark fins parting the water with surgical precision. They swam on all sides of my kayak, an aquatic police escort, smoothly disappearing on one side and resurfacing on another, often with a sudden, startling chuff. I have paddled with dolphins count-less times in the Pacific waters off my California home, and they never fail to lift my heart and my spirits. They are curious creatures and seem to grasp the idea of fun. Many times I have seen them explode from the water, corkscrewing briefly in midair before falling back with a happy splash.

These dolphins followed me for thirty minutes. They were indis-tinguishable from their St. Augustine brethren, so I could imagine, in egocentric delusion, that they were the same pod, gently usher-ing me north.

At an inlet a mile or two north, tiny waves fanned out in a broad arc as they touched the shallow shoals. On a beach just to the south of the inlet, I could see a mass of gulls, wheeling and dropping. Something about their numbers and their frenzy drew me into the beach. When I pulled the kayak onto the wet sand, they lifted from a dark form and flew overhead screaming madly.

The form was a dolphin, lying on its side. It took me a moment to realize it was still alive. A watery eye half tracked the movement of my kayak paddle as I passed it slowly overhead, and now and again the dolphin gently shuddered. In summer a crowd would have gathered, horrified and offended, shooing the gulls away and calling animal rescue.

But there was nothing to be rescued: little life, less hope, and pain only the dolphin could know. I stood quietly. My presence kept all but the brashest gulls away, and a wave of my paddle discouraged them. These bolder gulls lighted in the sand just out of reach and waddled about peevishly. The birds had every right to this offering, I knew, but I couldn't bring myself to let them feast until a more appropriate time. That time came twenty minutes later, when the dolphin exited this life with a last great quiver. Paddling south, I could see strings of gulls winging down the beach, summoned by the happy shrieks of their brethren.

Instinctually, the dolphin understood its end. Dolphins are play-ful. Sleek and powerful swimmers, they will toy with their prey, nudging, prodding, and darting about the frantic fish, extending the hunt far longer than need be, before finishing it.

It is a harsh and dangerous place, the ocean. And if you take a hard, honest look, the shoreline is no better, though man has man-aged to sanitize this fact. Henry David Thoreau wandered Cape Cod's shoreline before bulldozers, animal control, and safer modes of shipping cleaned it up, and his take was as blunt as the ocean's edge itself.

"It is a wild, rank place, and there is no flattery in it," wrote Thoreau. "Strewn with crabs, horse-shoes, and razor-clams, and whatever the sea casts up,—a vast morgue, where famished dogs may range in packs, and crows come daily to glean the pittance the tide leaves them. The carcasses of men and beasts together lie stately upon its shelf, rotting and bleaching in the sun and waves, and each tide turns them in their beds and tucks fresh sand under them. There is naked Nature—inhumanely sincere, wasting no thought on man."

On St. Simons, George Baker had told me the story of a 1912

tugboat accident. The tug was pushing a huge wooden barge in heavy seas. A boiler explosion killed part of the tug's crew instantly. With their ship sinking beneath them, the survivors yanked on the cork lifejackets of the day and jumped overboard. The last of their bodies were recovered days later. "None of the men had drowned," said George. "Most of them had had their necks broken in the surf by the impact of the cork lifejackets' high collars."

Haints, those devil creatures of voodoo, will not enter a blue opening of a house because blue is the color of heaven. Blue is also the color of water, but that doesn't always make it heaven.

In the face of the hard and capricious tolls that the ocean's edge often exacts, again and again the coastal folk I met turned bad to good, exhibiting a wonderfully twisted outlook along with their toughness and fortitude. South Carolina's residents were no different. On September 22, 1989, Hurricane Hugo struck the coast with a ferocity that turned fishing boats into airplanes and wiped entire towns off the map, most notably McClellanville, where a quick-witted mother tied her two children to a tree with an extension cord to keep them from being swept away. The next day Philip Wilkinson and Mary Mac were married at Belin Methodist Church in Murrells Inlet in a twenty-minute candlelight ceremony. "This is not what I had in mind a week ago, but you just have to roll with the punches," Philip told a reporter. "It won't be much of a honeymoon because we'll spend it getting the tree off the roof of my house."

One morning, when conversation at the Coffee Club turned to hurricanes, I nodded in somber sympathy.

Harry's eyebrows went up. "Hell, everybody around here prays for a hurricane," he said. "Right after a hurricane, the fish go apeshit. Of course, in the perfect scenario the hurricane passes a hundred miles out to sea, so we get to keep our homes and still get the fish."

The ocean itself exhibits this same glib schizophrenia, stepping casually back and forth over the line between beauty and horror. As I paddled the kayak back from the inlet, my mind was filled with the suffering dolphin. At first I didn't notice the freshening, frosty wind, but after a time the drop in temperature became obvious. Returned suddenly to my surroundings, I saw long tendrils of fog appear as if by magic, snaking smokily just inches off the ocean's surface. There were dozens of them, running away from me like streamers. Each remained distinct from the others, and as they rose higher above the ocean's surface, the wind broadened and sheared them, so that they took on the appearance of ghostly mountain ranges, each with its smooth valleys and smoky-wisp peaks. On the horizon I could see a wall of fog, and in about the time it takes you to read this sentence, the fog was upon me, and the shoreline and the horizon disappeared. For a minute the world was cocooned in gray. Then the sun punched through, and sea smoke and fog were suffused with a golden light, as if, briefly, a portal to heaven had been thrown open. It was one of the loveliest things I had ever seen and, I thought, a fitting exit for a dolphin's soul.

※

EARLY THE NEXT MORNING I made a beeline north along 17, passing through Wilmington, North Carolina, and then, as fast as I could, away and across the Cape Fear River. I repeated this kind of transition again and again on my trip: after holing up in a tiny town inhabited mostly by wind and sand, the roar of civilization came as a shock, the traffic torrents, the automaton drivers, the equally faceless succession of Wal-Marts and Home Depots. It was as if Americans always had a project to tend to, but they never got to it because they were always stuck in traffic.

I found brief sanctuary in Surf City and Topsail Beach—beach towns hung only with drifting birds and the sound of carpenters' nail guns—but I continued to push north with a destination in mind.

I had taken the ferry from Cedar Point to Ocracoke in winter several years before, and it had been like a ghost ship, the only sign of life a dozen gape-mouthed passengers sleeping in their cars, tonsils dangling. So when I called to reserve a spot on the ten A.M. ferry, it seemed silly to make a reservation.

"We're full up," said Bill, who answered the phone.

"You're joking."

"Nope." Bill had a friendly, down-home voice, but I could tell immediately he was no joker.

"Okay. Well then, how about a spot on the one o'clock ferry?"

"Full up," he said amiably, if not, I thought, a touch proudly. "The ferry holds around fifty, and there's no spaces on the seven A.M., ten A.M., one P.M., or four P.M. ferry."

I looked at the calendar on my watch just to be sure. Wednesday, November 27. For a moment I was stunned. This was like finding a line at a Milli Vanilli reunion.

"Why would you be full on a weekday in November?" I asked when I found my voice.

"This is the time when people who own homes on Ocracoke and the islands come over and close them up."

I had hoped to be on Ocracoke Island before nightfall. Apparently this wasn't going to happen unless I was prepared for a bracing swim.

"Thanksgiving fills up, too," said Bill matter-of-factly.

That was bad news, since tomorrow was Thanksgiving.

"This is the last hurrah," Bill kindly injected with a note of optimism. "After this weekend there will be no trouble getting a ferry."

I was doing some mental figuring, but Bill made his living by the clock. "If I were you, I'd book a place now for the seven A.M. ferry tomorrow," he said. "Be there by six-thirty, or we'll give your reservation away."

Suddenly I had more time on my hands than I wanted. I could have left the van and crawled to the ferry in time for the seven A.M. departure.

I spent the night in Morehead City. When I got back on the road at four-thirty in the morning, it was black and cold, but I was excited. My trip felt like it was gathering momentum and purpose, assuming a cohesion I had believed in, yet doubted, from the beginning.

Travelers must be filled with equal parts optimism and pessimism. Both are required to foment a successful journey: optimism, so you take that first daunting step out the door; pessimism, to keep you stepping, a sort of prove-it attitude that forces you to venture around corners and into unfamiliar places you might normally bypass. I have traveled a great deal, and people are always telling me how wonderful that must be. But travel—excluding the self-absorbed, facile travel of vacations—is not easy. You must face strange places and strange people and risk being lost and ignored. Walking alone into a wary, clannish, small-town bar isn't pleasant, even for the most gregarious traveler. Hardest of all, you have to face down your own ugly negative thoughts: that these places will be dull, and the people and events within their borders uneventful. These thoughts, and their countless pessimistic permutations, keep many people at home or, if they do venture out, keep them from poking about in the places that can offer enlightening, and sometimes life-changing, experiences. Travel can bestow gifts beyond measure, but it can also be vaguely threatening.

I should know by now that my own pessimism is mostly pointless worry. Again and again in my travels I have found people to be welcoming and beyond gracious; their hometowns and lives are filled with a fascinating overabundance of interesting stories. Yet before every trip I hesitate, and this one had been no exception. Sitting at home in California, maps spread before me, the East Coast had seemed impossibly vast and foreign. *Beyond this point lie monsters.*

On this frigid Thanksgiving morning, I felt the old familiar optimism seeping in. Florida, Georgia, and South Carolina were behind me, each liberally spitting in the face of pessimism. The coastal refuges I had visited had offered both surprise and story. The people I had met were gracious to a fault. Better still, in these people and their places, I felt I was fingering the first thready beats of a larger, common pulse. I was picking up clues and a semblance of stride, and I was anxious to see where both led.

Driving north in the darkness, I made my way along two-lane Route 70, wandering the edge of Core Sound toward Cedar Point, passing aptly named streets (Peaceful Place) and towns (Sealevel). It was Thanksgiving morning, and all was holiday-still. In the cold silence I passed signs of the season: doors hung with wreaths, porches draped with holly, and a church sign proclaiming, "True Thanksgiving happens every day." Driving down one black stretch, I had to blink. A tractor sat in the middle of the field—a tractor I would have missed in the velvet dark had it not been draped with strings of brightly colored Christmas lights. From a distance, it looked like some alien spacecraft. Up close, it appeared splattered with neon rain.

Route 70 became Route 12, more than a name change, because suddenly the road seemed to be heading resolutely toward the ends of the earth. As the first light of dawn touched the eastern seaboard and the gray clouds stepped out of the night sky, the road shot arrow-straight across a prairie of marsh; the only signs of civilization were a line of telephone poles, wires undulating toward a tantalizing horizon, and the one phone at the edge of the world.

There are times on a trip when the road becomes a song. The notes rise from the road and infiltrate your heart, but they don't stop there—they continue to rise, and your heart, entranced, goes merrily with them, a village maiden eloping with a passing minstrel with nary a backward glance or note. It was, by any definition, a lonely road, yet at that moment there was no place else I wanted to be.

Ahead lay the palpable presence of winter. It warmed my soul.

8
THE WORLD ACCORDING
TO O'COCKERS

BILL DIDN'T HAVE to give my spot away. I arrived at the Cedar Point ferry with an hour to spare; time enough to pick up some last-minute turkey-cooking tips, courtesy of the *Gam,* a Beaufort newspaper proudly proofread by Cy the One-Eyed Cat.

The tips, from local kindergarteners, ranged from the brief—"Fri the trke 8 mnts, 500. Et the trke."—to the incriminating: "Me and my dad go to Food Lion and get a turkey. Mom doesn't know where Food Lion is"—to the potentially explosive: "I would put the turkey in the microwave for 8 hours."

Promptly at seven the ferry—with me aboard—throbbed away from Cedar Point for the two-hour-and-fifteen-minute trip to Ocracoke Island. Thanksgiving Day was gray and cold. The ferry dipped and rose as the sun poked above a wall of clouds on the horizon. Gazing out at Pamlico Sound, I saw waters that, for the first time, smacked of winter, white-capped, seething, and moving with dark, thick purpose.

✥

THE OUTER BANKS are a fascinating place, a people and landscape full of surprises, especially in winter, when both step lively front and center. In summer the barrier islands groan under the weight of thousands of vacationers who pour across the Currituck Sound Bridge, raft-wielding, bug-repellant-spraying Huns swamping Kitty Hawk, Nags Head, and Buxton, and, fervor undaunted, streaming across Hatteras Inlet to the lovely village of Ocracoke. Like any tourist destination in summer, these towns are less like themselves: gussied-up pretty, but their true character is suppressed, like a tomboy at a cotillion.

In winter the frilly dress and heels are stuffed into the back of the closet, and the Outer Banks shine, chewing snuff, swearing lively, and blaring soulful notes of life into the chill, briny wind. And nowhere does surprise step livelier or lovelier in winter than on Ocracoke. Some neighbors believe the island's residents—O'cockers, in island parlance—would prefer that it remain winter year-round.

"Those people down there, the world could fall away as far as they care," a Nags Head shop owner had told me on a previous visit to the Outer Banks. Perhaps because Nags Head receives far more visitors, the town sees itself as more worldly. Whatever the snobbery, the store owner didn't fancy sharing it. Leaning forward he whispered, "You don't get normal people down there."

In my mind that was as good a reason to visit as any, but I found others. In a book titled *Ocracoke Portrait,* residents gave their own assessment of island life. Many spoke of winter.

"I like the winters," Al Scarborough told the author. "You can walk around the island and not see anybody. You can go out on a winter night a mile and a half away from the ocean and you can hear those waves roaring and look up and see billions of stars in the sky."

An elderly matron was more socially inclined: "In the winter, the colder it gets, and the later in winter it gets, that's when you begin to hear a little more about the gossip, things that are going on."

It seemed to me that winter on a small island provides all the necessary ingredients for salacious happenings, real and imagined: idle time for rumination, much time in a confined space, a spouse with whom you are sick of sharing the confined space, possibly another spouse with whom you would like to share a confined space. I was hoping she would go on and share some specific social indecency, but she didn't.

Another visitor was told that the islanders had no wish other than "to be left alone to fish and fornicate," proof, in my mind, of the O'cockers' rock-solid sanity and equally sound sense of priorities.

Ocracoke Island, was actually once a continuation of Hatteras Island to the north, but the Atlantic Ocean has made things right for the O'cockers, cleaving it free from Hatteras and setting it adrift. The Banks are geologically young—a mere five thousand years or so—but they have suffered more than their share of abuse. Over the years the Atlantic has had its wanton way with the Outer Banks, washing over and through the islands with whimsical abandon. A casual glance at a satellite photo explains why. First you see nothing but water; only when you squint do tiny threads of sand appear, in many stretches no wider than the press of a fine-tip pen, bowing out into the ocean like a rounded arrowhead, with Hatteras at the east-ernmost tip. Factor in the traditional paths of hurricanes and nor'easters, and you have the geographical equivalent of a house in the middle of a railroad track.

At our point in geological time, the Atlantic has carved inlets to the north and south of Ocracoke, so you have to ride the ferry to get there. In summer this saline buffer does little to protect the island. Ocracoke bursts with tourists, who loll on its fine powdery beaches, address waitresses as "hon," and pedal bikes about the village as if they were four years old, strung out on Valium, or both.

This blatant disregard for traffic has influenced the very lan-guage of Ocracoke. "A ding-batter is the one you see riding real slow right down the middle of the road on a bicycle with a whole string of cars behind 'em," explained a burly man buying coffee at the Vari-ety Store one morning. He shook his head as if hoping to purge the memory. "God damn. They're worse than Republicans."

I had been to Ocracoke before, one long-ago September. I hadn't ridden a bike, though at the time I'd sorely wished I had one. In the late 1970s I had come across on the ferry from Hatteras with a col-lege roommate. We had a car, but I convinced my roommate to leave it behind so we wouldn't have to pay the vehicle fee. There was no fee, and the fact that my roommate kept reminding me of this fact made the fourteen-mile walk from the ferry slip into Ocracoke even longer.

While Ocracoke sees a torrent of summer visitors—and fall and spring have their share, too—few outsiders come to the island in winter. It becomes a jewel of isolation, sixteen miles of wave- and wind-scoured sand with seven hundred residents scrunched at the island's southern end.

Fortuitously, I arrived on Ocracoke in time to see both the tourist and the winter worlds. The long Thanksgiving weekend is the outside world's last hurrah. After driving off the ferry, I arrived at Edwards of Ocracoke and checked in. When I told the manager, Bert Clark, that I had been to Ocracoke long ago, he tidily encapsulated the passing years. "It's the same as it was twenty years ago, only there's more buildings," he said, handing me my key.

The early morning gray had given way to bright blue, and the town was a beehive of activity. People ducked in and out of quaint shops where summer's fixed prices were off ("Everything for Sale!"), and when they were finished shopping, they filled the local restaurants with the happy jangle of ringing cash registers. O'cockers who didn't have businesses dragged their junk out into their front yards and erected "Yard Sale" signs. It felt just like the last gasp of commerce it was.

"On Sunday it will die here," said Buffy Warner. "People will pull the plug."

Buffy knew something of commerce. A big man with a politician's firm handshake and charm, Buffy was not a native O'cocker, but he had lived on the island for thirteen years, managing with his wife, Ann, Ocracoke's most popular restaurant. Howard's Pub is open until two A.M., 365 days a year. I knew this because an enormous sign just outside town told me so. "Welcome to the Village of Ocracoke," it read in part. "Home of Howard's Pub."

Seeing it then was like driving across the George Washington Bridge and seeing a giant sign that reads "Buddy's Tattoo Parlor Welcomes You to New York." When I asked Buffy how his establishment had come to enjoy such choice exposure, he was forthright.

"I bought the property and put up the sign. People argued for years about who was going to pay for a sign welcoming people to

Ocracoke, and where it was going to be, and I got tired of it. I'm a shameless self-promoter. It really pissed a lot of people off when I did that. They said, 'How can the pub be more important than the town?' Well, you can read that sign however you want to." Buffy laughed. "But it does say 'Home of Howard's Pub,' doesn't it?"

Like everyone else I met on Ocracoke, Buffy answers questions bluntly and then some. I'm not sure why. Maybe because, in a town of seven hundred, people will find out how you think soon enough. This lack of circumspection was refreshing and in Buffy's case surprising, seeing as he'd come from an arena not known for straight shooting. "He used to be a politician," said the bartender who put me on to Buffy. "A state senator in West Virginia. He's got the gift of gab."

Perhaps because of this previous occupation, I was not the first outsider to ask for Buffy's input on the island.

"We've gotten our share of attention," he said. *"Good Morning America* and the *Today* show did stories on the island. CNN came here, and I gave them a hand. They ended up calling us 'refugees from reality.' "

Later I discovered there was some resentment in town that Buffy, a newcomer, spoke for Ocracoke. Buffy was aware of the resentment and put little stock in it. "I'm a politician," he said. "If you ask me to talk, I will."

Buffy had unseated an incumbent of ten years to win his first four-year term in West Virginia. He had been running unopposed for reelection when he withdrew and moved to Ocracoke. He reckons he is still practicing a form of politics ("Owning the only bar in town, you're still keeping the populace happy"), though he said he did miss waking up in the morning and reading his opinion in the paper.

From what I saw and heard during the five days I spent on Ocracoke, publishing everyone's opinion in the *Ocracoke Observer (Your Voice in the Village)* would have made it a struggle just to pick the newspaper up off the table. In a country politically corrected into caution and frightened silence, O'cockers speak out with abandon and flourish. Environmentally incorrect bumper stickers ride on rusted bumpers ("The only good turtle is a turtle in the pot, with potatoes and onions."), and an enormous sign on the side of Albert Styron's General Store urges customers to "Get Your Ass in Here." Letters to the editor tell politicians to kiss off and complain loudly about everything from ferry fees to church bells. Even death can't quiet the song of the Ocracoke soul. "You Ain't Heard Nothing Yet!" crows the tombstone epithet of Edgar H. Howard. Why go quietly into the day or the night? It's as if Hunter S. Thompson had founded a School of Tact and Concession, and O'cockers were his magna cum laude class. I loved it.

There's no telling from where such a firm sense of self arises, but O'cockers may feel it because they've been beholden to themselves for a long, long time. "Hell, this village was here before the United States was here," said Buffy. "The people are descendants of people who were here before this country became a country."

One story does not an island make, but on my second night on Ocracoke I heard one that comes close. The story involves Cleveland Gaskins. Cle, who died in 1963, once took a fancy to some toilet paper he saw advertised in a friend's Sears, Roebuck catalog. Cle couldn't read or write, but he had a daughter who could, so he had her pen a short missive. "Dear Sears, Roebuck. I would like to buy a dozen rolls of toilet paper. Please send the toilet paper to my home on Ocracoke. Sincerely, Cleveland Gaskins." Cle put the note and the money on the mail boat. The days spilled along, and no package came. Finally a letter arrived from Sears, Roebuck. "Dear Mr. Gaskins. We don't sell toilet paper by the dozen. Please consult our catalog for the quantities we offer." Cle wasted no time crafting his response. "Dear Sears, Roebuck. I recently ordered a dozen rolls of toilet paper. Instead I got a letter telling me to order directly from the catalog. Gentlemen, I can assure you, if I had one of your catalogs, I wouldn't need your damn toilet paper."

Cle's story was recounted by Philip Howard at the Ocracoke Music and Storytelling Festival, held Friday night at the Ocracoke Community Center. Driving around town, I had seen posters advertising the festival. Then while poking through the historical displays at the Ocracoke Preservation Society Museum on Friday morning, I met Jenny Scarborough. Jenny was working in the gift shop. When I told her I was trying to get a feel for her island, she smiled warmly. "Then you should come to the festival tonight," she said. "All kinds of people will be there."

I had seen the list of performers. It was long and comprised of violinists, guitarists, banjo-pickers, fiddlers, songwriters, and story-tellers, several of whom had appeared on National Public Radio, *Nightline,* and CNN. I thought the booking agent deserved kudos, getting so much talent to cross Pamlico Sound in winter, so I said so. "It's great you can get so many different performers to come down here," I told Jenny. "It's not exactly around the block."

"Well, it is for most people," she said, not unkindly. "Everyone lives here except for Wes, who lives on Hatteras."

Ding-batter. Noun. Non-native.

The festival began at eight P.M. I arrived fifteen minutes early, cautiously driving the black streets under a ceiling of glittering stars. Ocracoke doesn't splurge on street lighting. Unless a resident opts to pay for a street lamp themselves, there isn't one, and judg-ing from the roads I drove, O'cockers prefer nighttime as Nature makes it. My eyes are good, but several nights, driving around town, I had to stop in the road and press my nose against the cold windshield to ascertain an upcoming turn. Even the locals, I was told, have trouble. Now and again bicyclists crash headlong into each other.

Driving to the community center, I caught the movements of my fellow festival-goers beside the road, bundled bicyclists and pedes-trians moving silently through the dark. There was a surprising num-ber of them, and more appeared as I neared the community center. Despite their number, I wasn't worried. The building appeared to be large enough to house a good-size crowd. And unless the whole island turned out, a good-size crowd would be hard to find.

At 7:50 P.M. a line of twenty people ran down the wooden walk-way that sloped up to the front door. A few minutes later word came that the show was sold out, but tickets were still being sold to those who didn't mind standing.

An elderly gentleman in front of me harrumphed and turned on his heel. "I ain't standin'," he said to no one in particular. "I've seen this damn show fifteen times already."

Most everybody else bought a ticket, including me. Almost no one took a program. Outside it had been cheek-stinging cold; inside it was cozy with body heat and murmur. A sea of fold-out chairs, all taken, lined the wooden floor in tight rows, pushing right up to the small stage. Middle-aged daughters sat beside wheelchair-bound fathers, and children sat cross-legged in the aisles, laughing and pushing at one another. The walls were hung with quilts, and refreshment tables stood in the back, fat with homemade delicacies: peanut brittle and brownies for fifty cents, hot coffee, and Ocracoke fig cake ("Baked by the emcee!") for the raffle. A few older gentlemen, dewy-eyed and craggy-faced, wore coats and ties, but most people were dressed casually, the men in jeans and untucked flannel shirts, the women in plain long dresses. The performers would have been indistinguishable from the audience if they hadn't held instruments.

You didn't need a sign to know it was a community center. People waved quietly to one another from their chairs, and latecomers hugged and shook hands near the door.

I stood in the back, feeling watched and out of place. If there were other tourists in the community center, they were disguised in flannel. I had spent the past two days exploring the town, asking questions of the people I ran into. Without exception they had responded politely, if not a little distractedly, occupied, as many of them were, with selling whatever wasn't nailed down. Already I recognized many of the faces. Perhaps I was exaggerating my own impact, but I thought I saw a few glances cast my way. Someone offered me a chair, but I felt funny sitting while women stood, so I declined.

At just past eight the lights dimmed and the performers began playing. They played and sang in duets, in quartets, and on their own. The music settled over the room like a warm fog. A man named Martin Garrish played a song on his guitar, and then he called his Uncle Jule to the stage. Uncle Jule sat on a stool, hands folded neatly in his lap, a brown ball cap on his head.

"Jule is a vet from World War II," Martin told the audience. "He was in the navy. He said this was the most played song on the jukebox."

Jule didn't move, but as Martin began to strum, a voice issued from between the brown ball cap and a red check shirt. " 'There's a star-spangled banner waving somewhere,' " crooned Uncle Jule. " 'In a distant land so maaaany miles away . . . There's a star-spangled banner waving somewhere, and that's where I want to go when I die.' "

When Jule finished singing, there was only the sound of Martin picking "The Star-Spangled Banner." Each chord drifted through the room, delicate and clear, like the tinkle of fine crystal that lingers in the brief silence following a toast. Only here the silence continued until the vibration of Martin's last chord faded away, and then the audience erupted. It was one of the loveliest renditions of "The Star-Spangled Banner" I had ever heard.

Philip Howard took the stage and told the aforementioned story of Cleveland Gaskins, and everyone laughed, though I suspected many already knew the story. Captain Rob Temple came to the stage, and his wife Sundae Horn, and Gary and Kitty Mitchell.

"Kitty teaches at Ocracoke School," ponytailed emcee David Tweedie told the audience. "And what grade do you teach?"

"All of them," said Kitty.

Song and strum rang from the stage, ballads written by Merle Haggard or daughters of local fishermen, wistful songs about love, and loss, and fishing—and sometimes all three—and foot-stomping tunes about small-town life: " 'We're gonna howl at the moon, shoot out the light. It's a small-town Saturday night . . .' "

During intermission I walked over to Philip Howard, where he was standing beside the refreshment tables. The festival program had said Philip traces his lineage back to the time of Blackbeard. He is a slender man with a bookish, intelligent look, bald, wearing glasses and drooping jeans. I introduced myself.

"I loved that story about Cleveland Gaskins," I said. "Did he really do that?"

"I only tell true stories." Philip smiled. "Well, some facts change a little over the years, but basically it's a true story."

Philip has been collecting island stories and history and writing them down for years. Wednesday nights in the summer he tells Ocracoke stories to audiences at the Deepwater Theater.

"The talent here is incredible," I said.

I wasn't trying to butter Philip up—I meant it. I had expected a local talent show where people missed chords and lines and their friends fell about themselves as if Pavarotti had just taken his final bow. But the performances had been seamless.

Philip regarded me bemusedly. He reminded me of a kind, yet watchful, monk. "Most people who've never heard us play think, 'Well, how good could a bunch of islanders be?' " he said.

For a nauseating moment I thought Philip was reading my mind. I changed the subject. "I saw in the program where it says your roots go back to Blackbeard."

Philip nodded to a face in the milling crowd, then turned back to me. "My family has been here since 1759. My great-great-great-great-grandfather bought the island. He may have been the same William Howard that served as quartermaster for Blackbeard."

During the week I spent on the Outer Banks, more than a dozen people claimed to have had relatives aboard the infamous pirate's ship. Blackbeard and his vessel, *Queen Anne's Revenge,* roamed and homed on this slice of North Carolina coast and elsewhere between 1716 and 1718. Gas station attendants, movie ticket takers, K-mart clerks—they all traced a genealogical beeline to swashbuckling pirates. I'm certain more would have 'fessed up had I raised the subject in larger quarters. After a time I began to wonder if Blackbeard might have commanded not the tiny *Queen Anne's Revenge,* but the massive *Queen Mary.*

Philip's claim seemed more legitimate than most, if only because, unlike the others, he didn't state it as irrefutable fact. "I'm not sure it's true, but I think it is," he said. "Blackbeard was only a pirate for about eighteen months, and William Howard, his quartermaster, was captured in July 1718. He was born in 1700. The day before Howard was to be hanged, he received a pardon from the King of England, and he was set free. And then a William Howard shows up again in Ocracoke in 1759. Some people say that the William Howard who appeared on Ocracoke was too young to have been Blackbeard's quartermaster, but he would have been eighteen, and boys went off to sea from Ocracoke when they were ten years old."

O'cockers milled around us, pillaging the refreshment table with happy gusto, having their way with various baked goodies.

"Now, that's not proof that it is him," continued Philip. "But you've got this isolated little island, and a William Howard shows up later and buys it. How likely was it that two people named William Howard found this place back then?"

I liked Philip. He was soft-spoken and mild-mannered, and it was obvious, even from our short conversation, that his island home meant a great deal to him. There was more I wanted to ask, but the audience was taking its seats and Philip moved to go with them.

He nodded to me. "Come to my store tomorrow."

After intermission Roy Parsons took the stage. From the program I saw that Roy was born on Ocracoke in 1921 and had since become "the island's yodeler of renown."

Roy played three songs on guitar and harmonica, and I had the impression that, had the other musicians not joined him onstage, he would have played a few more. The pace of the songs waxed and waned, but there was no doubt that Roy still possessed plenty of wind. After the third song he remained sitting on his stool.

There was a long silence.

Gary Mitchell knelt beside him.

"So," said Gary, "what did you do for Thanksgiving, Roy?"

"I had some turkey, and lots of pie and collards," stated Roy.

"I didn't get any collards," said Gary amiably.

"Well, you should have come around, I'd have given you some." Roy returned to sitting ramrod straight and silent.

"Well, Roy," said Gary, after a pause. "Way back when, what were Thanksgivings on the island like? Did you eat turkey?"

"We didn't have any," said Roy tartly. "We didn't know what a turkey was. All we had was fish and clams and crabs. That's how I lived so long."

There was another pregnant pause. I could imagine Roy at home, spending the day neatly laying out his clothes, gathering his guitar and harmonica, considering and reconsidering his song list, waiting patiently in a favorite chair until evening purpled, then darkened, his windows.

In our youth-obsessed culture the old rarely take the stage anymore, except to extol the virtues of various laxatives or the positive assets of denture cream. These are not positions of respect.

Nobody rushed Roy, or filled the silence with a joke at his expense. The audience waited patiently.

"Do you have any Thanksgiving memories from long ago, Roy?" Gary finally asked.

Roy considered this for only a moment. "No," he said flatly.

When the show ended at ten-thirty, the trucks and bicycles evaporated into the night. In a snap the street was silent. It was as if everyone had merrily ridden off the edge of the earth, leaving me behind. Overhead the stars shone. Across the street Christmas wreaths glowed in the dark storefronts of the Variety and Hardware Store.

I stood for a moment, undecided. Then the dark road beckoned, and I answered, and that is how I found myself standing on the beach beneath an impossible dome of stars. They spilled across the sky as if pitched from vast stellar buckets; torrents that wove and intermingled so that the end result was a ceiling filled more with stars than sky. The sky was obscenely clear, so clear it was as if Nature were without secrets. I felt as if a mild stretch would allow me to reach up through the nearest stars and grab the dim ones from the deepest recesses. Beneath the sky the Atlantic stretched smooth and serene; stars fell past its black rim to sparkle some lower horizon.

It was exactly as Al Scarborough had said, only instead of the roar of surf, the night rang with the memory of full-throated laughter. Backlit by the stars, I saw Roy Parsons's smile, coming slowly to his face as dawn lightening water, as he realized the joy his paucity of Thanksgiving memories had wrought.

꙳

THE ATLANTIC, of course, isn't always at peace, just as life on Ocracoke wasn't always a Norman Rockwell painting, as Philip reminded me the next morning.

I met him at his store. A dozen shoppers wandered through the Village Craftsman, inhaling the smell of incense and cedar and admiring handcrafted pottery, glassware, and intricate sugar pine carvings of black-necked stilts.

Philip was busy, so I waited out on the porch. I didn't want to interfere with his last chance for serious commerce until spring.

After fifteen minutes Philip stepped outside. "Did you enjoy the show last night?" he asked.

"It was magic," I said. "I loved the whole thing—the music, the feeling of community, everything. It made me think I could live here."

Philip's smile, it seemed to me, had a touch of fatherly patience. "You know, no place is perfect."

Few roots burrowed deeper into Ocracoke's soil than those of the Howard family tree. I sorely wanted to talk to him about life on the island, but it appeared this wouldn't be easy. His schedule rivaled the pope's.

"Well, today I'll be pretty busy at the store," said Philip. "Tonight I've got dinner and weekly poker. I don't want to miss that. And tomorrow night I'm hosting a potluck at my place." He smiled apologetically. "Winter is when we socialize. It's a very busy place."

Suddenly I knew exactly what I was, an interloper with no friends and fewer people who cared. "A traveler has no power, no influence, no known identity," writes Paul Theroux in *The Happy Isles of Oceania*. "That is why a traveler needs optimism and heart, because without confidence travel is misery."

I felt miserable, though I tried not to show it.

For the second time in as many days I wondered if Philip could read minds.

"Say, listen," he said. "Why don't you come to the potluck tomorrow night?"

⁂

ONCE THE HOME of Indians, pirates, and debtors-turned-escapees, the Outer Banks and Ocracoke are now civilized, but they still bespeak wildness at every turn. On Madison Avenue it is easy to shunt Nature behind a partition; less so on a narrow rope of sand in the sea.

After leaving Philip that day, I drove north along the two-lane Irvin Garrish Memorial Highway, the sole road running the length of the island. Immediately the world fell away to scrub and sand. Only the southern tip of Ocracoke is developed; the rest is part of the Cape Hatteras National Seashore.

A few miles up the road, I pulled off at a small turnout. It was a damp day, cold with a stiff southeast wind. The sky was a leached blue, as if it weren't quite in the mood. Leaving the van, I walked toward Pamlico Sound along a rutted, frozen dirt road, my boots crackling the ice-glazed tire tracks. The road ended at a marsh. The tide was low. Mudflats ran out two hundred yards to meet the deep blue sound. Birds rode the buffeting wind at the mudflats' edge.

Despite the wind, the smell of mud hung as dank and heavy as a fresh-dug grave, downpour-wetted. In summer, I knew, this place would be very miserable, but now it was lovely and bug-free. Had any insects arisen, the wind would have whisked them off to Wisconsin.

Winter makes you listen. Standing at the marsh edge, I heard the fidgetings of a living island. The wind carried the ocean's rumblings. Close at hand, tufts of dead grass chafed against one another, their sound like a restless sleeper in straw. Sand scurried before the wind, snaking through the grass in grainy rivulets. The pines creaked. Though it is often depicted as such, Nature is rarely still. Stillness equates with death, and Nature is death's antithesis, always fiddling and twitching, moving, changing, adapting, ensuring that life, not death, wins the day.

Few places toss and turn more than the Outer Banks. In

complex geological terms the whole damn place is moving slowly westward, migrating out from under man's feet like a tablecloth pulled by a slow-witted magician.

Before my trip I had read with interest a magazine article on coastal erosion on the Outer Banks. Orrin Pilkey, a professor of geology at Duke University and one of the most respected students of the science of barrier islands, had accompanied the journalist to Shackleford Banks, the southernmost of the Outer Banks' barrier islands. On the beach Pilkey picked up a battered black oyster shell. Oysters are not found in the open ocean—the intense salinity would kill them. But they are found in the brackish waters of the sound. The shell, explained Pilkey, was a fossil from a marsh that had once stood where the beach was now.

Pilkey told the writer he wasn't overly concerned about these particular islands. No, he said, with the current rise in sea level, in a few generations the Outer Banks and most of the rest of the eastern seaboard's barrier islands would be abandoned; the serious sandbagging would be taking place in Manhattan, Boston, and Miami. In the interim engineers, of course, would build groins and sea walls to accelerate the erosion. Pilkey had already implemented more practical measures to account for the rising seas: a length of rope extended from the chimney of his Durham, North Carolina, home, ending at an anchor buried deep in his lawn.

I had walked the beach on Ocracoke the previous afternoon. The waves weren't big, maybe four feet, but each one fell on the sand with a hearty thump, clawing at the shore like a front-end loader. And they never stopped coming.

Coastal erosion is nothing new, but it has become a problem ever since man began building right at the ocean's edge, an edge that is continually moving inland. Before World War II beach houses and resorts covered just 10 percent of the islands along the Atlantic and Gulf Coasts. By the early 1980s development was swallowing up these barrier islands at a rate of six thousand acres a year.

Most of this erosion proceeds imperceptibly, which explains why real estate agents on barrier islands can sell oceanfront homes to folks from Idaho that locals wouldn't touch even if they could afford them. But some change is sudden, and few places see more sudden changes than North Carolina's barrier islands. The history of the Outer Banks is one of storms. Positioned as they are, the islands are a catcher's mitt for oceanic nastiness, especially in winter. Tropical depressions, hurricanes, nor'easters—they possess a touch both brutish and artful. On September 5, 1996, Hurricane Fran sent a twelve-foot storm surge across the northern end of Topsail Island, wiping away homes, roads, and people. It set out a silver tea set, a perfectly made bed, and a scattering of intact lightbulbs across the beach, should anyone find a working light fixture.

Everywhere you turn on the Outer Banks there is water, stretching uncaring and implacable to the horizon. It doesn't take much imagination to see it rising up and overrunning the place, especially in fall and winter, when storms march ashore as if God has fallen asleep with his hand on the havoc button. Even the vegetation seems aware of its precarious position. Bushes and trees bend low in obeisance, as if hoping the Big One (the massive hurricane that, eventually, is guaranteed to make landfall with horrific consequence) will lumber past unaware of their presence, moving on to bash some haughty, nose-thumbing, high-rise of a place like New York City. Don't scoff. To their own surprise, hurricane researchers, conducting the mandatory storm-evacuation studies required of all large communities on the East Coast, have found that New York is uniquely situated for a serious ass-kicking. Among other humiliations, computer models of a category 4 hurricane (winds of 131 to 155 miles an hour) have put John F. Kennedy International Airport under twenty feet of water and, surely for the first time in history, rendered New York cabbies directionless. Driven by the screaming winds, the storm surges will pour into the Holland and Brooklyn Battery Tunnels, as well as subways throughout lower Manhattan.

There is also a plain eerie weirdness to the Outer Banks. The shoals just offshore are well known as the Graveyard of the Atlantic; in December 1862 the "invincible" ironclad USS *Monitor* went down off Cape Hatteras in a gale. But fewer know of the *Carroll A. Deering*, a hulking five-master out of Bath, Maine, found aground off Hatteras on January 31, 1921, her sails set, the crew's food in the galley, and everyone vanished. Sudden disappearance can also lightning-strike a party of one. Anglers, fishing for the monstrous offshore tuna that frequent the Banks in winter, have been plucked overboard. Only God knows their last thoughts as they whirligig for the deeps still strapped to their fishing chairs.

Traveling the Outer Banks, I continually felt this spinal sense of danger. It was like admiring a sleepy lion at the zoo and knowing that, should the glass disappear, a good nap would suddenly be the last thing on both your minds.

"The sea-shore," wrote Thoreau, "is a sort of neutral ground." I would disagree. It is entirely Nature's place. Man exists there through ignorance and doggedness.

❧

THE BLACKNESS of the winter nights lent an uncivilized air to Ocracoke. I have been in darker places, but they were in the Peruvian Andes or Australia's Outback. It was odd to experience similar darkness but with take-out pizza right at hand. Still, pepperoni's proximity didn't relax my sense of vigilance. In the velvety night of Australia's wilds you may inadvertently step on a deadly brown snake, but on Ocracoke you may just as easily see a bicyclist's profile suddenly mashed against your windshield.

Driving to Philip's potluck on Sunday night, I eked along the dark roads, unable to count on the taillights of other drivers. That afternoon I had watched the final wave of visitors leave the island. When I stopped at the variety store to buy some supplies, the dirt parking lot had been clogged with cars. Inside the store moms supervised final purchases ("No, Jimmy, you can't have a soda, soda makes you pee"), while out in the parking lot swearing dads tried to find a place to stuff them. It was the same exodus you see on Labor Day, but instead of damp towels and sandy buckets mashed to the back windshield, now there were mittens and down jackets.

Tonight the parking lot was empty. A new sign was affixed to the window: "Beginning December 1 now closing hour early 7 P.M." The wind hunted down the empty streets looking for someone to sting.

It was anything but dark inside Philip's home. When I arrived at six-thirty, there was already a crowd of people inside, and more soon emerged from the darkness, like moths heading for the warm light. As kids played in the living room, their parents clustered in the small dining room and kitchen. The dining room table was piled high with food: garden salad, bean salad, creamed spinach, the eternal Jell-O dish. In the kitchen a heavenly aroma of beef stew rose from an enormous pot. Only one person had been crass enough to bring store-bought items, but Philip accepted my donation of pizza and beer graciously.

Laughter filled the air, fueled by the ample cluster of wine bottles on the kitchen counter. It seemed to me, though, that more than fermented grapes was at work. I was reminded of grade-schoolers, when the teacher leaves the room.

When I mentioned this to Philip, he smiled. "I think I can safely say that almost everyone on this island is really glad when this time of year comes, and you don't have to be onstage all the time."

The potluck was being held to honor everyone who had contributed to the *Ocracoke Observer* that year. I had already picked up November's issue and read it through. I liked the paper. It was newsy, with heartfelt editorials—"Why do they build on every #$%*& inch?" asked an editorial on developers—and it was an equal opportunity employer. Along with the requisite writers, the paper's masthead listed staff dogs (Buck, Kasey, and Jackson) and kids (Emmet and Caroline).

Philip introduced me to Linda Rippe and Sundae Horn. Linda is the *Observer*'s publisher, Sundae its editor. Sundae also has a lovely voice. I knew this already because I'd heard her sing two nights earlier at the music and storytelling festival. I have worked with plenty of editors, but I have heard none of them sing. There is likely a good reason for this.

When I told Sundae she was one of a kind, she laughed. "I'm not a newspaper editor by training," she said. "I kind of got talked into it. One of the great things about living here is you get to be a big fish in a small pond. I came here from Cleveland. If I walked into the *Cleveland Plain Dealer,* I don't think I'd be the editor."

Linda had also fallen into this labor of love. Like many of Ocracoke's permanent residents, she had first visited the island as a summer tourist, coming here for two weeks with her dog. During those visits she befriended the couple who owns the *Observer*. When they decided to stop publishing it, they suggested she take it over.

"It was all I could think about all the way home on the ferry," said Linda.

When she finished thinking, she packed up her things and left her software job in Raleigh. It hadn't been easy. Her first year on the island, she worked at one of the hotels, cleaned houses, and worked at Philip's store.

"A lot of people here have to work more than one job," she said. "You just do what you have to do to live here." We stood amid the merry crush around the dining room table. I smiled into strange faces and tried not to knock anyone into the creamed spinach.

I told Linda how I had watched the island empty in the afternoon.

"You should come back here in January and February," she replied. "It's virtually a ghost town. It's wonderful. The wintertime is really our time to do things like this. People have potlucks. You can go out on the beach and be the only one there. There's nobody. Nobody."

I thought this last word sounded a bit wistful. I had seen a picture in the *Observer* of three new mothers holding their babies at "their first Ocracoke School Halloween Carnival." They all looked tired but happy. Linda was single and looked to be in her fifties. It struck me that an island of seven hundred could be a very lonely place without someone to share your nights.

When I asked her about the drawbacks of living on the island, she didn't hesitate. "Well, there's no dentist, doctor, or hospital. There's still no place you can buy regular shoes and underwear. People go to Hatteras to do their major shopping." She shrugged. "But I knew about all the things that weren't here before I came. And after two years it doesn't matter."

Linda's gaze happily wandered the room. It occurred to me that foisting our own sensibilities on others isn't always fair or accurate.

If she was lonely, she didn't show it. Her eyes came back to me, but the joy hadn't left them. "It's hard to describe what happens to you when you come here," she said. "I never dreamed I would find a place like this. I really literally feel like kissing the ground each time I come back here."

Someone came up to Linda, asking about a recent editorial. Not wanting to monopolize her evening, I moved off. Standing alone, I saw a heavyset woman come through the back door. She nodded matter-of-factly to a few people, then tucked directly into the food. It appeared as if she hadn't eaten in some time.

I must have been staring.

"Joyce is the Methodist minister," said a slim woman standing beside me.

I was grateful for this information. When interacting with certain types—IRS auditors, card sharks, organized crime bosses, ministers—it's best to know their occupation from the outset.

I felt like I knew Joyce already. The peal of her church's bells carried across the island. I had even heard them that afternoon as I kayaked in Pamlico Sound.

When Joyce looked my way, I smiled at her. "I hear the lovely sound of your church bells all over town," I said.

Two men across the table guffawed. Joyce's eyebrows arched slightly between bites.

Sundae, moving past me, deftly leaned in close. "The bells were new last year," she whispered, "and they were kind of controversial." She continued speaking, now loud enough for Joyce to hear. "They didn't tell the community about the bells, and the first day they went off was the day after 9/11. It startled a lot of people."

Joyce forked up beans. Between bites she said to me, "Actually, they've been turned down. They were louder. We went from ringing them ten times a day to four times a day, and we turned the sound down."

Her words spoke of concession, but her tone wasn't conciliatory. It seemed to me a touch resentful, as if she and God had had to make an unnecessary sacrifice. I could see Philip watching me from the kitchen. It suddenly occurred to me that on a small island even the smallest of talk could have repercussions. The two men across the table were still enjoying a good chortle.

Joyce gazed at me, and her eyes narrowed. I was suddenly afraid she was going to ask me if the bells had drawn me to church this morning.

I was saved by a loud, blurting honk. Had a goose gotten loose?

"Uh-oh," said the woman beside me. "He's playing the trombone."

Sure enough, a stocky man was standing in the living room pouring his soul into a trombone. His cheeks puffed, his face flushed red, and his dark eyebrows arced with each note, which, after a series of unrecognizable blurts, became "When the Saints Go Marching In."

"Russ has been practicing, I can tell," the woman said appreciatively. "He plays on the ferry. You can see him on the very back, all by himself."

What Russ Newell lacked in polish, he made up for in enthusiasm. Best of all, he offered no excuses. "Never played anything in my life," he drawled, offering me a meaty hand. "Bought the thing for twenty-five bucks. I've only had two lessons, but I'm always practicing." He regarded the trombone with genuine fondness. "I'm gonna learn to play the damn thing if it kills me." He said it more to the trombone than to me.

"Do you really play on the ferry?" I asked. It conjured up a romantic picture, a solitary figure on the ferry's stern, trombone turned to the heavens, tone-deaf gulls wheeling overhead.

"Yep," said Russ. "I go to Hatteras about three times a week. You're supposed to practice thirty-five minutes, and it's a thirty-five-minute ride. They make me play on the back. They don't let me play up front."

"Why on the back?"

"Well hell, the back's where the engines are."

I felt an instant bond with this man. For a short time I had played the trumpet in elementary school. My parents were supportive, but they weren't deaf. I practiced in my room with the door shut.

That his own song was absorbed by throbbing diesel engines didn't offend Russ in the least. To the contrary, he took great pride in his fitful learning curve.

"One day one of the party fishing boats came up beside the ferry. Evidently they weren't catchin' any fish. So I played for them, and then I said, 'I've only had two lessons.' And everybody on that boat, in unison, said, 'You need two more!' " He beamed. "How are you liking our little island?"

Outside it was black, cold, and three thousand miles from my family. Inside it was warm with bodies and sociability. Aside from narrowly averting Methodists' wrath, I felt at home.

"I can't believe how nice everyone is," I said.

Russ didn't bother to lower his booming voice. "People here ain't normal," he said. "They don't appreciate good music, either."

✾

AFTER THE PARTY was over I sat down with Philip in his upstairs apartment. It was late, and he was tired. It had been a busy week-end. Friday night he had attended the music and storytelling festi-val, Saturday evening there had been a get-together and sing-along with friends, plus several full days at the Village Craftsman. Seeing he was tired, I had tried to bow out, but he dismissed my concerns. "I like to talk about Ocracoke," he said. "Besides, maybe someone will clean up while I'm up here."

Philip's apartment is small and tidy. Family pictures hang on the walls, and an antique lamp purses soft light through the room. Neat rows of books line the walls. There is no TV. Before he sat down, Philip shooed out a large, affronted cat who returned the insult by spending the next thirty minutes scratching at the closed door.

Philip is a bachelor. His wife has remarried. She and her hus-band were downstairs at the potluck, and she had played the piano at the sing-along the night before. "She's a really good pianist," said Philip.

I asked him about the pluses of living on the island. He repeated the refrain I had heard several times before: the sense of community, the natural beauty, the palpable sense of history one gets when one's antecedents are buried, literally, right outside the door.

During the potluck I had been nagged by a sense of something odd. Watching the easy mixing of the partygoers, Russ's spontaneous trombone recital, and even the minister's unabashed buffet bashing, I felt something amiss, but I couldn't put my finger on it.

Philip did it for me.

"One of the nicest things about living on Ocracoke is there's very little pretension. Everybody knows who you really are. I don't know what evening get-togethers are like off the island anymore, but I suspect they're kind of stiffer. Here it's more like family. You're not trying to impress anybody about anything because everybody knows you."

I thought of parties I'd been to; strangers often react to one another by subtly, or not so subtly, marking their place, mentioning their job (neurologist), or their children's accomplishments (elementary school neurologist), or maybe how they once saw the top of Oliver Sacks's head moving across the airport concourse. It was like dogs peeing on trees. On this night I had been spared this uncomfortable ritual. People accepted me as I was and offered themselves as they were. I had enjoyed it immensely.

Perhaps O'cockers retain this firm sense of self because, no matter where they are, they always have a place they call home.

Like many of the men on Ocracoke, Philip's own father had left the island to find work. He went to Philadelphia in 1927 at sixteen, promptly making an impression in the City of Brotherly Love. "His mother always told him to be polite to people, and when he passed somebody on the street to say hello," said Philip. "He said when he got to Philadelphia, it about wore him out walking down Broad Street saying hello to everybody." Philip's father lived in Philadelphia for almost forty years, although he never planned on staying there. He returned to Ocracoke in 1966.

In Philly, Philip informed me wryly, his father nearly came to an early end. "My father had never been off the island. He'd never seen an electric lightbulb. In the room he had, somebody had unscrewed the lightbulb, and he stuck his finger in the socket."

That Philip would recount a story of such sweet childish naïveté to me, a stranger and a writer, was charming. When I said as much, Philip regarded me bemusedly. Suddenly I felt like a child.

"We still have our secrets," he said.

I had seen a bumper sticker circulating about town. It read, "Republic of Ocracoke—An Island State of Mind." When I asked Philip if he would define an island state of mind, he rested his chin on his fingers and gave the question quiet thought. I looked out the window, a pointless exercise since there was nothing to see. Ice traced the window edges. The cat scratched at the door, and Philip's family members waited patiently on the wall for his answer.

Finally he shook his head. "There really isn't an answer to your question," he said. He thought a moment more, then smiled softly. "You know, one day it just kind of occurred to me there's a real small pool of potential partners on an island like this. But it's really, really difficult to think about finding somebody off the island because they don't have an island state of mind. I can't define it. It's just a different way of looking at life and thinking about things. When I go off the island, I can feel it. I don't really know how to describe it, but I feel it. We're just different."

I suddenly remembered two snippets of earlier conversations. The first was with a woman during intermission at the music festival. "Is there a movie theater in town?" I had asked.

"No, there isn't," she had said with a smile.

"Is this a substitute for a movie theater?" I asked.

She had looked at me puzzled. "I would say that movies are substitutes for this," she said.

The second was with Senator Buffy. "Life here in the winter isn't for everybody," he had said when I asked him how quiet things got. "There are people who literally freak out. It's a claustrophobic thing."

My mind swooped like a bird through the darkness, over the small cemetery just outside Philip's window and across the tops of the pines, then skimmed low past the silent community center and out along the Irvin Garrish Memorial Highway, running its straight and empty two-lane beeline beneath the stars. I looked at my watch.

It was eleven P.M. In summer, at the edge of town, Howard's Pub would be blaring light and music into the night, and on down the road couples would be walking the water's edge, fishermen would be casting lines, and teenagers would be looking for a dune where they could smoke pot and drink warm beer. Tonight the world beyond town was wax myrtle, yaupon, and brown seagrass, pressed with silence and frost.

By most people's definition there was nothing out there.

Philip sat serenely before me, a man in his place.

"We're different," he said again.

※

WHEN I RETURNED to my room, I read some back issues of the *Observer* in bed, the wind rattling the windows and the cold seeping through the walls. I read about a local man imprisoned for cruelty to animals after police discovered that his goats and chickens were given no water (they drank the polluted water on his wetlands property) and had only the shelter of an old van, which lost its allure after several animals crawled into it to die. On returning from prison, he dug a trench on his property, put food in it, and shot the goats when they came to eat. I also read Philip's full-page letter complaining about the Methodist church's new bells, which chimed in a direct line to his apartment windows. According to Philip's letter, the church's board of trustees initially turned the other cheek so that they might present their deaf ear, sending him a letter stating that "we do not feel that there is a need to try to reason with your criticism of Ocracoke United Methodist Church's Chimes."

When I finished reading, I still couldn't sleep, so I bundled up and walked Ocracoke's silent streets beneath a squinty-bright silver moon.

I thought about the conversations I'd had. I thought of Linda leaving an established life and job for a new life and jobs unknown; of Buffy, turning his back on the power and perks of politics to become a publican with the best sign in town; of Philip's father, strolling down Philadelphia's Broad Street startling strangers, knowing that his footsteps would eventually return him to an island where everyone waved back; of Russ and his trombone blurting their song to heaven and engine.

Which is real, life on an isolated winter island or life in the hub-bub of a city center? I had asked that question of many people I met on Ocracoke. CNN had called Ocracoke's residents "refugees from reality," but that assessment could be discounted because the media often look for a pithy catchphrase, even if it subverts—or sacri-fices—the truth. Philip, who had heard countless vacationers bemoan their inevitable end-of-summer return to the real world, believed the tourists had it backward: the unassuming lifestyle of Ocracoke was reality, and the world of high heels, neckties, and Palm Pilots was fiction. Buffy, who had strode the halls of Washing-ton, presumably in a necktie, told me Ocracoke life was fantasy, which was precisely why he found the island so attractive.

I walked for a long time just thinking and then found myself climbing a rise through the dunes. The sand was blue in the moon-light. The sea grass stood still, and the stars hung equally frozen. The ocean moved. The waves, dark creases, rolled in from the sea. As they neared shore, they rose and gathered the moonlight on their sloped backs and glittering faces. The waves came to shore like God's own pageant queens, sequined and sparkling and perfectly spaced. The foremost wave would rear in final, full-fledged preen, then arc forward and disintegrate in a turmoil of white that zippered down the beach, cracking and hissing as it went.

There was, as everyone had said, nobody on that beach.

Watching the unfurling waves, the words of a song I'd heard at the music festival drifted into my head: " 'Bobby told Lucy the world ain't round, drops off sharp at the edge of town . . .' "

Islands are synonymous with escape, but that is only wordplay. Ocracoke is not idyllic. People shoot goats; they snipe at and divorce each other; and the church bells violate your sanctity. There is no escaping reality, because we carry it with us. But we do choose the version we wish to live with.

On the news the next morning, CNN reported that a woman in San Jose, California, had been trampled in a Thanksgiving weekend shopping melee.

9
THE OUTER BANKS
Blackbeard Lives

ON THE OUTER BANKS I fell under the spell of Edward Teach. Or Thatch. Or Thach. Or Thache, depending on which historical account you read. History often becomes confused with time, especially if that history involves a man as multihued as Blackbeard.

Blackbeard was famously famous—fictionalized by Robert Louis Stevenson (*Treasure Island*) and immortalized in poem by Benjamin Franklin, an impressionable young printer's apprentice in Boston during the height of Blackbeard's piratical career, from roughly 1716 to 1718:

> *So each man to his gun, for the work must be done with cutlass, sword and pistol.*
> *And when we can no longer strike a blow then fire the magazine, boys, up we go.*
> *It is better to swim in the sea below, than to hang in the air and feed the crow, sang jolly Ned Teach of Bristol.*

Franklin settled on Teach, and the editor of the Declaration of Independence likely spelled better than most. Still, in all the writings on Blackbeard, few agree on the pirate's true name, or even where he came from. Bristol, England, according to most scholars. London, says one. Philadelphia, says another. The man has been pinned to more places than Elvis.

Most historians do agree that Blackbeard made a base on Ocracoke Island, and from there he sailed, causing considerable pains to colonial authorities and, probably, to the sailors he and his men fell upon. On one occasion Blackbeard purportedly removed and boiled an adversary's lips, then made the man eat them. Some historians pooh-pooh this account, but it's just like academics to bleed the fun out of everything. Even if Blackbeard didn't make the man eat his own lips, there is enough historic fact to indicate he would have appreciated the idea.

Whether the remaining bits of trivia I happened upon in my readings are true or not doesn't make them any less fun. Blackbeard had fourteen wives. He stuck lit cannon fuses in his beard before battles. He shot off the knee of one of his crew. He went into the hold, had pots of sulphur lit, and stayed in the smoke until everyone else fled. His skull was made into the bottom of a large punch bowl, last seen during the candlelight initiation rites of a University of Virginia fraternity. This last item may sound ridiculously far-fetched, but there is precedent for it. Plutarch and Herodotus both recorded similar skull-to-goblet conversions practiced by the Teutons, Scythians, and Tibetans. Plus, I attended the University of Virginia for four years, and I can confidently say the undergraduates there will drink out of anything.

The true event of Blackbeard's propensity for violence and mayhem remains unknown. Several historians believe he was less a lusty pirate than a shrewd intimidator; folks who feared they might end up digesting their own collagen had less stomach for a fight, often surrendering before a blow was struck. David Moore, one of the most respected Blackbeard scholars, claims that though "Blackbeard cultivated a 'demon from hell' look," there is no evidence he ever killed a man until the final battle that cost him his life.

According to Moore, Blackbeard operated far more fairly than the governments of his time. Ship's officers aboard the *Queen Anne's Revenge* were elected. The entire crew was involved in "general consultations" regarding itinerary and strategy, and everyone got a share of the loot, though the captain got two shares.

Whatever Blackbeard's propensity for bloody violence might have been, his joy in sticking it to the bewigged authorities of his time cannot be doubted. My personal favorite incident occurred off Charleston, South Carolina, in May 1718. With his crew short on medicine, Blackbeard and the cannon-bristling *Queen Anne's Revenge* hunkered outside the city's harbor, plucking hostages from incoming ships, many of them Charleston's most prominent citizens. Deliver a chest of medicine, Blackbeard demanded of the townspeople, or receive the hostages' heads. The medicine was delivered, and the hostages were returned, "sent ashore almost naked," wrote South Carolina's governor in an indignant letter to London.

It is easy, and pleasant, to visualize the scene: Charleston's haughtiest citizens delivered ashore to the waiting townsfolk as only their mothers and wives knew them. There's no better cure for self-absorption than a good stripping.

Politicians were as humorless then as they are now, and this incident marked the beginning of the end for Blackbeard; within six months his severed head was hanging from the bowsprit of the sloop commanded by British lieutenant Robert Maynard after a fierce battle in Ocracoke Inlet.

To my mind, Blackbeard was a man to be admired. True, he didn't kowtow to authority, but he was fair and you knew where he stood. No surprise, O'cockers admire him, too. Along the road edging Silver Lake Harbor I saw a historical sign: "Lt. Robert Maynard. Of the Royal Navy. Sent by Gov. Spotswood of Virginia, in the sloop *Ranger*, killed the pirate Blackbeard off shore, 1718," it reads, though some of those final words are riddled with buckshot.

✻

BEFORE LEAVING OCRACOKE, I paddled the waters once split by the *Queen Anne's Revenge*. Historians believe Blackbeard operated from the southern end of the island, anchoring in a shallow channel on the Pamlico Sound side near Ocracoke Inlet. From there Blackbeard could see passing boat traffic before it saw him. "Teach's Hole" is clearly marked on modern nautical charts.

Teach's Hole is also where Blackbeard met his end. Few historians debate the violence of the November 21, 1718, battle that saw

Blackbeard absorb some six gunshot wounds and twenty cutlass slices before someone finally thought to lop off his head.

I eased my kayak into Silver Lake Harbor one blustery afternoon; the blue sky hung with fast-moving gray clouds running with the chill northerly wind.

It takes only a few minutes to paddle the length of Ocracoke's tiny harbor to where it opens up to Pamlico Sound. Paddling toward the harbor mouth, I could see an uncountable army of whitecaps frothing into the distance until they disappeared from sight.

Another kayaker bobbed at the harbor mouth. I saw him before he saw me. His head was down. I could see the waterproof chart, likely a nautical chart, spread across the deck of his red kayak. He had a compass, too, and was nattily covered in various waterproof gear.

I suddenly felt as naked and embarrassed as Blackbeard's hostages marching along the quays of Charleston. It was true, I had thought to wear a wetsuit, but I still felt like a child leaving home with matches and a bag of licorice in his backpack. I have never been much for equipment or planning. Ours is a wondrous age of technological doodads: thumbnail-size camping stoves and global positioning systems that pinpoint the animal droppings you're standing on. But I lose equipment, and I usually don't know how to work the equipment I manage to hang on to. I realize it is unwise to head into a wild place without even a compass, but I would surely get lost wandering around trying to find where I put it. As for planning, it smothers spontaneity; or, to be honest, it requires too much work.

My fellow kayaker was bristling with equipage, and, judging from the focused look on his face, he knew how to use it. I considered paddling quietly past—perhaps he wouldn't look up—but this seemed both cowardly and alarmingly antisocial. Plus, you never know what you'll learn if you speak to people.

"Beautiful out here, isn't it?" I said.

His head came up slowly, as if reluctant to leave the chart. He appeared to be in his fifties, though it was hard to tell, as only a small portion of his face emerged from the bubble-wrap of protective gear.

"It sure is," he said, absorbing my bare skin and minimalist equipage with a practiced glance.

Being short—roughly eight feet—my kayak is maneuverable, but it is also easily buffeted by wind. In the exposed harbor mouth, the wind had assumed new velocity. I had to dig my paddle into the water to keep my bow from swinging around and the winds from shoving me unceremoniously sideways back into the harbor.

My companion's kayak was the traditional model made for long oceangoing paddles, nearly twenty feet and annoyingly stable. His paddle rested beneath the chart, and his bow remained precisely pointed into the wind.

"Where are you heading?" he asked.

It was a polite inquiry, though I thought I detected a trace of professional concern. Few things rankle me, but one of them is people who assume a superiority of competence, even if it does exist.

"I don't know," I said.

This was largely true. I knew I was turning left once I exited the harbor, though now this didn't seem like much of a navigational plan. I certainly wasn't going to tell him I was thinking about paddling to Teach's Hole. If it was a nautical chart spread on his deck, he would quickly calculate the distance and my idiocy.

We floated in the water, the wind beating between us, and exchanged pleasantries. His name was David. He was from Cary, North Carolina. He'd come to Ocracoke for the long Thanksgiving weekend.

He didn't smile as we talked, but his tone was amiable. I had drifted close enough to see that he had a small plastic orb affixed to the shoulder of his jacket. Technologically speaking, it resembled one of those Christmas snowglobes, only instead of swirling snowflakes, it contained a winking light.

His eyes followed mine. "I'm one of those people who like to plan," he said. The statement was unapologetic and his face remained expressionless, but it seemed to me a humorous nod to his own personal quirk.

I appreciated his honesty.

David asked where I was from, and when I told him California, he said his wife's family lived in California. "My wife died about a year and a half ago," he said. "Of cancer."

The water slapped at the sides of my kayak, and the wind blew in from a horizon without color.

It is impossible to find the right words for sorrow like this, so I said what I felt, and the words sounded pointless and trite: "I'm so sorry."

Then I realized David was finishing his voyage, not beginning it.

"I was just paddling in a sluice back there," he said almost absently. "There were herons and egrets. It probably goes back two miles. You know, I was paddling back there and I'm thinking, 'This is one of the most beautiful places I've ever seen.'"

The wind had gathered strength. A quarter-mile of paddling in the open sound was enough to convince me to discard my search for Teach's Hole and duck into David's sluice instead. Sheltered from the wind, the sluice, little wider than my paddle in most places, meandered toward the interior of the island, through straw-colored marsh grass and a few scattered guano-stained trees. The water was less than a foot deep in some places, the tide was running out, and beneath the water's marble-clear and smooth surface, I could see tiny bird tracks in the mud bottom, fine, graceful etchings that sang of flight.

Out of the wind it was warm. Birds sang, and egrets, snow-white and silent, swooped low, dropping below the brown grass line to their own secrets. The bow of my kayak created ripples that made their reluctant way to the mud bank, where they were absorbed forever.

When I finally turned around, I stopped paddling and closed my eyes, and the tide's delicate tug drew me slowly back to the sound.

It was lovely, but it was hung with sadness, too, this beautiful place given to me by a man who couldn't plan for everything.

✳

THE NEW PIRATES of the Outer Banks are the developers.

I left Ocracoke on a Monday, crossing Hatteras Inlet by empty ferry to a Cape Hatteras I didn't recognize. The 208-foot-high

Hatteras Lighthouse, 9.6 million pounds of granite, brick, marble, brass, iron, and bronze, is still there, though it has been moved back a half-mile from the beach, wholly intact (reaching a top speed of one foot a minute) to save it from pitching into the sea. (When the lighthouse was first built, just after the Civil War, it stood eighteen hundred feet from the sea.) The unfettered dunes that curve along the length of the National Seashore remain, too. But in dunes where development has not been stymied by federal decree, enormous homes rise into the gray sky.

Homes is not the proper term for this new development on the Outer Banks. Three to four stories high and equally deep and wide, these monstrosities are too big to be homes. Twenty years before I had seen cottages, ramshackle things, weathered to the blandness of the dunes, fronted with a loamy drive and equipped perhaps with a washer-dryer and a fish-cleaning table. The new places I saw as I drove north from the ferry landing were bright-colored and many-windowed. Where they hadn't required the complete removal of the dunes, they ground them underfoot, squat lords gazing imperiously out to sea. I found an old copy of a local newspaper, advertising one of these summer rentals: seven thousand square feet, seven bed-rooms—five with a Jacuzzi, one with two Jacuzzis—a game room, three home theater systems, and a heated pool. "Ocean Dream," the ad said. *Why even bother with the beach?* I thought.

These homes were empty now, which depressed me even more. They sat under the bleak gray sky, their windows as black as cat's eyes. They were soulless and emanated vague threat.

The threat was vague to me, but not to those who live in Hat-teras. Another newspaper article described the fast-changing times: in late 2002 a half-acre lot in Hatteras Village was selling for $875,000. It's no surprise that every available inch of that half-acre has been smothered, then raised again into the sky. The article focused on a proposed forty-five-unit condominium complex, and local resistance to that project. "We are not going to back up now," stated the developer. "It has become a matter of principle." "You can't adjust to development like this," opined a local. "These guys literally and figuratively bulldoze their way to whatever they want . . . It's the extermination of a place, and a way of life."

This was civilized discourse on the printed page. But the Outer Banks are still inhabited by cuss-tough sorts who are not easily quoted or bulldozed. On Ocracoke I had heard the story of a Hatteras fisherman who had inherited some stock. He wanted to cash it in and buy land and a dock, so he called a broker.

Sell the stock, he told the broker, and send me the cash.

You'd be crazy to sell, the broker said. It's a gold stock, it'll only go up.

I want to sell.

I can't let you do that.

How about this? I don't give a damn what you think. Sell it, or I'll come down and shoot you.

"He would have shot him, too," the storyteller told me.

With people with spine like this, perhaps some hope remains. I drove slowly north along Highway 12, entertaining myself with happy visions of rogue citizens' gangs torching the monolithic structures and putting the developers to sea in small rowboats.

But the reality is different. There aren't enough rowboats. The homes are just as big, and more numerous, in Nags Head and Duck. I kept driving, finally reaching the end of the road at a sign identifying the ensuing stretch of beach as Currituck Banks.

"Part of the North Carolina Estuarine Research Reserve," read the sign. "Home to Atlantic bottle-nosed dolphins, red-tailed hawks, and osprey."

All of which were probably preparing to flee in the face of the ever-coming lumber trucks. At the very edge of the reserve stood another new neighborhood of summer homes, presumably for families who practiced the same birth control method as the Waltons. Apparently, too, procreation was the only fun they could count on—signs proclaimed the enclave to be "The Villages of Ocean Hill. A Private Community Governed by Restrictive Covenants." Apparently people with more porch space than sense needed restriction.

I walked down to the beach that fronted the reserve. Here the dunes were empty. The seagrass lining their ridges was pressed on only by sky. Unimpeded, a west wind raked over the dunes. Like a powerful river, it swept up and over the ridge, and when it descended again to the beach, it set off swirling sandy eddies along its edges. It whopped in my ears, pushing so hard against my back that I had to dig in my heels to keep from being marched toward the ocean.

It is impossible to live in the past; our own needs make it so. I myself have spent summers in cottages that were once nothing but restless sand. My money and my need to be near the ocean have helped see to a small part of Nature's demise. But what I saw here on the Outer Banks was unnerving and different. When taste gives way to size, and foresight to the lust for profit, a place of salt and wide sky is obliterated almost entirely. When all our shoreline looks the same as our interior, it will be difficult to turn back the clock.

Before I left the Outer Banks, I made one last pass through Nags Head. I drove cautiously along Beach Road ("The speed limit says twenty-five, and cops here don't have anything better to do in the winter," a gas station attendant had warned me), past silent beach cottages and closed-down motels, their parking lots inhabited only by fluttering caution tape.

I stopped to stretch my legs. The skies had turned dark, in the roiling outer edges of the worst ice storm in North Carolina's history. To the west, four people had been killed; nearly 1.3 million were without electricity, and in Charlotte sidewalks were roped off as skyscrapers calved giant icicles. To the north, in New York, Connecticut, and Maine, feet of snow were falling, and schools and businesses were closing up like clams on an outgoing tide.

But here the Gulf Stream is the great moderator. The sky was ominous, but the temperature was close to balmy, in the mid-fifties, and the sodden air carried a false hint of spring. I walked along the water's edge watching small waves jumble and bump one another before crumbling lazily to shore. A hopeful gull followed my progress, soaring sideways on the breeze, its head swinging in nervous tics, alternately peering down at me and scanning the beach in search of coolers and trash.

It had rained hard the previous night. Close to shore the ocean was muddied. The waves had deposited great gobbets of brown foam on the beach, where they quivered and, now and again, leaped suddenly sideways in happy, amoebalike skips. My heart did the same.

It was early December now, but I walked in spring. I took off my shirt, spread my arms to the wind, and for no good reason shouted "Yes!" to the sky.

It is fun to spit in the face of convention. There is a little pirate in all of us.

10
VIRGINIA'S EASTERN SHORE
The Curious Case of George Avery Melvin

FEW PEOPLE RETURN from the dead, but George Avery Melvin did, and he did so dressed to the nines.

"An interesting case, the Melvin family," Jerry Doughty told me without emotion, when we first met on a Monday morning, two weeks before Christmas, on Virginia's Eastern Shore. "It was a spectacular news story around here."

I had spent several days holed up in a cheap motel, writing, in Virginia Beach, an unremarkable place of asphalt, high-rise hotels, and condominiums. "Winter Rates Are Blowing In, Name Your Price," read the sign out front, and variations of this plea were everywhere. The smell of pot and cooking drifted into the dim hallway from the other rooms. When I stayed in similar motels up and down the coast, I found they were often home to construction workers, in town to pick up cash during winter's preparations for summer. Along with these single men, there were families. I saw kids going off to school, and in the evenings their worn-looking mothers slouched home with single bags of groceries. I rarely saw fathers, and I never saw these families together. Everyone came and went from their rooms quickly, and no one smiled. I wondered where they went in the summer.

The motel was a block back from the beach, and twenty dollars a night cheaper than similar establishments twenty yards to the east. At night, outside my ice-edged window on the fourth floor, a three-story Christmas tree winked and sparkled where 26th Street runs into the boardwalk. It sat there cheerily between the Holiday

Inn and the Seahawk Motel, the ocean providing the perfect black-curtain backdrop. I imagined the motel children gazing at the glittering tree and wondered if their parents could afford more than groceries.

Outside sirens howled.

I called home.

Cullen was building a California mission for school. Kathy had bought tiny golden bells, black shoe polish, and a heaping supply of macaroni noodles.

"We put the shoe polish on the bells to make them look older," explained Cullen. "We're boiling the noodles right now. When they're soft, we'll cut them in half and then let them harden again. Then we'll use them for terracotta shingles."

My wife is an elementary school teacher, and her capacity for innovation never ceases to amaze me, though like any child, Cullen took parental genius for granted.

I could see him looking toward the kitchen where his mom stirred a steaming pot.

"I'm not sure *where* we'll make the farm animals," he said wistfully.

When Graham came on the phone, he was quiet. I extracted a hello from him. Then all I could hear was his soft breathing.

"How are you doing, little friend?"

"I'm doing okay . . . well, not too good."

"Why not?"

"You're gone," he said, and I realized how lucky I was.

Outside the motel the wind moaned, anxious to be let in out of the cold. I had been gone for two months, but I had made plans to fly home for two weeks at Christmas. Children are seven and nine only once in this life, and I wasn't going to be cheated out of the most wondrous of childish holidays.

"I'll be home in nine days," I said, for once sounding as cheerful as I felt. "That's not long at all. We'll blink, and I'll be hugging you."

"I blinked," Graham said bleakly.

Often when I called, Graham would wander around the house as we talked. He kept the phone pinched between his shoulder and his ear so his hands were free to pick things up. I knew this because now and again during our conversations I heard a beep as his chin pressed a button.

Suddenly he assumed a happily surprised tone. "Hey! I've got something in my ear!"

The phone beeped twice in rapid succession, then hit the ground with an eardrum-rupturing *clack*. My ear, thankfully, still worked. Though three thousand horizontal miles and some four vertical feet separated us, I heard Graham's voice clearly.

"Ewwwwwwww. Part of a Q-tip."

⁂

HAD JERRY DOUGHTY found a Q-tip in his ear, or a javelin for that matter, he would have extricated and examined it without expression, and without missing a beat. Jerry has wild gray hair that he partially tames with a ball cap. He favors brown polyester slacks, a thin brown jacket, and worn New Balance sneakers, and when he isn't being addressed directly, he stands aside, quiet as stone, watching. Jerry was born on the Eastern Shore, in Nassawadox, in 1944. He has lived most of his life a skip away, in Willis Wharf. He never married. He taught U.S. history at the local middle school for over thirty years and took care of his parents until they died.

In the several days I spent with him, that represents almost everything I learned about Jerry. He eagerly answered questions about his Eastern Shore home and just as eagerly deflected questions about himself. Officially Jerry is now the docent at the Barrier Islands Center in Machipongo, a wonderful repository of Eastern Shore history, but he is much more than that.

We met at the Barrier Islands Center. I had driven from Virginia Beach across the Chesapeake Bay Bridge-Tunnel that morning. The balm of the Outer Banks was gone—a furious wind raked the bay. While driving across the seventeen-mile bridge, I felt the van lurch and buck. Seagulls, riding updrafts, whipped up suddenly from beneath the bridge and shot across the road, like clay pigeons sprung from traps. A few had appeared too suddenly; their broken bodies lay in the road.

Winter and silence had descended across the bridge. On maps, the bridge-tunnel connects Norfolk to the Eastern Shore. In real life, it is a wormhole. You leave Norfolk's citified jumble, clack across the frighteningly narrow bridge building speed, plunge beneath the water, and emerge to farms, woods, sweet air, and wide sky. Should you yank the car to the side of the road to fight down panic, you might be calmed by the sight of a curious deer, or the hypnotic chat of Atlantic brant, the birds issuing odd basso croaks, like frogs clamoring beside a creek.

I followed Route 13, the main and only highway up the Eastern Shore, past fallow fields, freeze-dried and cropped nearly to the ground, their brown stubble shorn crew-cut close. Now and again the fields were interrupted by a smoking-chimney farmhouse. Truck commerce rumbled along, accompanied by folks hurrying somewhere else, heading north to Ocean City, Maryland, or south to Norfolk. The side roads were a joy. Stoplights swung pointlessly in the wind—in 1970 Northampton County possessed two traffic lights, and thirty-three years later there isn't need for many more—and churchyard headstones pushed to the edge of the road, tilting forward to peer vainly for a ride.

"Here there is nothing to do, oh no," lamented an Indian hotel clerk. "There is no shopping, no malls. Unless you are busy with your job, the day is long."

I took to the place instantly.

I came to the Eastern Shore to see Hog Island. Twenty-three barrier islands lie off the Eastern Shore, the best known of which is Chincoteague; visitors can drive on to this National Wildlife Refuge to pick their way around pony droppings, though they are forbidden to do so in the buff. ("Nudity Prohibited," read a sign I saw when I visited Chincoteague later in the week, proving that federal regulators have not yet run out of imaginative avenues for repression.) But the majority of the islands—with singsong names like Metompkin, Mockhorn, Parramore, and Assawoman—are shielded from man and queer signage by the grand buffer of water, and all are protected by various entities: the federal government, the Nature Conservancy, and even the United Nations, which has declared the islands unique and beautiful enough to be recognized as an International Biosphere Reserve.

With due respect to the United Nations, I found another accolade more impressive.

"Finest damn beaches you'll see anywhere," said a chaw-chewing fellow seated in a pickup in front of the Great Machipongo Clam Shack. "Miles of nothing that make you realize you're nothing. You can piss into the wind and holler your heart out to the heavens, and no one will be the wiser."

He deposited a collection of phlegm and tobacco neatly in the cold gravel. It quivered there, steaming.

He squinted at me. " 'Course weather like this, your pecker might freeze solid."

The veracity of all this was beyond question. I have spent enough time in the outdoors to know why pissing into the wind leads to heartfelt hollering.

I yearned to see those beaches and stroll their empty reaches, but Hog Island intrigued me for another reason. In the early 1900s it was home to the village of Broadwater, a thriving community of some 250 people, with sixty-plus homes, a church, three general stores, a post office, and an ice cream parlor. Most of Broadwater now rests beneath the Atlantic Ocean. In the 1930s Hog Island simply walked out from under the village, Nature's wry answer to man's short-term hubris.

Jerry, I learned almost immediately, has a connection with Hog Island. "My family owned it," he said, offering nothing more.

I followed Jerry as he walked slowly through the Barrier Islands Center looking at the displays and pictures. Our footfalls echoed on the hardwood floors, and framed faces long gone frowned down at us.

"There were all kinds of classes on the islands," Jerry explained to me. "The rich, the famous, and the infamous came and did exactly what they pleased. We've been known for smuggling and blockade-running. My great-grandfather was a blockade-runner at fifteen. And during Prohibition a lot of local farmers were in league with the mob. Plenty of places for private landings."

We stopped before several caricature sketches of Union soldiers on Hog Island. In the summer of 1864 Union soldiers were garrisoned there to protect a lighthouse that had already been wrecked once by Confederate sympathizers. In one sketch the soldiers are merrily exploring; in another they enjoy a swim. In a third their faces are screwed in anguish, and mosquitoes swarm like dark basketballs.

Jerry examined me as I examined the drawing. "It was just like a George Lucas special-effects horror movie in the warm months," he said. "Almost every day the mosquitoes came down on them and just tore them up and caused their eyes to swell shut."

I thought I caught a tinge of satisfaction in his voice, though his face remained blank.

The local Indians were aware of the mosquitoes, steering clear of the island in the summer. They called Hog Island Machipongo. The singsong name likely fell prettily upon the Anglo ear.

"Machipongo means 'fine sand and flies,'" said Jerry.

Jerry stopped before another picture. Ten children surrounded a straight-backed, distinguished-looking gentleman with long gray hair. "That's my great-great-grandfather, Martin Doughty," he said. "It's the oldest picture we've found so far of a scene on Hog Island. I think it's about 1882."

Jerry gazed at the picture. Then he said dreamily, as much to himself as to me, "When I saw Hog Island for the first time in the fifties, I couldn't believe people had lived there."

❧

SINCE I WAS the center's only visitor, Jerry took me on a tour of Willis Wharf. We drove north on Route 13, forking off at Exmore, driving past the Exmore Diner ("Old-Fashioned Food, Old-Fashioned Prices") and the brick-fronted hardware store with a Christmas wreath and a Radio Flyer scooter in the window. Then we turned right again, heading down Willis Wharf Road, past the sign just outside town—"Welcome to Willis Wharf, Founded in 1854"— that has been a thorn in Jerry's side for years. "It wasn't founded in 1854." Jerry refused to look at the sign. "We go back to the sixteen hundreds. This is an irritant to me."

We drove toward the water, past weathered clapboard homes ringed by rusted metal fences, some with Nativity scenes in their brown yards.

It was a bleak day; leafless trees pronged hopelessly up into a cold, pale gray sky. Perhaps this affected Jerry's mood. We had already stopped at two cemeteries. ("They say all the best stories are in the cemetery," he observed.) He had also recounted several tales of woe, halting each story before revealing any particulars, though he did let it darkly drop that one calamity involved his own family tree.

The nature of the ruin varied, but the recountings all went something like this.

"They used to call that Satan's Three Acres," Jerry would say, nodding vaguely off to his left, at a parcel of land that could have been in Willis Wharf or, just as easily, in Dayton, Ohio. "It's a genuine curiosity. Everyone who lived there or pushed up against it got pushed back. Financial scandals, family curses, massive suicides . . ."

Tales of suicides, curses, incestuous relations—all were recounted to me in the same animated tone that flight attendants use to describe lap belt workings. After ending a tale prematurely, Jerry would regard me poker-faced. "You can't believe it. I wish I could tell you more, but I can't."

After a time I saw that Jerry possessed a dry-ice sense of humor. I wondered if his scandal-sheet game of cat and mouse might be a form of amusement; he dangled catnip before me, watching to see how actively I'd swat. I wasn't offended. He told me what I needed to know and what I would never know. Frankly, I didn't care. I felt sorry for the families that had suffered but felt no urge to broadcast their private sufferings to the world. Prime-time TV specials ably take care of that these days.

We drove slowly along Willis Wharf's waterfront. The barest of breezes blew in off Parting Creek, mucky and saline. A few small oyster boats bobbed off weathered docks. The waterfront looked like an odd mix of the Gaza Strip and *Close Encounters of the Third Kind*. Large stretches stood empty, unless you counted grass and weeds, jumbled piles of broken brick, and concrete slabs fractured and sliding into Parting Creek. Alongside these ruins stood tidy rows of long, low-slung buildings, each glowing dimly.

"Aquaculture," said Jerry. He shook his head slowly, an un-Jerry-like burst of emotion. "This doesn't look anything like it did when I was a child. There was all kinds of activity down here. You should have seen it when it was going full blast with all the packinghouses. It was really something."

We crossed a small creek, gray and still on the slack tide. Shortly thereafter we turned right.

Jerry motioned for me to stop.

We sat in the middle of the road. Jerry said nothing. I glanced at him out of the corner of my eye. He sat beneath his ball cap, monk-serene, staring out the windshield.

I was catching on. I said nothing. Through the windshield I saw a narrow gravel road running but a short distance before it ended. The road was lined on both sides with weathered clapboard homes no different from the others we had passed. A scarecrow sat in one front yard; an American flag hung listless from a tall pole in another.

The silence continued while I mentally wrestled for the lesson Jerry was trying to impart.

"Six or seven of these homes came over from Hog Island when they abandoned the island," Jerry said after a time. "Transported over here on barges. Sometimes there would still be a fire going in the fireplace. You could see the smoke coming out the chimneys as they came across the bay."

I looked at the street sign: Hog Island Lane.

❋

RICK KELLAM had been to Hog Island recently. Not only that, he was willing to take me there, which was how I came to witness a piece of heaven and learn the true particulars behind George Melvin's resurrection, Rick being his great-grandson.

Rick, like Jerry, has family roots that plow deep into the soil of both Willis Wharf and Hog Island. By his own estimate, Rick's first ancestor set foot on Hog Island in the mid-1700s. Rick, like Jerry, is courteous and helpful to a point almost past belief, though while Jerry is stoic, Rick is boisterous. Rick, unlike Jerry, visits the Eastern Shore's barrier islands, Hog Island included, frequently. He has worked for the Virginia Marine Police for eighteen years as officer in charge of the area. He has written several books about the islands. These days he runs his own company, Broadwater Bay Ecotours, taking tourists out to the islands in a twenty-four-foot Carolina skiff.

When I called him, he straightened out one popular misconception right off the bat. I had assumed large parts of Hog Island were under water. I envisioned an island that was but a shadow of its former self.

It's true, Rick said amiably, that most of the village of Broadwater now rests beneath the Atlantic. But Hog Island itself is roughly the same size it has always been—about six miles long and a mile and a half wide. Now it is simply located farther west.

When I mentioned my plan to paddle to Hog Island, Rick was polite. "Waaaall, I wouldn't recommend taking a kayak out there," he drawled tactfully. "It's pretty far. Plus the waters can be kind of treacherous if you don't know them. It could be done, I suppose, but it wouldn't be wise."

I have been around enough nautical sorts to read between the lines: *Go on your own and if God is on your side, they may find your bloated body washed ashore in the Azores.*

"Will you take me out to Hog Island?" I asked.

Simple as that, it was done.

⁂

ON THE DAY we went out to Hog Island, we met for breakfast at the Exmore Diner. I had eaten at the diner the night before. To keep costs low, I generally divided my dinners between chunky soup cooked over a small propane stove in my motel room, taking care to cook far away from any curtains, and fast-food restaurants, where I could get my weekly allotment of cholesterol for less than two dollars. But at the Exmore Diner, a five-minute drive from Willis Wharf, I could afford to splurge. Stuffed shrimp and crabcakes went for $8.95, fresh oysters were $7.95, and, for the fearless and budget-inclined, a bowl of lima bean soup was $1.70. At mealtimes the diner was ringed with an Indian headdress of pickup trucks, and the small interior resounded with the happy clamor of locals getting a good meal at a fair price.

Breakfast was just as pleasing: steak and eggs for $4.50, creamed chipped beef with home fries $3, hotcakes with melted sharp cheese $1.50.

"Unbelievable, isn't it?" Rick laughed.

The town, as its name implies, is grounded in the water. Since man first took up residence along Parting Creek—in the 1600s, if you believe Jerry; since 1854, if you favor signs—oysters, clams, scallops, fish, and crabs have provided meals and livelihoods. But like many of the coastal towns I visited, this one had changed. At one time Willis Wharf and the rest of the Eastern Shore had bestowed shellfish on the world just as the Renaissance had produced art. On Hog Island alone, clams were collected from the beach by the canoeful.

Rick had oystered for a time, and he was frank. "We'd harvest five hundred to seven hundred bushels a day, every day except Sunday," he said, sipping hot coffee. "We harvested a lot of oysters, and they were the juveniles, the spawning oysters. We were wiping them out, but all we saw was dollar signs in our eyes. And we weren't the only ones. It was being done all up and down the coast. We were taking what would have kept the oyster business going. We thought there was no end."

But there was an end. Oysters, clams, and scallops, made Nature's way, are now pretty much done. The new face in town is aquaculture—vast rows of water-filled troughs and buckets, overseen by Ph.D.'s, where happy shellfish live in perfectly moderated waters, eat all the algae they want, and, in their feisty robustness, shoot spumes of egg and sperm. Imagine a brackish Club Med.

There were four aquaculturists operating in Willis Wharf, said Rick, and if Nature didn't interfere, they were capable of productivity that rabbits would envy. "There's one building that can produce up to six hundred million small aquaculture clams a year," said Rick. "They don't, they produce about three hundred million, but it's still an amazing thing."

This new world order for the watermen proceeds in much the same fashion as the old, with a few twists. The eggs are fertilized indoors under the watchful eye of aquaculturists. After an appropriate passage of time, the watermen take these seed shellfish from the farms and out into the wild, planting them in mud banks and flats and tending them lovingly until they are large enough to harvest. Then they haul them back to dock, the big companies market and sell them, and the watermen get their cut. It is by no means an ever-tidy process. Even lovingly tended shellfish have small chance in the wild—roughly five clam eggs out of a hundred survive to maturity. In recent years parasites with punk-rock names like MSX and Dermo have devastated the local oyster crop.

Earlier in the week I had gotten a glimpse of aquaculture at Cherrystone Aqua Farms. Mike Peirson, a marine biologist and the man who has pretty much built the operation from the ground up, showed me around. I watched uninhibited clams in long tubs, their siphons extended, expunge white clouds of sperm and eggs to begin the process. I peered into large vats where, if I squinted, I saw near-microscopic dust motes whirling on invisible microscopic currents: roughly 20 million clams in a single vat. There were lots of these vats. In fact, there was lots of everything spread across the greenhouse-warm buildings: troughs, vats, cylinders, and enormous plastic bags hanging like IV drips for sperm whales.

It was all about numbers, and the numbers were astonishing, a work of incontrovertible diligence and genius.

"This is a nine-million-dollar-a-year business in gross sales," said Peirson with deserved pride. "We now ship fifty million clams a year. Our goal is a hundred million seeds going out."

This was impressive, but what was really impressed upon me were the numbers I could no longer see. The day before I had walked the waterfront alone, gazing out at Parting Creek, its waters placid beneath a gray, drizzling rain. The ground was littered with shells; every step I took, I felt their firm, insistent push against the bottom of my boots.

Before we parted, I mentioned this to Peirson.

He nodded. "All this is shell," he said. "What we're resting on."

Peirson ducked back inside—it was raining again. I remained where I was, watching a small boat pass low in the water along Parting Creek. I raised my hand, and the hooded fisherman returned my wave. It was cold and wet, but at that instant all I could feel were the shells beneath my feet. And I thought, *Why can't we apply ourselves before the fact?*

※

FOR SEVERAL DAYS it had been gray, rainy, and cold, but on the day Rick and I went to Hog Island, the heavens parted and graced us with clear blue skies, as if to properly showcase the place. It was sunny when we left Willis Wharf, and prettier still when Rick casually maneuvered his skiff into a shallow gut at the south end of Hog Island.

"This is Wharf Creek," he said, bending to settle the anchor in the muck.

The name meant nothing to me, and frankly I was only half-listening. A light wind blew refrigerator-cool across the golden-brown marsh grass, playfully cuffing its tops and pushing small ripples into the gut. It was quiet and soothing, and after four days of absorbing more history than anyone should, my head ached for mindless respite.

I noticed a series of pilings, two rows low in the marsh, neatly paralleling each other. Rick followed my gaze. "This was the Hog Island Hotel," said Rick, gesturing at the empty marsh. "That's part of the walkway that led to the hotel. That's all that's left."

The longer I looked, the more pilings I saw pronging from the marsh. "What about those?" I asked. I found myself talking softly, as if afraid I might wake the hotel guests.

"The remnants of houses," he said, nodding appreciatively. "Yep, when you docked here, it was quite a landing."

Rick handed me a pair of hip waders. At its edges Hog Island is still built low to the ground.

I eased myself overboard, squelched briefly through mud, and found my way to a firmer path heading for the island's interior. Again I felt oyster shells beneath my feet. My waders made a funny chafing sound.

"Walking up this road, you'd be walking toward Broadwater," said Rick.

As we walked, he pointed here and there into the brushy bramble of wild blackberry, wax myrtle, baccarus, and ivy, the wind whispering above it all, *Here were homes. Here was a store.*

Suddenly Rick grinned wide. "Ken, look at your boots."

My God, I thought, *were there ponies on this island, too?*

"They're not even wet," said Rick. "Correct me if I'm wrong, but you're not under water."

The island is still the same size as it was during the days of Broadwater, but its appearance has altered dramatically. Rick pointed out the paucity of trees: there were almost none, except for a few lonely clumps of small, wind-thumped black pines.

Sometimes the change Nature wreaks is shocking.

"This area was once smothered in a great maritime forest," said Rick. "The trees were forty to fifty feet tall, huge tunnels of them that blotted out the sky. They were called lovers' lanes. People could walk under a canopy of trees and not see the sky."

"Where did the forest go?" I asked. I knew the answer, but it was still hard to fathom.

"The ocean literally washed it out to sea."

Trees, of course, weren't the only items carried out to sea. Islands may be lovely places to live, but they are often impractical for eternal rest. The soil is not deep, and the water table often lies just below that loamy veneer. When a storm of consequence passes through, the veneer is washed free, and caskets pop up like whack-a-moles and bob off to wherever the storm surge carries them. On Hog Island, post-storm, the first order of business was to look for the living, and the second was to retrieve the dead, unceremoniously upended in the woods or bobbing jauntily at sea.

Most believe George Melvin died sometime before 1933. He was buried on Hog Island because that's where he lived, though frankly he was so frugal he would likely have preferred to be left where he dropped. "He was so tight he probably wouldn't have even wanted a box," Rick said merrily. "He was an irascible fellow who didn't like spending money."

But it is life's final twist that when you are dead you can't argue your cause, so his family buried him in a casket on Hog Island, where he would have remained had Nature not had other plans. The Great Storm of 1933 nearly washed Hog Island away, and George Melvin's remains were not found.

"It was in the fifties, on Rogue's Island, a half mile south of Hog Island. A Coast Guardsman and a local waterman were walking the backside of the island scavenging after a storm," said Rick. "They were walking along the inland marsh side of the island and looked down. One looked at the other and said, 'I believe that's George Avery Melvin.' He wasn't hard to recognize. He still had on his coat and tie and white shirt. The only thing that had changed was that his hair and his fingernails had grown."

Once again George couldn't be overlooked. The Coast Guard brought him to Willis Wharf. His family had no trouble identifying him, though they had a harder time swallowing the price of a second casket. When family members balked at the initial fee, the owner of the funeral parlor presented a workable option. George was already missing part of one leg up to the knee and was stiff as stone.

"They chiseled off the other leg and put him in a baby coffin," said Rick. "He was a short fellah anyway."

I laughed. In the final accounting, George Melvin had succeeded in cheating the system.

Rick looked at me intently. Suddenly I realized it is not wise to mock anyone's relations, even when they do.

"Think about how he was perfectly preserved," Rick said. "The answer is all around us."

I allowed a moment for my heart rate to drop and my mind to work. "Salt," I said.

"Yep. He was buried in an open pine box. From the day he was buried until the day he was found, he was probably immersed in salt water. His body had literally been turned to stone. He was petrified by the salt content in the water. The Smithsonian sent representatives who wanted to take his body to Washington to examine it, but my grandmother refused." Rick fell silent.

I said nothing. Best to let the man have a dignified moment to dwell on the passing of his great-grandfather.

Rick chuckled. "You know, he probably would have been just as happy to be left alone in that marsh without all the expense."

NOT EVERYONE who lived on the island was a miserly curmudgeon. One afternoon in Willis Wharf I visited Yvonne Widgeon, who had been born on Hog Island in 1937, though her family left the island when she was two. Yvonne had interviewed some of the Hog Islanders, many of them relatives, and compiled their memories in a small booklet. Theirs were lives of hardship, but they also had wonderful stories of beach oyster roasts, and young boys who stuffed pumpkins down toilets, and three young girls who stayed up all night to watch the sun rise over the water—simple moments, passed with little thought at the time.

There were accounts of the Great Storm of 1933, too, churning floodwaters that poured across the island and brought more than George Melvin to light. "We looked down in the water," recalled an islander. "Everywhere we looked there were little snake heads sticking up out of the water."

Now the island was serene and dry. Ten minutes of walking put us atop a dune ridge overlooking the Atlantic. Delicate waves unfurled, their tops blown back in vapor-trail wisps by the light offshore wind. The ocean was deep blue; a hint of sea tang tingled our nostrils. The beach was as smooth as velvet and ran emptily into the distance as far as we could see.

Rick stood right beside me, but I almost didn't hear him. "There really is heaven on earth," he said.

The Union soldiers, the contradictory historians, even the bugs—they were gone. Rick and I fell upon the beach like giddy drunks, making the only footprints.

"Oh man, look at all the coolers and boom boxes," I said.

"Look at the parasailers!" said Rick. "You see the parasailers?"

"Oh geez, and the huge homes on the dunes. What an eyesore!"

"Yeah," said Rick, carrying on our game of make-believe. "Pretty soon they'll have to put lights on the top so they're not hit by aircraft."

"Or the parasailers," I said.

It was a pleasant visual, a frantic parasailer crashing through a fourth-floor window, squashed like a bug against a home theater system or landing amid hot tub intimacies.

Rick bent and scooped up a handful of shells, wafer thin and tinted gold. "Know what these are?"

"Change dropped by the hot dog vendor!" I nearly shrieked, until I saw Rick was no longer playing.

He shook the shells in his hand. They made a familiar sound. "They're called jingle shells. When the Hog Islanders went to the mainland, they didn't want the people there to think they were poor and destitute. They'd put these shells in their pockets, and when they walked around, they'd shake their hands in their pockets."

How little we change. I found this need to impress touching, but sad, too.

We strolled north beneath a gauzy-pale half-moon. The tide was dropping fast. As the ocean receded, the hidden flats appeared, dark brown and sensuously scalloped with geometric precision, as if an armada of child angels had descended, working meticulously with buckets and shovels to sculpt a masterpiece of otherworldly perfection. Above the high-tide line the sand was as smooth and light as dry snow. The wind wrapped coolly about our bare necks and corkscrewed down to our feet. Before us the shore curved away in a great white cusp.

The beach was empty, but I saw the ghost shapes of young girls and boys crowded around a bonfire, roasting oysters on wires; men digging for oysters, and three bleary-eyed girls huddled together on a log watching the sunrise. It is Nature's way to move forward, and human nature to look back and pine for joys we initially missed.

"The men worked on the water, and the women did the house-work and cooked three meals a day," Yvonne had said that afternoon in her living room. "Everyone went to bed early because they worked so hard. It was just day-to-day living, I guess." She paused; in the quiet I heard several clocks ticking. Then she said, "To me the ulti-mate lesson of Hog Island is to not forget, to remember and cherish how precious things can be."

It is true. We leave this world making too few moments count.

I try to live by this lesson, but it's even harder to do so in our rushed times. While walking Hog Island's edge, I tried to absorb everything: sight, sound, scent, sensation. But the tide was also falling away from our boat, and it would be a frigid overnight on the island.

"We'd better head back," said Rick.

I knew he didn't want to go, because for a few minutes neither one of us turned around—and because we didn't, we received a pre-cious treat. Rick shouted and gestured to the north. I followed his finger into the distance, where the sand curved out toward the sea. At first I saw nothing but pale blue sky. Then, in a snap as sudden as a magician's unveiling, a shimmering white veil appeared high in the sky. Its surface caught the sun delicately, producing not glare but the subtlest glint of sheen and sparkle, like a single sequin glimpsed at the bottom of a green pond. Just as my eyes registered its appearance, it winked out. I waited a few hopeful heartbeats. The invisible hand produced the handkerchief again, snow-white and as unspoiled as a child's dream.

Again the birds wheeled as one, and the sky returned to blue.

"Might be a flock of snow geese," said Rick, his voice hushed. "When they turn, their white undersides catch the sun."

It was like the brief flicker of a door opening to heaven. It was not hard to imagine, on the door's other side, a crowd of Hog Islanders peering back, more than a few of them coveting our steps.

When we idled back into the dock at Willis Wharf, it was black night. The few waterfront homes were dark. The barking of dogs rang out under the cold stars. Rick winched the boat onto the trailer, while I piled our gear neatly in the gravel lot, lit by the now-bright moon.

My hands felt the night's sting, but my mind was back on Hog Island. I had seen the ocean turning deeper blue in the afternoon's falling light, the sky mirroring the change, and Rick's words came to me again: "It wasn't really the 1933 storm that put an end to Hog Island. The main reason people left Broadwater was modern conveniences: electricity, heat, running water, movie theaters. They were beat down and tired of not having what everybody else had. That's human nature."

His gaze had gone to the moon.

"Technology was what destroyed Broadwater."

※

THAT NIGHT I bought Rick dinner at the Exmore Diner.

There are times when I wonder if my job as a writer wears on people. It is not easy to spend a day with a stranger, facing a torrent of questions, not all of them incisive. By the end of the day, I sometimes think, my subjects would like to see me facedown with a pen in my back.

This worry is largely unnecessary. More often, I know, the reality is the exact opposite. Three hours, three days, a week—the time you spend with a helpful source can be oddly intimate. The people you visit tell you things they haven't told their lifelong friends, largely because their friends never ask. In an unintentional peace offering of sorts, I often find myself revealing intimacies to them. Under such circumstances friendships are forged quickly. It may be presumptuous of me—you would have to travel in my footsteps and ask the people I met—but I believe, in many cases, I made new friends along my winter's wander.

※

AFTER DINNER Rick and I stepped outside.

I am awkward with good-byes, often feeling as if everything has been said, so Rick beat me to the punch, extending his hand.

"I'm actually going to miss you," he said, and I felt the same way.

The next morning, before I left the Eastern Shore, I drove back to the Barrier Islands Center.

Jerry was there, standing quietly, wearing the same light-brown jacket.

I had no more questions. "You made my visit," I said.

Jerry took my hand without expression. "You made my day," he said, and this time nothing was left hanging.

11
TANGIER'S SOLITARY
WATERMAN

TANGIER ISLAND, VIRGINIA, is a low scrape of sand in the Chesapeake Bay, roughly three miles long, half again as wide, and dwindling fast. To tourists, Tangier is a curiosity. To its 650 or so residents, the island is something beyond home. Ask an islander how long they have lived on Tangier, and they might ruminate for several pensive beats—few on Tangier rush into anything—before saying, "Eight generations."

"Here," a Tangierman once wrote, "everything is weighed in the light of eternity."

In winter eternity might also be how long you wait to get on or off the island. In summer enormous ferries throb like clockwork out of Crisfield (Maryland) and Reedville (Virginia), pouring tourists onto Tangier's narrow streets like salmon. In winter only the mail boat comes out of Crisfield, and sometimes not even that. It is twelve miles from Crisfield to the Tangier dock, but when the Chesapeake Bay freezes over, it might as well be twelve thousand.

Though it didn't seem possible, the mid-January weather had taken a right turn for the worse: a savage cold front was plowing down from Canada, portaging winter's rude brutality on its back. Cape Hatteras was bracing for a record ten inches of snow. Arctic air had graced Miami with a low of thirty-nine degrees, forcing retirees to hitch their socks even higher than their knees. On the Chesapeake Bay it was a cold like steel laid on bone.

Perhaps the cold felt more bitter because my blood had thinned and my spirits were low. I had flown home to California for Christmas, two glorious weeks of family and sunshine; then, sooner than I had thought possible, I'd boarded a plane back to Virginia, my heart a fist of loneliness and half-hearted resolve. Leaving once had been difficult; twice, far worse. Knowing I would be gone until spring didn't ease the hitch in my throat, heart, and mind.

On the plane to Virginia I read John Steinbeck's *Travels with Charley*, partly because I enjoy Steinbeck's take on the world and its people, but also because I hoped his thirst for travel would jump-start my own. Traveling alone provides countless opportunities, but if you are lucky enough to be loved without reservation, it also wrings the heart; even Steinbeck had a family he passionately missed. It is a roller coaster of highs and lows, and the ride is wholly unpredictable. High and low can strike at the same moment; the electric thrill of new places and faces, and the realization that both are strange to you and wholly indifferent to your presence. An adventurer who is forever striding, upbeat and indefatigable, across the Sahara lies unless he tells you how the grit between his teeth annoyed him to madness and how, in a phone call abruptly ended by bad reception, his wife's voice sounded sadly distant. Anything else is fiction, and not travel at all.

Lifting off from Los Angeles, I felt dead in the water. But as I traveled America with Steinbeck and his sidekick poodle—his canine anchor to familiarity—I felt the smoldering of a spark. By the time Steinbeck crossed into Maine, noting "a sweet burned smell of frost," I was regaining my enthusiasm.

On Tangier the sweet burned smell of frost was delivered up my nostrils by blowtorch.

I drove to the island on a Sunday, passing over the Chesapeake Bay Bridge-Tunnel, then down Route 50 through Easton, Cambridge, and Salisbury, Maryland. Snow geese rose in unison from white-blanket fields, barns wept brown rust from their windows, and billboards promised the seemingly impossible ("Springfest Is Coming May 4!"). Winter's hand was beautiful, viewed from the proper side of the windshield.

When I arrived in Crisfield, however, I had to get out of the van. As soon as I stepped outside, the wind raked my face, its nails polished to precision points. I lurched up to pull down my wool cap, one of those North Dakota fashion statements with drooping beagle-ear muffs. When I raised my hands to jerk down the cap, the Arctic blast, in a clever bit of subterfuge, rushed up my untucked shirt. It was like being caressed by George Melvin after his twenty-year bob at sea.

Back in the van, heater blasting, I wormed myself into every warm item I could find, stopping only when I realized I had to fit back out through the door. This cold was unlike any I had yet felt on my trip. It both humbled and scared me.

I lumbered down to the dock, duffel bag in hand, and stood there searching, teary-eyed, for the afternoon's scheduled mail boat.

A man at the dock turned to me. "Mail boat's frozen in," he said, emitting great gobbets of steam from his mouth.

Eight-inch icicles hung from the warehouse edges of H. Glenwood Evans and Son Peelers and Soft Crabs. Clumps of ice the size of trash-can lids drifted aimlessly about the harbor like ponderous gray jellyfish. A sign on the dock forbade swimming, perhaps to keep people from fracturing their ankles when they jumped in. A half-dozen illiterate ducks paddled in the dark green channels that snaked between the floes. When the ducks found their way blocked, they bumped up and across the ice, as if lifting off into the dense, frigid air required too much energy.

The man regarded the ducks. "We're goin' duck hunting on Tangier," he said without enthusiasm. He was already dressed in full camouflage regalia, perhaps to prevent advance duck scouts from drawing a bead on him. "Ducks seem to like the foulest weather possible. In fine weather they'll pass over a decoy without a glance, but for some reason in foul weather they'll come right down. I'm not sure why they like such rough weather, but there's no changing their minds."

We both stared mutely at the ducks paddling merrily before us as if part of some mocking carnival game. For not the last time on my trip I was struck by how ably the creatures of our planet manage cold and, for that matter, adverse conditions of any sort. Ducks are superbly adapted to their world. I, on the other hand, was nearly paralyzed by the bubble-wrap of insulation I was required to wear to stay warm. Had a runaway truck careened along the dock at that very instant, I couldn't have leaped out of the way, at least not without three weeks' notice, though if the truck had struck me, I probably would have bobbed back up unharmed.

The hunter regarded me curiously. "You got any clothes left in that bag?"

A boat was tied up just off our boots. I had watched it come in off the gray-water horizon of the Chesapeake Bay, sending up furrows of white that dissipated reluctantly with an odd sludgy peel. It was a common fishing boat—42 feet long, sturdy, built low to the water, with a single small cabin forward and open deck aft. But it was different, too. Large parts of the boat appeared to be coated with a donut glaze, which, after scant examination, I identified as ice. At first I thought it might be a mirage, like a desert oasis, only in this desert the sun had been unplugged. But a man was knocking ice off the boat's railings with a plastic paddle.

"Going to Tangier?" I asked.

He stilled his chipping for a moment. "Waaaall, that's why my boat's named *My Tangier* and not *My Smith Island,*" he said.

His words drawled out slowly. The accent was like nothing I had ever heard before. There was plenty of the South and a touch of Old England. Imagine Billy Carter failing miserably as Macbeth.

I had already read a bit about Tangier's language. The island was first settled permanently by Cornishfolk in the late 1600s. After that, isolation and perhaps a sense of good fun saw to it that Tangier's islanders developed a language all their own. So it is that a Tangierman might say, "Run sooks'll be runnin' soon. When the grass is greenin' up, they starts crawlin', and really starts wanderin' when lilacs and snowballs bloom," and only a handful of people on the planet will respond, "Hey-yuh. They ain't a-crawlin' yet."

The boat captain, Dave Crockett, wasn't much interested in linguistics. "I wouldn't normally be running today, but these men"—he nodded to the long-faced hunter beside me—"hired me special." Dave eyed the ice floes pushing up against the side of *My Tangier* like suckling kittens. "Don't like this ice. Normally I'd just touch and go, but a woman called me up in Salisbury. She's visitin' her mother in the hospital. So I'm waiting for her. She comes, we go."

I secured a berth for ten dollars When we left Crisfield at three-thirty, seven passengers were aboard; myself, the three hunters, a prim elderly woman, and a mother and her teenage daughter. Outside the harbor the ice gave way. Crisfield fell away, too, its crab-festooned water towers deflating like balloons leaking air.

My Tangier rolled and dipped. Loose bits of PVC pipe rattled about in a milk crate near my feet. A thick plastic curtain separated us from the exposed stern. A heater pulsed from somewhere, but still the cold crawled under the plastic—I could feel it through my boots, like icy water seeping in from a slushy puddle. The Chesapeake Bay surrounded us, its gray waters leaching into an equally gray and sodden sky. It was a stellar day for ducks.

I find it hard to ignore someone whose thighs are brushing mine.

I turned to the prim woman beside me. "Is it usually this cold?"

"This is one of the coldest winters we've had in some time," Rita said peppily. "But this is nothing compared to what it can be. One time the bay froze up solid for six weeks. The only way in and out was by plane. We had one funeral. They had to fly the body and the flowers to Crisfield."

Rita had married a Tangierman. They had moved off the island, settling in Pennsylvania. When her husband died, she had returned to the island. Tangier had been her home now for eleven years.

"I'm still a foreigner, but the people are real friendly," said Rita. "They treat me real nice."

When I had told Rick Kellam of my plans to visit Tangier, he had nodded. "Be prepared to know they're very, very clannish people. It takes a while for you to get to know them. Sometimes it can never happen. People have lived on Tangier their entire life and never been accepted."

☙

IT HAS BEEN said that Tangier Islanders' lives are intertwined like the branches of a grapevine. "If one suffers, all suffer," an islander once noted.

Tim Marshall may be the sole exception. He was born and raised on Tangier, is related to half the island, and knows the other half just as intimately, yet he lives largely alone. He wouldn't call it suffering. He's practical—he knows clearly where he walks. He chose his job, and when he did, he knew its rules and demands. Predawn mornings, when he rides straight-backed through Tangier's black streets on his bike, passing the Double Six where the fishermen start their day with hot coffee and sausage biscuits, most of the men standing outside regard him mutely. For the island's watermen—that is, most of Tangier's able-bodied males—the Double Six is the social hub. Long before sunrise they crowd inside its narrow confines, downing coffee and buying grilled cheese and chicken salad sandwiches for a lunch to be wolfed down later on the water. Evenings, when they come off the water, they come to the Double Six to trade stories and lies, talking football and fishing, occasionally playing dominoes (hence the name), and generally ignoring the sign on the wall that reads "Lord fill my mouth with worthwhile stuff and nudge me when I've said enough."

Tim never goes inside. "It wouldn't do to socialize," he says. "I might hear something that would upset me."

Tim grew up with these men. They plunged off the same docks, chased through the same woods, studied in the same class; in two cases they lived under the same roof. Tim's brothers fished for crabs, clams, and oysters; for a time Tim worked alongside them. Fishing is what Tangiermen do. Four-year-old boys prog for crabs in the muddy shallows. Twelve-year-old sons spend summers on their fathers' boats. When they are old enough, the boys go to the water full time, though these days this progression is no longer hard and fast.

Tim Marshall polices the fishermen, his neighbors, and his kin. He has worked for the Virginia Marine Police for eighteen years. In a community that lives and dies by the water, this is a heavy responsibility. The fishermen rely on the waters of the Chesapeake Bay (to the west) and Tangier Sound (to the east) to provide for their families, and things are not getting easier. On Tangier, religion and a strong sense of moral conviction run deep. But if you have a family and the crabs have wandered up into Maryland waters, where it is illegal to dredge for crabs, and you're sitting on water empty to the horizon, what are you going to do? No one doubts the aggressiveness of the Tangier fishermen, least of all the fishermen themselves.

"Eastern Shore and Western Shore fishermen don't like us much," one fisherman told me. "We've got to be aggressive. On this island, fishing is all you got."

Over the years Tim has caught plenty of folks on the wrong side of the law. He has boarded oyster boats, found undersize oysters, and, following the letter of the law, forced the offender to dump the whole day's work—legal and illegal—over the side. He has served citations with heavy fines to uncles, cousins, neighbors, and, yes, brothers.

To the happy day-tripper, Tangier is nostalgia: Mayberry RFD hung with a salty breeze. Century-old clapboard homes sprout American flags, crab houses line the water, kids roam anywhere they like, and residents buzz about town in golf carts. (On an island three miles long, most of it sand and marsh, cars make little sense.) But behind this Norman Rockwell tintype, life is hard. Haul up a lick of mud, eelgrass, and not-nearly-enough oysters from winter's waters; the muddy mess pouring onto the deck ices up around your feet, making stinging cold a fact of life, and the slippery deck a threat to life. Fall overboard into freezing water, and your focus narrows quickly. In winter, in a good week, a waterman might make $600. Break the law, and an $800 citation stings.

Tim is fifty-nine. He was a strict father; he is a pushover as a grandfather of six. His hair is gray, while a fastidiously trimmed mustache, still shaded with the brown of youth, rides neatly above his lip. He resides between heavy and trim, the frame of a man who has held off aging's sag despite lifelong back problems, numerous sprains and wrenches, and now painful arthritis. On the job in winter he wears olive-green slacks and a same-colored fleece jacket with "T. Marshall" inscribed in neat white letters on the right breast, in the highly unlikely event that someone doesn't know who he is. Tim sees the humor in life, and when he smiles, his green eyes light up and his face goes soft and he looks like the doting grandpa he is.

When he is serious, his face goes chalkboard hard and blank. He looks like a cop who will throw you in jail, which, in the case of jail-less Tangier, would require a trip across the water to Accomac.

Some on Tangier have no qualms about breaking the law, and not just on the water. Drugs have come to Tangier; dealers are selling Valium, marijuana, and—the latest mindbender of choice—OxyContin to their fellow islanders. But mostly Tim deals with watermen who know the difference between right and wrong, only now and again need forces them to turn their backs on their conscience. One summer Tim gave a brother two citations. On the water it was not pretty. When his brother was finished ranting, Tim looked him square in the eye: "If I was in your position and you were in my position, I never would have forced you to give me a ticket." That night his brother called and apologized. Tim has since served the same brother additional citations. There are more providers than saints on the water.

In his mind Tim has no choice but to see things clearly. "If you take a step back, then you might as well throw your badge away," he told me the morning we met. "Once they know they can back you down, they won't respect you. These people I work with, I'm related to most of 'em. It's not always easy enforcing things. But there's one thing for sure: all the watermen in Tangier are treated alike. And if I can give 'em a break, I give it to 'em, and they know that, too."

I met Tim my first morning on Tangier, after spending the night at Shirley's Bay View Inn. Waking before dawn, I walked across the dark island beneath a ceiling of stars as clear as a harp's chord. Lights glowed in a surprising number of windows. A full moon, white-bright, remained high in the sky. The watery channels meandering through the marshes at the island's center caught the moonlight, glowing with the foggy luster of solid ice.

All that night I had lain in bed listening to the wind moaning in fitful bursts and the steady trickle of running water from the bathroom sink, left on so the pipes wouldn't freeze. As I walked to meet Tim at the dock, that same wind, unencumbered by wall or window, ran across the frozen marsh, sweeping up an icy chill as neat as a broom and throwing it full in my face. My eyes watered, the air stung my lungs. The tips of my fingers, tucked into mittens, ached.

It was lovely and shocking. Oyster season had been under way since December 1. It was oyster boats primarily that Tim was policing now. Crab-dredgers were on the water, too, but many of them were far from home, gone for a week or more, down south around Cape Charles. That men worked on the water in these conditions was astonishing. A head of lettuce or a Chesapeake Bay oyster—we give little thought to the origin of the food we fork into our mouth. This short walk, I thought, would forever change the way anyone looked at an oyster.

Carefully negotiating the snowy dock, I passed *My Tangier*. She was hung completely—bow to bulwarks—with yesterday's spray. Ice coated the railings, glazed the sides, and draped from the wooden edges of the cabin's square, flat roof like strings of Christmas lights. Oddly, it looked like the boat was melting. I half expected to see Dave Crockett cryogenically preserved in midchip.

Tim was easy to find. Apart from the light in his cabin, there was no other sign of life on the dark docks. Roughly two dozen boats sat black and quiet. Across the narrow channel, crab houses and more boats sat silent. The channel was chocked with jigsaw-puzzle chunks of ice, the ice topped with a wispy, powdered sugar coating of snow.

Tim had already warmed the cabin of the thirty-one-foot Bertram—also named *Tangier*—with a portable heater. Mornings when he had the early shift, he rose at four for prayer. Now he surveyed the black, silent world. "A lot of the watermen didn't even get up this morning," he said.

It wasn't the cold; it was the ice that was keeping the watermen off the water. Ice, sucked into a boat's cooling intake system, can wreck an engine. Still there was always the chance the boats would head out.

"Watermen's like a bunch of cows," said Tim. "When one leaves, everyone leaves. They'll watch a boat headin' out the channel, and you can hear 'em on the radio saying how stupid he is headin' out, followin' a gale. The next thing you know, all the boats are followin' him right out."

Whether the boats went out or not, Tim's presence at the dock needed to be noted. "The oystermen cain't start work until sunrise, and they cain't leave the harbor until half an hour before," he said. "Some of 'em try to sneak out early." This year when oyster season opened, he had to reacquaint the boys with the rules. "Had to block the channel off one morning and tell 'em to wait. I come on the radio and said, 'Anybody leaves the dock early, I'm going to take their license.' That ended the problem right there. You have to babysit 'em. If you didn't say nothing, they'd leave here two hours before sunrise."

Apparently there wasn't universal agreement on what constitutes sunrise. "Soon as she starts painting the water, that's sunrise, and that's when they can start up." Tim adjusted the volume on the marine radio, which at this moment emitted only sporadic crackle. "You'd think it was pretty simple. But I've had fishermen say, 'Yeah, but she's up somewhere else.' I said, 'Yeah, but you ain't somewhere else, you're in Tangier Sound.'"

The sun was pushing its way over the horizon now, though today there was no painting, only a reluctant lightening to gray. Several slips away the *Elizabeth Kelly*, a crab-dredger, throbbed to life. A man moved about inside the cabin, studiously keeping a broad back to us.

Tim chuckled. "That boy don't want to look at me. I got a summons for him. He's my cousin's son. He got caught up in Maryland just last week. It's like he won't get the summons, if he don't look at me."

Several other crab-dredgers had been caught on the wrong side of the state line in the same sweep. One lives next door to Tim. Shortly after the bust Tim and the crabber found themselves walking down the street together. "I got that summons for you," said Tim. "You want me to come and get it?" said the crabber. "Waaaall, if you want to."

On Tangier there is no place to hide, which fosters blunt honesty and an oddly casual manner of law enforcement. Once Tim was out on his deck watering his tomatoes and looked up to see a boat thief walking down the road.

"Well, you did it again."

"Yeah, Tim, well, you know how it is. I had to get the drugs, and I needed a boat to do it."

"I suppose you did."

In the time I spent with Tim, I saw that he wielded power and kindness with deftness that our world leaders would do well to emulate. He made concessions where he could and stuck to the letter of the law when he had to. Virginia state law requires fishermen to pay a tax on each day's oyster catch. It also requires they do so before they deliver their oysters across the state line in Maryland. To ask an oysterman two miles off Crisfield to return ten miles to Tangier, then backtrack again across winter waters, was just the sort of nonsense government trafficked in. Tim talked to his supervisor on the mainland. Tangier's oystermen now sell their oysters in Crisfield, then pay their taxes at Tim's house and walk home.

"Why keep them away from their families any longer?" Tim shrugged. "They're out on the water long enough as it is."

My personal favorite piece of legal adaptation involves the bicycle Tim currently rides about town. I noticed it the first morning on the dock, a splendid green Huffy whose silver fenders sparkle gloriously, thanks to Tim's loving applications of wax. His previous bike had come to a soggy end. Occupied with the arrest of one man, Tim had been forced to watch as the man's friend heaved Tim's bike into a watery ditch, then, for good measure, retrieved it and tossed it out farther. By the time Tim returned from the county jail in Accomac and pulled his bike from the water, its finish was ruined.

Tim proceeded to the bike-tosser's home. "I'm not going to arrest you, but I want a new bike just like the one I had, and I want it tomorrow." Tim received his new bike and gave his water-sopped one to the offender.

"If I had arrested him up, he'd have gone to court and had a fine put on him, and he probably would have had to reimburse me for my bike anyhow," Tim explained to me. "That whole process would have taken a couple months to go through court. I saved him some money and the courts some time, and I got my bike a lot quicker."

Not that concession matters much. People remember slights long after they forget kindnesses.

"It is funny," Tim said, disinterestedly watching his cousin's face-less son move about the cabin of the *Elizabeth Kelly*. "You can give one a break and come back the next day and give 'em a citation for the same violation, and he'll get mad at you and won't speak to you. You meet the wife on the road, and she won't give you a word. I always speak to them, but a lot of them won't speak." He shook his head. "The officer's always wrong."

These weren't jaywalkers. These were fishermen, fiercely inde-pendent and plenty tough. Since its settlement in the late 1600s, Tangier has seen only a handful of murders. One of them was the town policeman, C. C. "Bud" Connorton, shot through a window in the early 1920s by an assailant who was never caught.

"Do you ever worry about someone coming after you?" I asked.

"Naaawww. It's true, they're upset when I first lay a fine on 'em. Generally I let 'em do the fussin' because they're aggravated. I give 'em a few minutes to rant. Then I tell 'em, 'You say another word, you're going right to jail,' and they shut up. They know how far they can push. I ain't never took too much off of people. 'Bout the only threat I've ever had is 'I'll knock your head off.' That's as far as it gets."

Tim's face had gone lawman hard. Now it relaxed to something between sadness and resignation.

"It ain't easy policing your relations," he said wearily. "But I couldn't live with myself if everyone wasn't treated the same."

A mooring line creaked. I could hear ice chewing at the pilings. The ice was thickening. In a few days cows would be able to walk out through this channel.

"They do say some hateful things," said Tim quietly. "You don't ever get used to it entirely."

Undersize oysters and shot-putted bicycles are one thing. In recent years, lawbreaking on Tangier had taken on a far uglier bent. "We got a real bad problem with drugs and alcohol around here," said Tim. "Right now we've got seventeen drug dealers and two bootleggers on this island. It ain't no big secret around here who they are. We got one seventy-three-year-old sellin' drugs. Right now he can get twelve dollars for one Valium pill. He was makin' $1,200 to $1,500 a month when the pills were eight dollars. From what I understand, a lot of our teenagers are doin' pills. Drugs are a real thorn in my side. I hate what they're doin' to our kids."

It wasn't just the kids.

"Some of the watermen, too. They say they're doin' it all day, smoking pot and things. The thing is now they go to a doctor and get Valium and all this mess, and there's nothing you can do. It's all prescription."

Tim looked out the cabin window. To the west, away from North Channel, there was nothing but water, the vast emptiness of the Chesapeake Bay. Then his eyes came back to me. "Was a time we used to be to ourselves here in this bay, but no more," he said.

Though I had been on the island for less than a day, Tangier's problems were not entirely news to me. Sunday night I had attended the seven o'clock service at Tangier's Swain Memorial United Methodist Church, vainly trying to find a place to hang my coat on the jammed coatrack. Midway through the service, which was attended mostly by middle-aged and elderly couples, the minister invited a woman to sing. She stepped to the pulpit and stood silent, her head down. The congregation waited quietly.

"I don't want to sing," she said finally, her voice quavering. "This is not a good time for me. My children, they seem to have no love for Christ at all." She began to cry. She kept her head up, tears running down her cheeks. "The devil's havin' a heyday with me."

A community entwined like a grapevine is now up against a grapevine world.

"I was looking on the Internet the other day, trying to learn more about OxyContin," said Tim now. "I was clicking on symptoms and such. I kept on clicking right on down to where you can put your credit card number in and order all you want."

※

As SAD A place as Tangier was, I loved walking around the island, and the lower the thermometer dipped, the prettier Tangier got.

At night I strolled beneath the star-filled sky, the frosty air so heavy I half-expected my passing to make it crackle. Nighttime afforded me solitude; this is a community that works the water beds early. Most nights I saw no one, which allowed me to snoop about town freely. Most of the island's homes lie on its eastern and western edges; these points are connected by several wooden bridges that cross the marshy center. The homes sit tight together, separated by narrow lanes. At night I walked the silent lanes, gingerly picking my way across the Zamboni glaze of ice; miffed cats huddled on gateposts stoically marked my shuffling. Single candles shone from dark windows, signs hung from front gates ("Prayer Changes"), and bicycles lay jumbled about doorsteps as if dropped from the sky. The air came to my lungs sharp and pure, and a thermometer atop a doghouse read a wishful eighty-five degrees. Down by the water stacks of crab pots lined the docks—inside their wire mesh confines snowball prisoners glowed ghostly white. The water in the channels was as still and dark as velvet.

During the day I walked past front yards where kittens pounced on snowflakes and, out over the water, snow swirled indecisively. On the streets people nodded friendly hellos and even looked out for me: "Travelin' north? You're headin' the wrong way."

If Tangierfolk were clannish, they didn't seem to know it. Everyone I met exhibited a friendliness as genuine as it was easy.

One morning, while I was walking to meet Tim, a golf cart whirred up beside me in the darkness. The sides were hung with plastic, sealed shut with a zipper. A voice came from inside: "Roid."

I was both surprised and touched that a stranger would instantly share so personal a problem. I searched my mind frantically for the appropriate cream to ease the man's suffering.

A meaty paw pulled the plastic curtain aside. The voice, patient and affable, repeated the question: "Wanna roid?" My friend Chris gave me a warm smile. "I'm going to get me some breakfast at the Double Six," he said. "Buy you a cup of coffee."

I smiled back. "Thanks, but I'm supposed to meet Tim Marshall."

Chris swung the golf cart left, away from the Double Six, erasing my protests with a nod. "I'll take you to Tim," he said. "Too cold a morning to be out walking."

I often walked the beaches. One cloudless blue afternoon I walked along Tangier Beach at the island's southern end. It was a lovely day, twenty degrees, but still. No surprise, the beach was empty. There were no homes, only sand and low dunes. The Chesapeake oozily nudged the shoreline, the half-frozen water slushy and milky gray. Just back from the tide's edge, the sand was coated with an icy varnish that crackled beneath my feet. I crouched and peered close. Wind and water had delicately deposited individual sand grains atop one another in the tiniest of drip castles, the ice shellacking them in place. Hundreds of these tiny turrets sparkled under the bright sun, shining fairy-tale cities.

Tangier is noted for its strict religious beliefs, though not everyone speaks of the islanders' convictions in complimentary terms. When the town council unanimously rejected Hollywood's request to film *Message in a Bottle* there—objecting to "drinking and blasphemy" in the script—a location scout for Warner Bros. groused, "It's like *Children of the Corn* over there. There's no separation of church and state."

Everyone defines reality in their own terms. I thought it funny that the location scout defined Tangier with a movie reference, as if what took place on the screen were reality and the rest of world banged about deaf, dumb, and clueless in the theater lobby.

Religion is your own business, but traveling winter's shore, I found it hard to ignore the ample evidence of a hand greater than man's. One evening I walked across the brittle brown grass edging the airstrip on Tangier's western flank. Slowly a sunset like none I had ever seen unfolded in the west. It was less a sunset than an explosion. Blood-red and burnt-orange veins coursed jagged through the sky, scorching the bottoms and singeing the edges of towering cumulus clouds. The deepening blue diffused into these colors so that the skyline appeared smeared with smoke. When the sun finally fell into the Chesapeake's black waters, its yellow scrim remained just above the horizon, treading water doggedly, reluctant to leave its creation.

⁂

THE SAME SUN set on Clyde Pruitt's life, producing both sadness and complication.

Tim told me of Clyde's passing at dawn the next morning as we slowly throttled out through the North Channel. "The man with the cancer on his face I told you about?" he said. "He died yesterday evening."

Tim had told me about Clyde Pruitt the day before. A respected waterman, Clyde had worked the sound and bay for nearly fifty years. He had serious heart problems, but skin cancer killed him.

"He always had sensitive skin," said Tim now. "He started getting this little blotch on his face. Eventually the whole side of his face was eaten up. Smelled awful, too. Never heard him complain about nothing."

Now Clyde suffered no more, though his bereaved wife had added concerns. Colder weather was forecast. If Tangier froze in, she would have no way to get her husband's body to his gravesite in Crisfield.

Most islanders dearly want to be buried on their island—"I'd rather be washed ashore than buried there," an island saying goes— but these days that was becoming nearly impossible. Tangier folk have been laying their loved ones to rest on the island for more than three hundred years; making matters worse, the island is shrinking. Currently the only thing scarcer than an autobahn on Tangier is a plot to bury the dead.

Tim, among others, finds this worrisome. "A lot of families have bought plots in Crisfield," he said. "I want to be buried here even if they stick me in a ditch." Alongside us crab houses scrolled past, their lights throwing quavering ribbons on the dark water. "I told my wife I hope I die before they sell all the lots here. I love my island. I was born here. I hope there's room for me."

Ahead of us, the living were concerned with making a living. A conga line of oyster boats was spreading out into Tangier Sound: the *Carol Marie,* the *Miss Donna,* the *Miss Sandra,* and the *Patti Page.*

A voice crackled over the radio. *"It's cold, my blessed. Twenty-eight degrees."*

"Wind had a been blowin', it would be a lot colder," said another voice.

Droplets of water etched sludgily down the glass in front of us. We moved into Tangier Sound. Seventy-five yards off our starboard side, backlit by smoky red sky, the *Miss Donna* throbbed slowly through the water.

"That's Alfred Dise," said Tim. "He's runnin' really slow. He's got time. The catch is not as good right now. They were getting forty dollars a bushel. First time in history that oysters have ever been above thirty. Now that the New Year's rush is done, they're getting twenty-five a bushel."

No doubt Alfred could see us as clearly as we could see him. Scanning the sound, I could see the other boats scattered about us, some of them several miles away. One thing about oceans and bays: subterfuge is hard to pull off. It struck me that, in our thirty-one-foot vessel, we were only slightly more conspicuous than a private investigator standing in the middle of the street in his underpants.

I didn't want to be rude, but I couldn't think of any other way to say it: "Doesn't everyone know you're out here?"

"Yep." Tim grinned. "They're watchin' every move I make. Plus all the boats have CB radios. Crab-dredgers started with it. Now just about every boat on the bay has a CB." Above our heads the radio's marine frequency crackled oddly empty static. Tim nodded. "All the way over here they've been talkin' on the other radio. I don't guess the talk is mostly aimed at us, but it's also true they know we don't have a CB."

Standing in their underpants with corks in their ears.

This didn't trouble Tim. He was mostly interested in counting the boats that were out and, playing to our strength, letting our presence be known.

Tangier Sound is sprinkled with oyster rocks. We moved from

rock to rock. At each one boats milled in circles, dragging dredges, then hauling them out and dumping the scraped contents on their decks. Tim would watch the proceedings casually, kindly providing me with commentary: "That's my uncle working up forward there. Seventy-seven years old. . . . That one there is my brother and nephew."

A voice crackled over the radio. *"I'm standin' in ice,"* said a fisherman. *"Every time I pull the dredge aboard, there's ice on her. I'm thinkin' it may be too cold for me."*

Tim's face went blank. "That's not good. He's working by himself. He's got ice around his feet. It's dangerous and all from slipping."

❧

TIM ONLY HAS one brother now. His other brother, Ted, died in a fishing accident. Tim had been there beside him—one instant on the deck, the next in the water.

"February 12, 1968. Twenty minutes after three." Tim was quietly recounting the details one morning as *Tangier* rocked gently at the dock.

Tim and Ted had been dredging for crabs down off Cape Charles, near the mouth of the Chesapeake. Tim remembers the time because Ted had just asked him to check it. They were getting ready to quit for the day. The catch had dropped off. This was their last lick.

When Tim stepped back from the cabin, the dredge was coming up, spilling frigid mud, water, and eelgrass. The air was in the mid-twenties, a chill wind blowing out of the southwest. Ted had one leg up on the dredge and was reaching to grab the chain to pull the load over into the boat. Tim joined him. When Tim bent out to reach for the chain, their collective weight sent the men and the dredge into the water.

Tim was thrown clear. When he first came up, he saw nothing but gray water—no Ted. The sudden shock and stomach-punch cold may have robbed him of his sight; more likely his brother was fighting for his life beneath the water, hooked somehow to the dredge. Then Ted popped to the surface.

The boat was still in gear. It moved methodically away from them as the chain spooled out.

Ted surfaced a few feet from his brother. He still had plenty of wind left. Other boats were crabbing nearby. The brothers waved and shouted at the nearest boat, which was manned by their uncle and his son, slowly making their own drag. But the boat, only fifty feet away, kept about its work. A second boat, also dragging, swung near. The brothers shouted and waved, but that boat too was occupied with crabbing. Above the waterline everything appeared normal. The Marshall brothers' boat moved slowly through the water, making its lick.

"My brother said, 'Don't they see us?' I said, 'No.' He said, 'Boy, this is somethin.' " And that's the last thing he ever said to me."

Finally the entire length of chain, roughly 230 feet, spooled out. The dredge now acted as an anchor. The boat, working vainly against the weight, began kicking up a froth of foam off its stern. The other boats knew something was wrong. Tim turned and saw his brother going down.

He grabbed Ted by the collar, but the shock of the cold, their clothes, and his brother's dead weight clawed to pull him down. Tim shouted for God to save them.

Quick as men can move, the other boat—his uncle and his cousin—was on them. A hand reached down and grabbed the hood of Tim's sweatshirt. Tim heard the captain, his uncle Charles, shout, "Where's Ted?"

Tim had hold of his brother, and when the two men above him tried to pull him up, Tim waved them off. If they hauled him aboard, he knew he wouldn't have the strength to hold on to the weight below him.

No. Get Ted.

Tim was yanked aboard. They pulled him by the arms into the cabin, sat him on a kerosene heater, and made for shore. Tim remembers little. He could see his brother on the engine box, watching him.

"How is Ted?" Tim asked.

"Ted's all right."

There was the ride to shore, the foggy background crackle of radio, an ambulance waiting, and a press of hands and faces in the emergency room. A doctor spoke to him: "You're a lucky young man that you didn't drown with your brother."

Tim spent the night on his uncle's boat. He didn't sleep much. He kept getting up to look for his brother. Ted was thirty-six, the father of four children.

For fifteen years Tim didn't talk about the accident, not to anyone. He tried to go back to the water, but he couldn't. One day he sat down with a pen and a notebook. He wrote down every last detail, from the decision to crab down off of Cape Charles, to his return to Tangier, to his frantic mother who had already lost a husband (to pneumonia) and thought she had lost two sons. There was crying for Tim, too, down in the woods. After the writing and crying, things got better.

Between the beginning of the nightmare and the end—though there is never really an end—a strange thing happened. While Tim was in the water, holding his brother, a face had peered down at him. It wasn't his cousin; he would arrive a short time later. It was the face of his three-year-old daughter.

Often people caught in a life-threatening circumstance recount a curious surge of energy just before what they believe is the end. They attribute this to various things: an odd flush of physiology, a mind unwilling to give in, reptilian survival instinct. Often it is what saves them. Pinioned in the dead numbness of February water, staring at his three-year-old daughter, Tim experienced his own odd surge, and he is certain it saved him. His face was turned directly up, a final precursor to going under. Tim had another daughter, too, a one-year-old, but it wasn't her face he saw.

Life has taken its natural course. Tim has six grandchildren now. They all give him joy—he plays no obvious favorites. In the time I spent with him he mentioned them all, again and again. But one name came up just an iota more, and when it did, it seemed to me that Tim's eyes took on a slightly brighter light. Josh is four, a year older than his mommy was when she saved Grandpop's life.

Boy, this is somethin'.

When Tim was finished talking, there was silence. It was our last morning together. Outside the sun was painting the horizon. The ice atop the dock pilings glowed orange. The boats sat still. No one was going anywhere. The channel was frozen in. The ice stretched a mile out into Tangier Sound.

I felt a wash of gratitude and embarrassment. I had asked Tim to tell me about his brother's death. Now that he was finished, I felt guilty that I had made him recount something so painful.

"I'm sorry to make you relive that," I said.

"It's okay," said Tim. "It does me good to talk about it."

✻

WE CRISSCROSSED the sound for a little over an hour. At one point we pulled within shouting distance of the *Victoria Faith*, a clammer. Her skipper, a burly fellow named John, was standing, legs braced wide, on the deck.

Tim pulled his window aside. Rude cold leaped in. "How ya doin'?" shouted Tim.

John smiled but said nothing. Maybe his tongue was frozen.

"Cold, ain't it?" said Tim.

John's mouth moved. "Yeah, cold," he said.

"Whar you goin'?" Tim asked.

John turned up his hands good-naturedly. "Dunno. Whar you goin'?"

This seemed an infinitely practical question to ask a lawman.

Tim didn't duck it. "Goin' in for fuel pretty soon. Then callin' it a day."

John suddenly began hopping about and swatting himself briskly. Perhaps he was excited about having a lawless sound to himself. He shouted something. It sounded to me like *That ought to be hot if I get my sleeves wet.*

Tim laughed. When he shut the window, he turned to me. "That means 'it's gonna be cold.' Ain't no one in the world talks like us."

Heading back toward Tangier, he regarded me bemusedly. "I

know it seems funny, this manner of policing, but we really don't have many problems. When things drop off, you have a handful of trouble with some people, but that's pretty much it."

※

MRS. CLYDE PRUITT'S dilemma was the talk of the island, or at least I think it was, because frankly on Tangier it is pretty much impossible for a conventional English-speaker to tell what is really going on.

One afternoon I sat on a long wooden bench inside the Tangier Oil Company, a combination marine supply store and grocery. A half-dozen men in their sixties and seventies sat quietly on the bench, engaging in fits and halts of conversation. They were watermen most probably, spare men in flannel, though I didn't ask them. I just sat listening. But I looked at their hands. They were rough, square, and brown. Where their sleeves were rolled up, their arms had the same texture, like wood left to the elements. They looked as if they were turning into their boats.

When the men spoke, they looked straight ahead at the neat rows of varnish remover, antirust gloss enamel, engine paint, and not at one another. Opinions were kept short.

The language is lovely and quaint, but it is like listening to Dr. Seuss on acid.

"Fuuuuhrrr, isn't it?"

"Said it be down to fourteen tonight."

"Sounds like ice."

"This is gone be a hot day."

"Yep."

"The island don't want Clyde to go."

"You can't see."

"We're running out of room on the island for the living and the dead."

"Streeek. You better go cuttin' the bushes down."

I'm sorry I can offer no translation, but in the end what the men said didn't matter. Nature would take her course as she always did. Tangier, and Clyde Pruitt, would be frozen in. An ice-cutter had to be called in to lead the ferry, with Clyde's quilt-draped casket at the stern, back to Crisfield. His weeping widow would stay behind, watching him leave Tangier a final time, the ice closing in behind him.

I left Tangier several days before Clyde, in the afternoon, on the last mail boat out before the deep freeze.

Tim and I had parted that morning. We stood near the county dock watching a seagull drift skyward, drop a conch to the snowy dock, then descend to pick at the intact shell and try again.

One survivor regarded the other. " 'Fraid he's gonna have to come to the road to break that," said Tim.

I watched Tim ride off in his olive-green jacket and brown dress shoes, fenders glinting brightly, down King Street, past the Double Six, pedaling home to see Josh.

The gull gave up, beating off across the marsh into the stony cold.

When Tim is buried, on island or off, it's hard to know what the fishermen will have to say. But while riding back to Crisfield on *My Tangier,* I got an idea.

My Tangier rose and fell, again collecting icy spray. In the wheelhouse a man sat across the table from me. "Spendin' some time with Tim, whar you?"

His blue eyes searched my face. Odds were, in eighteen years this man had suffered at Tim's hand. I said nothing.

He waited a time. "Tim's fahr," he said. "Tim's fahr."

12
RETREAT AND REVIVAL ON
THE JERSEY SHORE

I PASSED QUICKLY along the edge of Maryland and Delaware.

While Maryland's coast is largely a ruined place, Delaware's shoreline is quaint. You can see the demarcation clearly, standing on 146th Street, where Ocean City, Maryland's, wall of oceanfront high-rises abruptly ends and the low-slung beach cottages of Fenwick Island, Delaware ("The Quiet Resort"), begin.

Ocean City's beachfront view may be obliterated by towering condominiums with haughty names like Excalibur and Fountainhead, but humble Maryland folk still have their say. One afternoon I watched a dog pointedly crisscross a narrow alley between two grand structures, liberally peeing on their armada of "No Parking" signs.

The weather remained frigid. At night snow fell quietly. During the day people hustled along the sidewalks as if an air raid were imminent. "It was so cold this morning," quipped a radio deejay, "there were penguins on my bird feeder."

Sleeping in the van had made sense in the South, but this economical arrangement was fast becoming both risky and potentially litigious. Wal-Marts in the North were less understanding. Where the southern establishments had welcomed me and my RV kin in their parking lots, when I pulled into a Wal-Mart outside Ocean City, red-letter signs declared that loiterers would be fined five hundred dollars, an inflated rate for accommodations with a shared bathroom. In frozen climes I was faced with a second problem. With night temperatures sometimes dipping into the teens, many mornings I woke to a thin scrim of ice on the inside of the windows. Sleeping wasn't the problem (I still slept cozily beneath my down comforter), but getting back into my clothes the next morning was. When I slept in these parking lots, I always rose early, well before dawn, to avoid startling any passersby. But given the tensile attraction of cold surfaces and bare skin and the fact that, in changing, I often rebounded about the back of the van like a pinball, it occurred to me that, wrestling into my boxers, I might suddenly find myself affixed to a window in a compromising position that could hold until the noon thaw. I imagined slack-jawed children rooted outside my van until their mothers, turning curiously from their shopping carts, gave the nippers, with their hysterical shrieks, a real fright.

I slept in the van for the second-to-last time to the west of Ocean City, near the only slightly misnamed Assawoman Bay. The next morning I stuffed my comforter away for what I thought was the last time and drove north toward Lewes, Delaware, to catch the ferry across the Delaware Bay.

With time on my hands, I stopped to walk the Rehoboth Beach boardwalk. It was a blustery day. The wind blew cold and hard off the ocean, under a white-bright sun. The beach and boardwalk were empty except for a few solitary walkers.

I stopped to read a plaque, a tribute to Frank "Coach" Coveleski:

The Tide Recedes but Leaves Behind
Bright Seashells in the Sand
The Sun Goes Down but Gentle Warmth
Still Lingers on the Land
The Music Stops and Yet It Echoes
On in Sweet Refrains
For Every Joy That Passes, Something Beautiful Remains.

It was a touching tribute to a man who had obviously touched others. But as I stood on the desolate boardwalk, with the Atlantic sparkling as merrily as an unwrapped Christmas present, it struck me that the poem could as easily be an ode to winter's shore, the shy but no-less-lovely sister whose subtler charms are overlooked.

While the tourist pines for seaside summer, those who live at the ocean's edge appear to grasp the gift in all the seasons. All along my coastal journey I came on lovely passages that tried to define man's place alongside sea and shore. I love these scribbles and musings, and once I started looking for them, they popped up everywhere—on plaques, in small-town newspaper poems, in a sweet ballad sung by a fisherman's daughter. On the wall of a coffee shop in Ocracoke, I saw a lovely phrase that expunged the seasons in one breath, spelled out with those word magnets people affix to their fridges to etch silly and inspirational messages:

> *Yet summer is over watch fall whisper as languid winter urges spring will flood beauty in the symphony of sweet drunk summer . . .*

Our species is driven to label, identify, and place, perhaps to keep ourselves from being overwhelmed by the immensity of it all. Few things are more immense than the sea. Faced with this force that can snuff us out without thought or interruption, we feel a lacing of fear. Wrote Herman Melville, "There is, one knows not what sweet mystery about this sea, whose gently awful stirrings speak of some hidden soul beneath."

Fear, of course, is not what attracts us to the sea and its shore. Roughly 60 percent of the world's population lives in coastal zones, and everyone has their own reasons for being there. In Fenwick, Delaware, John Dux, the ponytailed owner of the Quail Restaurant and Pub, told me, "I was going to college and driving a cab in Baltimore and somebody stuck a gun in the back of my head, and I was down here the next day watching the sunrise."

More than anything, the ocean offers escape. I once stumbled on a haunting Slovene ballad that expresses this better than anything I have seen:

Fair Vida by the seashore washing,
Her sick child's linens on the shore,
Looked up to see a Blackmoor sailing
And heard the words the sea wind bore:
"Fair Vida, why are you no longer
As fair as once you were before?"
"How should I still be fair and lovely
As fair I was once before,
When my old husband sits at home
When my sick child can't be alone?
All day my old man coughs and moans,
All night my sick child weeps and groans."
The Blackmoor brought his boat to shore,
"Come with me, leave them all behind,
Come with me, be fair forevermore . . ."

Some people, once they escape, don't want to be found. In the Strathmere post office, Elizabeth Bergus fixed me with a no-nonsense stare and said flatly, "We don't want people to know where Strathmere is."

I'd come to Strathmere, New Jersey, across a muddy-brown Delaware Bay strewn with car-size lily pads of ice. As the ferry neared the Cape May shoreline, the ice pads knit together in a solid white Antarctic sheet. The ferry's engineer had eyed the ice with disdain. "So much for global warming," he said.

Thirty-five miles up the coast, inside the Strathmere post office, Elizabeth Bergus's gaze was no warmer. "Why would you want to write about Strathmere?" she demanded.

The question wasn't rude, only firmly stated. I would find, in the course of our acquaintance, that Elizabeth spoke authoritatively, with a raspy growl: the growl the product of cigarettes, the authority the product of a lifetime. She was seventy-six, and I doubt if she had kowtowed to a soul in any of those years.

There was no short answer to her question, but a short answer was required. My brain locked, and my tongue went with it. I took a step back. I was a bit intimidated, but it's also true that Strath-mere's post office is only slightly larger than the stamps it sells, and I felt uncomfortable nearly pressing up against a woman I barely knew.

"Strathmere is the last of the old communities," continued Elizabeth. "We're different."

I discovered my tongue. "Why?"

Elizabeth smiled triumphantly. "Sewers," she said. "We don't have any. The minimum building lot is sixty by one hundred to allow for a septic system." She was already tall, but she drew herself up. "I will lie down in the middle of Commonwealth Avenue if they ever try to put sewers in."

Discounting frostbite, lying down on Commonwealth Avenue didn't seem like much of a risk right now. I could see Strathmere's two-lane main drag through the post office's lace curtains. The only movement was the wind-ripples moving across cold puddles. The last car had shooshed past ten minutes ago.

In the course of my three days in the Strathmere post office, I would learn a few things about Elizabeth—and plenty about Strath-mere's other residents, too. It might seem odd to stand in a post office for three days without Christmas packages in hand. But I assumed my place in the bathmat-size foyer—boxed in by lace curtains, a wall of post office boxes, the forearm's-length counter, and the front porch door—because, as I reasoned, there was no better place to touch the pulse of the town.

Strathmere's residents, I had been told, love their town and fight fiercely to keep it from being overrun—no mean feat on the Jersey Shore, which one day will issue a resounding crack and plunge into the sea, sheared off by the collective weight of joints selling pizza, cheese steak, and fudge and the boardwalk-ambling vacationers who consume it all. Tucked between Ocean City and Sea Isle, Strathmere—less than two miles long and only a few blocks wide—has no boardwalk, no amusements, not even a gas station where people might be tempted to stop, just rows of old-style Jersey Shore homes catching the smell and sound of the sea. The water tower is unmarked, and this is no accident.

Strathmere's post office sits near the north end of town, just before the road bends away to arc over Corsons Inlet toward Ocean City. If it weren't for the flag out front and the sorely weathered red, white, and blue wooden sign—"U.S. Post Office 08248 Strathmere"—you wouldn't know it was a post office. It looks more like the first floor of the two-story clapboard home it is. The postal service rents the downstairs from the owner, who resides upstairs. From there she controls the thermostat, which, in winter, she keeps at sixty-five degrees. This and the fact that the post office floor, once a front porch, isn't insulated explain why Anna Seltzer had a small floor heater hissing furiously when I first stepped inside.

It was a dreary Saturday morning, gray interspersed with freezing rain; the thermometer outside the post office door read twenty-two degrees.

Part of traveling and writing a book is requesting many odd favors. I have never gotten used to it, but kind souls like Anna, on duty behind the counter, make it easier.

When I introduced myself and told her what I hoped to do, she kept smiling warmly. "You want to stand in here?" she asked, just to make sure. "All day?"

"If your productivity goes down, you can tell the post office to blame me," I said apologetically.

"Oh, I don't worry about that," she chirped. "You either need stamps or you don't."

Anna, like Elizabeth Bergus, is in her seventies. Being in Strathmere in the winter is like being in a retirement home, only all the residents have been shot through with adrenaline. They have a spring in their step and steel-trap minds. I met very few people under sixty, and most of those who came in to pick up their mail were well past that. The salt air must suit them.

Anna has worked in Strathmere's post office for thirteen years, plenty long enough to know everyone. Our days together unfolded simply. I stood in the foyer. We talked until Anna's neck lengthened. Then I would follow her gaze out the window, watching as a bundled personage shuffled gingerly up the icy driveway. The door would bang open, accompanied by a blast of frigid air, and someone with lively eyes and a wind-chafed face would insinuate him- or her-self into the foyer, glancing curiously at me before accepting a fat package of mail from Anna.

Anna, kindly, was always quick to introduce me. The reactions varied. One of the first residents I met, Mrs. Smith, regarded me sourly.

"This man is writing a book about Strathmere," Anna said help-fully.

Mashed up against the post office boxes, I tried my winningest smile.

"It's full," barked Mrs. Smith. "There's no more lots. Nothing's for sale!"

She grimaced at me. She appeared to have all her original teeth. For an uncomfortable moment I thought she might affix herself to my leg.

Mrs. Smith filled my startled silence with more discouragement.

"There was a building moratorium here for thirty-five years. Nothing changed. You couldn't change the number of bathrooms that you had!"

She turned her back to me and became another person.

"Are you warm enough, Annie?" she said soothingly. "I could bring you another heater."

Elizabeth Bergus did not dismiss me as casually. Instead she began asking me questions. When I explained why I was cluttering up the post office, she nodded her approval. "This is our community center," she said. "Some few years ago they tried to take it away from us and move the post office to Sea Isle. But we fought and got it back."

That fight had been spearheaded by Elizabeth. Elizabeth didn't say so, Anna did.

"I call her the mayor of Strathmere," Anna said proudly. "If she wasn't here, nothing would get done."

Elizabeth didn't have it in her to look uncomfortable. "Oh, someone will take over," she said absently, leafing through her mail. "There's always someone who comes in after you. No one is indis-pensable."

Strathmere, I learned, falls under the jurisdiction of Upper Township, a sprawling assemblage of communities that for a long time cared little for little Strathmere.

Elizabeth shot me a wry grin. "Let's just say the township had ignored us for many years. They don't anymore."

"How many people live here year-round?" I asked.

"One hundred and fifty," said Elizabeth.

"I'd say about a hundred twenty-five," said Anna.

"Well, I have to count the children in," said Elizabeth. "About eleven."

Elizabeth saw the puzzled look on my face. I wondered why there were so few young folk.

"You're on a barrier island," she said. "Young people can't afford to buy on a barrier island. Conservatively I wouldn't put my house on the market for less than one point five million. And I'd get that in a second."

Elizabeth wasn't selling. She inherited her home from her father, who had bought it in 1915. Later I would see a fuzzy-grained picture of Elizabeth, age roughly three, in front of the family home, striding confidently down the sidewalk, leading a friend by the hand.

"My children are going to inherit my house," she said. "It's only right."

Actually, Elizabeth owned several lots in Strathmere, and she wasn't hurrying to sell any of them. One, next door to her home, she kept vacant for a simple reason. "Kids need a place where they can lie on their backs and look up in the sky," she said, cementing my friendship and admiration in a single phrase. "If you want to know more about our town, call me," she said, and, without further ado, she left.

※

TAKING ROOT IN Strathmere's post office turned out to be one of the brightest ideas I've had in a long time. A large percentage of the town clacked in for their mail. I learned many things, among them that few people get more mail. It was almost February, but I had to check the date on my watch to make sure it wasn't Christmas. Most everyone walked away with an enormous rubber-band-bound bundle. Sometimes this wasn't enough. One resident, I learned, sorted through his neighbors' trash to accrue more reading material.

Nor was Elizabeth the only one possessed of chutzpah. One afternoon a woman banged in, giving me a cheery nod. *"This,"* Anna told me, "is a galavanter."

Actually, Marion Ingram was a sailor. She had recently spent nine months sailing from New Bern, North Carolina, to the Bahamas. The final leg—from Key Largo to Gun Cay, near Bimini—had proved an adventure. They had pushed off from Key Largo at night in a driving rain. Her husband—at least I think it was her husband, she never did say—promptly got seasick and went below, rising only once to scream at Marion and a woman friend.

"I suppose we did get close to that cruise ship," Marion said thoughtfully. "We were having a great debate as to which direction it was headed. We couldn't see the lights that told us which direction it was going, but we could read the name of the boat on the smokestack."

I asked if, come morning, they had received any additional navigational advice from her male companion.

"Hell, no." Marion grinned. "We crossed the dreaded Gulf Stream all by ourselves."

As conversations unspooled, I saw again that winter is a special time. There were neighborhood parties. At an annual cabin fever party the hostess required each guest to provide some form of entertainment—a poem, a dance, a song. She, in turn, dressed in costume. One year the hostess morphed from nun to hooker in the course of the evening. The hostess has since moved, but her parties ceased before her departure, to be replaced by something less formal. "We got kind of tired of the pressure," an attendee told me.

The town draws close in winter. They share common troubles ("My toilet bowl water is frozen again," lamented one woman), and they look out for one another. If a regular doesn't come in for their mail, someone checks on them. Not that all is utopian: I was told

that once, in a first-aid class, one matron offered to apply a tourni-
quet to the neck of a local Realtor.

The days could be long, lengthening as slowly and soundlessly as
shadow, gray winds wandering empty streets, but everyone I talked
to liked it that way. "I hate the summer," Greg Bennett, a local artist,
told me amiably. "I hate the heat, the people, and the bugs. I don't
even like the light. It's too green. The gray of winter is much more
beautiful."

When I asked one woman what it takes to live in a place like
Strathmere in the winter, she had questions of her own. "Are you
odd? Are you different? This town's been known for that for years.
We don't fit into a pattern, and we don't particularly like people who
do. Which is lovely."

Such sentiments may seem queer and elitist. But if we are honest, there is some misanthrope in us all. Even within the treasured
confines of love and family, we often wish to be alone. After a time,
fair Vida would have pushed the Blackmoor overboard.

※

I VISITED Elizabeth Bergus one afternoon. She fixed me a cup of
coffee, and we sat at her kitchen table. She lives alone, now that her
husband, Donald, has passed away. Her children are grown and
gone. There are books everywhere.

"What have you found out about this little town?" she asked.

It seemed like a facile answer, but it was what I felt in my heart:
"That people care about one another."

Elizabeth smiled knowingly. "Don't they?"

We discussed various community matters. Elizabeth is a reliable
source. Among other things, she is president of the improvement
association, the only Democrat on the zoning board, a fire commis-
sioner, and, when required, a firefighter as well: "I can roll hose
along with anyone else."

I also learned something of Elizabeth's life. For nearly forty
years Donald served in the Foreign Service, in Beirut, Turkey, Saudi
Arabia, and Iraq. He was ambassador to Egypt and the Sudan.

Elizabeth had worked beside him, raising their children and performing the innumerable and invaluable functions of a high-level diplomat's wife. It was not hard to see where her natural authority and tough-when-required diplomacy stemmed from.

After a time we wandered upstairs to the second floor. The house was pin-neat, dark and heavy with wood. In a study framed and signed pictures lined the shelves. "With best wishes to Donald Bergus," read the inscription scrawled beneath the picture of Jimmy Carter. "To Don with all the best wishes, Nasser," read another.

From Elizabeth's bedroom window, over a fence and empty clothesline, I could see the dunes and the slate-gray Atlantic.

"I had the Nile, and now I have the Atlantic," she said.

I thought of Elizabeth rustling through town meeting notes in a soundless house, and there was no sadness in it.

"Which one do you like best, river or ocean?" I asked.

She smiled. "I can't choose. I'm always happy wherever I'm living at the time."

When I left Elizabeth, I walked to the beach, taking the same path she had walked as a child. It was a still afternoon; the sky was a yellowish gray. Down by the water wood pilings jutted from the sand, their tops toupeed with snow. The tide was drawing out, leaving wet-slick mudflats and the hearty smell of marsh.

I looked inland. Elizabeth's house, the post office, the whole of Strathmere was shielded by the dunes; only the anonymous water tower blemished the sky. It was a view that would please any of the town's residents greatly.

※

UP THE COAST Asbury Park cried out for attention, a soft bleating like a long-wounded animal.

For those who know Asbury Park, and even for those who don't, the Jersey Shore town resonates with colorful history. In its heyday in the 1930s, 1940s, and 1950s Asbury Park defined seaside grandeur and salty fun. All was larger than life: lavish restaurants and hotels—the Lafayette, the Montauk, the Marlborough; a grand oceanfront convention hall; the largest saltwater pool in the world—

so large that bands played on a giant platform that floated in the pool; and, of course, the boardwalk. New Jersey is to boardwalks what Detroit is to cars, and, in Asbury Park's glory days, there was no boardwalk finer.

The first blow to this vibrant place came in the 1950s, when New Jersey finished its Garden State Parkway, providing fun-lovers easy access to South Jersey's uncrowded beaches. Then the 1960s and 1970s saw the advent of the American shopping mall—conspicuous consumerism, under one roof—and many of Asbury Park's finest establishments, department stores where impeccably dressed clerks had once moved like Fred Astaire, went out of business or left town to meld with the mall. When things spiral badly, they often gather momentum. In 1970 three days of violent race riots brought Asbury Park national attention. Richard Nixon, blind to disaster in his own presidential office, declared Asbury Park a disaster area on national TV.

As a final coup de grâce, a nearby state psychiatric hospital closed down, moving some of its purportedly tempered clients into the crumbling boardinghouses and hotels along Asbury's beach. "You'd be up on the boardwalk and you'd see this guy with half his clothes off, smelling like urine, and swinging a stick, saying, 'I am God,'" an Asbury native told me. "These guys were all over the place."

This is not the God that parishioners or vacationers wish to see. Asbury Park's original architects were designers of heart; the city's streets flared out at the ocean to catch the sea breeze. Now it's as if the streets were retching, opening wide to spill their spoiled contents into the sea.

I pulled alongside Asbury Park's famed boardwalk on an appropriately bleak day. Clouds the color of a dirty Brillo pad hung low in the sky as if poised to scour the landscape clean. Skeletal buildings sat silent, and seagulls rose from Dumpsters in front of those buildings that still possessed life. I stepped from the van. In the quiet, tattered newspapers snapped against chain-link fences like pinioned butterflies.

I walked up to the boardwalk past a miniature golf course, its cracked cement buried in empty milk containers and brown weeds.

The boardwalk itself was much smaller than I had envisioned, paralleling the empty beach for roughly a mile. Asbury's boardwalk held such a place in my imagination that I had expected something grander. What I beheld was a narrow alley of weather-worn planking, flanked by salt-ruined railings that tilted out in places as if the boardwalk were striving to spread itself wider. It was like happening upon a favorite childhood place after many years, and seeing its sad shabbiness through adult eyes.

I walked from one end to the other, passing through cold ghosts of chill and creosote. Sand pooled in the doorways of boarded-up buildings scrawled with "dick" and "bitch" as if even the spray-paint poets couldn't bear to stay long. I peered through the salt-streaked window of a Howard Johnson's. A Christmas tree with a Hefty bag on top leaned in a corner. At its base, a tiny snowman lay on its back in a pile of trash, staring black-eyed up at the chipped ceiling.

Summer apparently was no charmer, either. A sign on the next building laid out summer's bathing rules: "Please do not enter the water if you are experiencing or recovering from diarrhea . . . Do not wash out diapers in the bathing water . . . Immediately report any 'accidents' to the lifeguard . . ."

The boardwalk was empty. Even God had forsaken the place.

I drove to find a place to stay. There were several decrepit motels near the boardwalk. They looked to fit my needs, cheap and empty, but when I pulled into the first one, a man shouted, "We have no rooms!" and his stone-faced little girl watched him shut the window in my face. It started to snow.

I had experienced desolate moments on the road, but this one stole the show. At that moment all I wanted was to be rid of Asbury Park. I left as fast as I could.

※

I SPENT THE NIGHT in Long Branch, six miles north, but I returned to Asbury Park the next day.

I came back for two reasons. One, I believe everything and everyone deserves a second chance; it was unfair to see Asbury Park through the prism of a single dreary day. Second, Asbury Park was, and occasionally still is, the stomping grounds of the Boss. Bruce Springsteen lived in Asbury Park. He used what he inhaled there—the boardwalk, Madam Marie's, every beach town's drifters and dreamers—to touch his first tentative fingers to the pulse of life at the Jersey Shore and, given man's common desires, beyond. He rocked Asbury's honky-tonk bars until the audience collapsed. His first album was given the only title that made sense: *Greetings from Asbury Park, N.J.* The songs on it were written in the back of a closed beauty salon, the floor below Springsteen's apartment in Asbury Park.

Music weaves a different spell on each of us. On the surface my personal connection with Springsteen is simple: he sings of a Jersey Shore life that I once lived, and a Jersey girl I still love.

I try to remain above adulation on any front; we are all too human. But to my mind, Springsteen is exempt from this rule. He's human, no doubt, but his songs are like no one else's. He sings from the heart, without apology. The ride is not always pleasant, but it is always unforgettable. I also like Springsteen's songs because, though the message may be dark, the songs almost always resonate with an undercurrent of hope, and without hope, there's no point in living.

I returned to Asbury because I wanted to walk in Springsteen's footsteps, even if they now ambled through memory and ruin.

It seemed everyone I met along the Jersey Shore had had some encounter with the Boss. It was if he had dedicated his early life to insinuating himself into the lives of strangers. I have to admit, it was hipper to have had a brush with Springsteen than to have an ancestor who served with Blackbeard's crew.

"I saw him on his thirtieth birthday," one man said happily. "He was sitting all by himself drinking shots in the middle of the afternoon. I was sitting about four seats away. At first I thought it was just another guy. Then some girl told me it was his thirtieth birthday. I wished him a happy birthday, and he's like, 'I can't believe it. Today I'm thirty years old. But I'm still beautiful. Ain't I beautiful?' "

The man nodded.

"Springsteen's just a regular New Jersey guy. People think of him as a rocker, but what he really is is a poet. You could take all the god-damn poems published in *The New Yorker* last year and just shove them. Springsteen knocks them dead."

He shook his head sadly.

"Springsteen is a poet," he said. "There's no real poets anymore."

TOM DESENO had his own Springsteen stories, but he knew plenty more about Asbury Park. Tom is thirty-nine, a lawyer with the firm of DeSeno & Kunz, and father of four. Equally important, he is third-generation Asbury Park, and he fervently believes in his home-town's resurrection.

I was glad I gave Asbury Park a second chance, because when I visited Tom, I saw a different place. It's true, the beach and board-walk resemble Disneyland after a nuclear strike. But it's also true that a mile inland the heart of downtown Asbury is buzzing with change, change that Tom and others believe will make its way to the ocean's edge.

"You're here at a time to see both the past and the future all at once," said Tom. "The gay community has discovered Asbury Park. The real estate market has really taken off. For some reason the gays are not afraid to go up to an old crack house and say, 'Look at that place. If we put a little money into that, that would be a castle.' Now one nice house goes in, and a straight family drives through the neighborhood and they decide they want to build right next door."

Asbury's renaissance is bigger than one house at a time—the beachfront is prepping for a wholesale face-lift. A New York devel-oper, Tom said, has invested $1.2 billion in a grand redevelopment that will see the dilapidated buildings along the beach torn down and replaced by retail stores, an entertainment complex, and three thousand–plus upscale condos.

Plenty of people are vehemently opposed to this razing of Asbury Park's once-glorious past, though most of them, said Tom, live some-where else. Springsteen is part of the problem. With his songs he created a familiar place for thousands who otherwise wouldn't know Asbury Park from Jurassic Park.

"There are lots of people who have strong feelings and memories for what's down there, and the thought of those memories disappearing hurts them," said Tom. "But what are we supposed to live on while they're reminiscing from New York or Seattle? Tourism is dead. We need quality year-round residential to save us."

Tom loves his hometown. His office is a shrine to the place. The walls are plastered with old pictures of Asbury Park. Some of the photos antedated him, but others didn't. In one early 1980s photo he mugs outside Asbury's Jefferson Bar with six friends and a familiar smiling face. "Me and Bruuuuuuuce!" reads the scrawled photo caption.

Tom has memories of his own, and they are real. He belongs firmly to the redevelopment camp, though now and again his resolve slips a notch. "I grew up here. There's a part of me that would like to see the beachfront stay," he said, then steeled himself. "But nobody is going to buy an expensive condominium by the ocean if they have to look out at that dump."

Tom took me on a walking tour of Asbury's downtown. He is a superb tour guide, enthusiastic and surprisingly knowledgeable.

My walking tour wasn't his first. "This past summer I started closing my office at two P.M. on Fridays to give people tours of the downtown stores," he said. "If the residents don't talk up Asbury Park, who will?"

We walked along Cookman Avenue. It was a cold and sunny-bright. The air sung with the whine of planers and the ring of hammers: workers taking advantage of a break in the weather. Cookman Avenue and its neighboring streets were an odd mix of bustle and decrepitude. One building would be vacant and graffitied, the next would be slung with scaffolding and workers, the next would be filled with pricey bronze and porcelain statuary. It was like watching evolution, aided by time-lapse photography.

We crossed Cookman and ducked into a store. Robert Legere Home brimmed with expensive furnishings, refinement, and taste.

A lean man came out from behind a counter, giving me a smile and an iron handshake. Robert is a gay man. Asbury Park is the last place he expected to be. He was a New Yorker. He'd never even been across the bridge to Jersey until world events and a special partner changed his mind. "Steve read this article about this great beach community where you could come down and buy a house and use a credit card for the down payment," Robert recalled. "Houses were that cheap."

Steve and Robert bought their house for a song, then sank $550,000 into its refurbishment. Robert believes firmly in Asbury Park's renaissance. They have a five-year lease on the store. "This is an amazing place," he exulted. "It's hard to believe that it just about fell away into the ocean."

From what I'd seen, the oceanfront looked to be far from out of the woods yet. But Robert is no stranger to sudden makeovers. "I was a fashion designer," he said. "September eleventh killed my business." His spark flickered for a moment. He looked out the window, though I don't think he saw the street. "It also killed my spirit and my innocence," he lamented softly. "New York is gone forever for me."

But he had made a fresh start. Robert drew himself up. "When you tell people in Manhattan you live in New Jersey, they're like 'Why?' I tell them I live in Asbury Park, and excuse me, it's a new thing."

When we stepped back outside, Tom turned to me. "You gotta believe," he said.

Nearby workers on a scaffolding hammered and planed a renovation. Beneath them a sign on a cracked plate-glass window read "No Trespassing. Police Take Notice."

Man creates and man destroys, and man, hopefully, never loses his belief in renewal. Robert wasn't the only person I met who was forever altered by the events of September 11. In Long Branch a man said to me, "A little while after, we could see this gray soot out on the water. And there were smells. Smells of burning plastic. And burning bodies."

Before I headed north, I walked the boardwalk a last time. The same trash chased around the buildings. At the south end of the boardwalk a gutted casino hunkered beside the Atlantic, a cold wind clawing its exposed innards. Painted on a wall nearby were the words "This Too Shall Pass."

This is indeed the one certainty. Beyond it there is no telling. For better or for worse, this sentiment endows our lives with both hope and horror.

13
LONG ISLAND
Santa's Helpers

THERE IS A PLACE where kindness and selflessness exist, a small glen, on the first morning I saw it, smothered with snow and cloistered by bare trees as quiet as monks. Despite winter's stinging press, the world sang. A bright sun sparkled the snow, and trilling bluejays hopped from branch to branch. Through this fairy-tale glen, cats padded, furry butterballs that tumbled and bounded over the crusted snow, now and again plunging into the softer drifts with a wild clawing flurry, emerging with small toupees of snow. It resembled a Disney movie, only without all the shameless trailers.

I could tell you the location of this place, but then I would have to kill you. It is somewhere on Montauk, Long Island.

"We don't tell people where this is." Jean Fischer gingerly picked her way through ten inches of new-fallen snow. "We just don't want more cats dumped here."

Jean and her husband, Herb, have cared for these feral cats, and their predecessors, for seventeen years. They moved to Montauk in 1983 after Herb retired from his job as a patent designer for Bell Laboratories. They wanted a quiet life, and Herb wanted to fish; Montauk offered both. The cat feedings were temporary, filling in for the elderly lady who cared for the cats full-time. Then she got sick, and the job was Herb and Jean's for good. Not everybody loves cats enough to care for them over the long haul. Dumped in the woods or left behind at summer cottages, the cats must fend for themselves. This isn't so hard on a resort island in summer, with brimming restaurant Dumpsters and soft-hearted tourists. It's tough, though, in February, when the tourists are gone and the Dumpsters are frozen shut and the winds billow in off the Atlantic like sodden freight trains, piercing the thickest fur.

Herb walked through the snow just ahead of us, carrying a green bucket and stacked paper plates spread neatly with dry and wet cat food. Several butterballs followed him, their tails up. One brushed against his white rubber boots. Herb didn't reach down. For one thing, his hands were full. For another, it made no sense. Jean often accompanies him, but it's Herb who comes here once a day, winter, spring, summer, and fall, driving ten miles round trip in his pickup truck, up the long rises with their vistas of gray, green, or blue sea. The cats know this serene white-haired man, but, like any canny animal, they mistake him for nothing more than a vending machine.

When we reached the glen, Herb put the bucket down, and the cats oozed away like the edges of a smoke ring.

"Right now there's only two cats I can touch." He smiled. "Not only can I not touch them, I can't get near them. They don't trust people, and I doubt they ever will."

In retrospect this might have been a subtle warning. I like cats, and these round sirens cried out for a cuddle.

I was crouching down toward one of the cats, a calico that hadn't moved off quite as far, when one cat inadvertently jostled another. The affronted animal issued a savage guttural growl and slashed out with a roundhouse swat whose speed was outdone only by its evil disemboweling intent.

Suddenly it was easier to envision that fervor affixed to my face. I straightened slowly, hoping Herb and Jean wouldn't notice.

Herb was busy spreading the paper plates around the glen, which was filled with what looked like oversize boxes. The cats' homes are simple structures: plywood roofs resting on bale walls of hay, resting in turn on a plywood floor. The insides are also generously lined with straw.

"Straw doesn't freeze like rugs do," said Herb. "It doesn't stay wet long, either. The main thing with a cat is they can stand a lot of cold, but they can't stand wet and cold. These houses keep them pretty well protected."

Though the morning was sunny and clear, the air was still hung with a trace of the dampness that always lurks near the sea. The bluejays tittered merrily, fidgeting like children watching the cutting of a birthday cake.

"The birders hate us," said Jean.

This was hard to imagine. Herb reminds me of a cross between a kindly J.R.R. Tolkien and Santa Claus. Jean reminds me of everyone's mom. I have spent time with birders, and they are indeed a fussy lot, but this ire seemed misdirected.

"Why would the birders hate you?" I asked.

"Sometimes the cats eat the birds."

Winter is tough on birds, too. Apparently the birds light down on the plates to help themselves to cat food. More often than not the well-fed cats pay them no mind, but now and again Herb returns to the plates to find scattered feathers and a cat who has enjoyed a two-course meal.

Most days the cats eat the same thing, though a few days are different. "They get chicken liver and hamburger for Christmas and New Year's," said Jean cheerily. "At Christmas we also put up a tree and hang some tinsel and put out some toys, catnip mice and little twisty things that they can play and jump with." She paused. "Although feral cats don't really know how to play."

The cats moved warily through the skeletal trees at the outskirts of the glen. There were others we couldn't see. "They're waiting for us to leave," said Herb.

I was grateful for Herb and Jean's presence. The longer I stood in the glen, the more the circling cats lost their hearthside snuggliness. They assumed menace and girth, transforming from puffballs to predators. Their eyes were fixed on me, probably because I was a strange figure, but I couldn't be sure. I imagined Herb returning to the plates the next morning to find notebook pages and fiberfill scattered everywhere. *Our secret dies with you.*

Herb laid out the plates with the efficiency you would expect of a man who has done so roughly six thousand times. Then he considered the grotto for a quiet moment, smiled at me—"The food isn't going to freeze today"—lifted his empty bucket, and crunched back down the snowy path whence we'd come.

When we arrived back at the parking lot, Jean promptly hopped into the cab of the truck and shut the door. At first I thought she was cold, but Herb grinned. "Jean's afraid of the seagulls," he said.

He pulled a large plastic bag stuffed with bagels and bread bits from the bed of the truck. In a blink a cloud of gulls had massed over our heads. I resisted the urge to jump into the truck beside Jean. Herb was wearing a hat, but I wasn't.

"This comes from the bread deliveryman." Herb was tossing bagels and bread bits out across the icy parking lot. "Since Montauk is his last stop, whatever he has left over, he gives to me. It's a very convenient arrangement for me and the birds."

The gulls—herring gulls, Herb told me—fell upon the feast with a madcap shrieking and whirling, their wing beats snapping time to their greedy pecking, shoving, and gobbling. It was like watching a group of congressmen react to the sudden appearance of a camera.

"You can't say much for their table manners," I said.

"All I can say about gulls is that they're survivors," said Herb. He tossed a last handful of bread bits. "Okay, guys. See you tomorrow."

As we pulled away, the gulls continued to fight over nothing. It is easy to mock them as mindless, but this is a mistake. Already a scattered few were rising into the icy air, winging gracefully toward the ocean.

Herb followed my gaze. "In ten minutes there won't be a gull in the parking lot," he said. They were now on their own. Until tomorrow, no one else would stop with bagels.

But they don't need us. The gulls are able opportunists, defying circumstance and death. When the bounty of spring and summer returns, they will be waiting.

※

To get to Montauk, I had driven from north Jersey through New York City, then out to Long Island. It was an odd journey. North Jersey and New York are clogged with civilization as we define it; an endless wall of dirty brick and smoking industry unspools beside the freeway, and people in icicle-hung cars cut one another off with merry abandon, conveying their mutual affection with horn blasts and hand signals. On Long Island trees reappear, though the westerly towns—Jericho, Deer Park, and Islip—are as big as small cities and equally thick with traffic. But as I drove east toward the tip of Long Island, the road pinched and pine forests slowly assumed dominance alongside the road. As night fell, I saw a deer standing at the wood's edge, and the homes melded with the woods, throwing blankets of warm lamplight across the snow.

Long Island ends at the Montauk Lighthouse, falling into the Atlantic and Block Island Sound. When I woke the next morning in Montauk, the world, with one notable exception, was simple low-slung buildings washed by brilliant blue sky. There were no smokestacks, and no one shot me the finger. It was as if man's angry blight had been sea-scrubbed away.

"Montauk is the most seasonal of Long Island's towns," an East Hampton resident told me. "When winter comes, the place just dies."

Perfect. I stayed at a motel just behind the dunes, the owner, swamped by a loud, happy bevy of kids, giving a fellow family man a kind discount. At night I lay in bed listening to the wind moaning past the dusty fronts of souvenir and T-shirt shops. During the day some of the stores opened, and a happy but minute fraction of summer's cars and hordes moved through town. By Herb's estimate, Montauk's summer population hovers around 28,000; its winter population is one-tenth of that.

I was comfortable in Montauk. It had no pretensions, unlike its close neighbors, and its residents didn't seem to give a damn about influencing or participating in the outside world. I was told the story of a local fisherman who, informed that a friend was traveling to Spain, replied, "Oh. Are you going to drive there?" Montauk's most famous fisherman is Frank Mundus, the real-life shark hunter whom Hollywood turned into Quint in the movie *Jaws*. Mundus caught a 4,500-pound great white with a harpoon and helped a client land a 3,427-pound whitey on rod and reel, earning himself the nickname Monster Man. He is as candid as any Montauk fisherman. *Jaws*, Mundus chuckled, "was the funniest and stupidest movie I've ever seen."

⁂

MONTAUK HAS NEITHER the chic nor size of a Miami Beach, though it very nearly became one. In the mid-1920s a developer named Carl Fisher bought 9,632 acres of Montauk real estate, much of it prime waterfront. Fisher reasoned that Montauk, jutting out into the Atlantic, would be the ideal port of entry for New York City, a grand resort town with luxurious hotels and amenities and trains running into the city. Fisher was a dreamer, but he had tangible successes in his pocket, too; by the time he cast his eye on Montauk, he had already created the Indianapolis Speedway and, yes, Miami Beach. Once asked why he built things, Fisher replied, "To see dirt fly." Fortunately dirt eventually flies over all of us. Fisher died in 1938, and his grand design for Montauk fizzled. But he did manage to erect portions of his vision before his passing, including a seven-story building that prongs up, Stonehenge-like, out of Montauk's quiet town center.

Thankfully Montauk never became Miami Beach. God knows how many cats would have been abandoned by heartless sun-seekers or misplaced by addled retirees. In winter it remains a place unto itself.

"Officially we're a hamlet in the town of East Hampton." Herb was driving me back to my motel after the morning cat feeding. "But really Montauk is a different world. The mindset here is not like the other communities, which are quite sophisticated. Montauk is raw bones."

East Hampton and Southampton have long been renowned as places where the wealthy escape—and so sport the requisite trendy affluence, with literary readings, pricey art galleries and boutiques, and establishments called simply "Brent's," as if only the great unwashed need to be told it's a restaurant. Montauk is a place where fishermen moonlight as landscapers to make ends meet and retired codgers gather most mornings at Ronnie's deli to sip coffee and chew the fat, or, as the deli owner good-naturedly described them, "a bunch of old farts who come in here and solve all the world's problems and get in the way." East Hampton, Southampton, Water Mill, they were connected to Montauk by the same lovely shoreline, but back from the sand they were worlds apart.

That afternoon I drove west into East Hampton, with no particular destination in mind. After a few misguided turns I found myself driving down Old Beach Lane and followed it just because I liked the name. I parked right in front of a sign that read "Egypt Beach. Parking by Village Permit Only. Permits Required May 15–Sept 30." It is a joy traveling a land where all the rules are off.

Snow covered Egypt Beach, a luxurious blanket that ran from the high-tide line up into the dunes. I walked in the snow, dry and soft, like velvet underfoot. In summer I always walk by the water's edge to be as close to the ocean as possible. But on this trip, when I walked the beach, I chose to walk in the snow. This moved me away from the ocean's edge—the waves were washing the snow away—but it didn't matter. I saw lots of snow on lots of beaches, and it never lost its allure, but walking in snow on the beach is more than strange. It is a rare and precious treat, almost illicit, an aberration, as if Nature has momentarily discarded her sane and proper self and thrown herself, beckoning and white-limbed, on sheets all askew.

On a more innocent front, I walked in the snow because it allowed me to make snowballs. I heaved them into the waves heartily and often, trying to plant them, just as a wave reared, in its smooth face, imagining myself sending arrows into the underbelly of a rearing dragon. Sometimes I juggled snowballs, one of many critical skills I learned in college. Once in a while, when the snow was dry but still packable, I would toss a snowball straight up into the air and, if fate would have it, let it crash down on my head. It was infantile, I knew that, but I didn't give a damn. It was fun, and there was no one around to see me. Let whoever hasn't made faces in the bathroom mirror cast the first stone.

I wandered mindlessly for a time, with only the sound of the wind whopping in my ears. When I regained consciousness, I found I had walked up the beach and through a breach in the dunes. I was drawn toward a long string of wooden cabanas, shingle-roofed, silent sheds that belong to the Maidstone Club. I crunched past a sign informing me I was in the Men's Sunyard and read the names above the cabana doors: L. T. Steele. A. J. Connick. A. D. Duke. Plastic lawn chairs sat outside the cabanas. On each chair sat a pile of snow, presumably male.

Behind the shelter of the dunes the sunyard was crypt-quiet. But it wasn't hard to imagine brown-skinned life pouring from the cabanas, the shouts of children heading for the water, and the half-hearted admonishments of sun-drowsed parents to swim near the lifeguard. Now the lifeguard stand lay on its side in a snowy dune. When I stepped again between the dunes, frosty wind filled my lungs. Beyond the toppled stand a single set of footprints worked their way backward down to the waves. It was a beautiful, bright sunny afternoon. The ocean sparkled enticingly. It could have been summer, but it wasn't, and this thrilled me. In summer I wouldn't have been alone. In summer I would have been shooed off, politely no doubt, or forced to shoulder the disdainful stares of members who recognized me as an interloper. Yet here I stood in the Connicks' and the Steeles' Sunyard, and, though not an iota of cabana belonged to me, I owned the place. Depending on my mood I could have recited Yeats, or hopped about naked, or invited a half dozen close friends to do the same. No one would have cared, no one would have known, no one would have been arrested. We are, most of us, proper in our actions, often at the price of stifling our hearts. It is a rare thing when society's tethers are loosed, and, even if you don't act on it, it is still fine medicine for the heart.

Had I been offered, at that instant, the chance to conjure summer with a snap of my fingers, I wouldn't have hesitated for a second: I would have done precisely what I did. Thrusting my hands in my pockets, I happily stifled any hope of a snap. I followed my footprints to the sea, though, truth is, I'm not sure my feet touched the ground.

※

THE NEXT MORNING I went again with Herb to feed the cats. Jean didn't come; maybe she wasn't in the mood for seagulls.

The routine was the same. We parked in the icy lot, and I walked alongside the bucket-toting Herb. Three cats appeared on cue, tails upright, trotting jauntily a safe distance away. The remaining four were aware of our presence.

Age, and the occasional summer road accident, had reduced the colony from nineteen cats to the current seven. This whittling saddened Herb, but it also served a purpose.

"I just hope I live long enough to see this colony go to nothing." Herb bent to put the plates down. "You don't want to put the burden on somebody else. You're on your deathbed, and you say, 'Now you've got to promise me you'll feed the cats . . .'" He shook his head. "They're tough, though. They'll probably outlast me."

"If they do outlast you, do you think they'll miss you?"

Herb chuckled softly. He knew his place in this pageant.

"They may feel a little more at ease with me because they know me. But if you showed up with a bucket of food, they'd like you, too."

Herb's birth certificate says Queens, but his ashes will be scattered over Montauk's waters. Each December until then, Jean and Herb will put up a Christmas tree in the glen. It is easy to close your eyes and see it on a still, frozen night, the tinsel catching the moonlight, cat shadows padding about, ignoring the toys beneath the tree, waiting for morning and the arrival of their Santa Claus.

14
CONNECTICUT
One If By Kayak, Two If By Ski

IT WAS THE WINTER that wouldn't quit.

The picture had been serene in the pampered cats' glen, but the rest of the country was hunkered beneath meteorological mayhem. There were floods in Texas, vicious lightning storms in the South, and snow pretty much everywhere else—not pretty Currier and Ives dustings, but blasphemous belchings. Garrett County, Maryland, collected forty-eight inches in one fell dump, enough to effectively bury everyone under the age of six. Newspapers ran pictures of street-side snowbanks of Everest proportions, into which thoroughly bundled citizens gamely thrust shovels, hoping to find their double-decker bus. Thousands of chickens were crushed when poultry houses collapsed in West Virginia, while drivers in Wilmington faced a maximum $2,500 fine for unnecessary driving. Airports looked like post-Woodstock, as rumpled zombie-people stood slack-jawed and sleeping strangers drooled in one another's arms.

Due to the ocean's moderating influence, the coast traditionally escapes the worst of the snow, but this winter the ocean seemed without influence. When I took the ferry from Orient Point across the Long Island Sound to New London, Connecticut, it was snowing again, gray flurries that dropped without protest into the brown water.

To cheer myself up, I sat in the van and listened to the news. There was a run on chocolate beer, the country of Liechtenstein was for rent, scientists were thinking about cloning woolly mammoths, and silicon supplies in Brazilian hospitals were exhausted due to a rash of breast implants preceding Carnival.

An announcement on the ferry intercom encouraged passengers to report suspicious activities to the crew. I wondered what, in these times, distinguishes strange behavior.

⁂

STEVE FAGIN is no stranger to strange behavior, and he owns up to it willingly.

Like any thoughtful man, Steve is also always correcting himself. "I like to do things that are kind of unique but not life threatening," he told me when we first met. Pause for consideration. "Life threatening being a relative term."

While exploring the Connecticut coast, I stayed in a friend's cottage in Ledyard. In another stroke of the serendipity that seemed to be padding alongside my trip, Steve lived next door. Steve is a newspaperman of thirty years, but, unlike others of his ilk, he has remained free of cynicism. To the contrary, he possesses characteristics I have always admired and tried to emulate. He is like a child: wide-eyed, curious, and willing to stick his finger in the flame to see if it really will burn him.

You can learn something of people by listening to the stories they tell; less from the bare facts than from how they are presented. Steve has lots of interesting stories. He paddled four hundred miles down the Connecticut River in a canoe, was nearly crushed by stampeding yaks in Nepal and mauled by an annoyed grizzly in Alaska, and once spent forty-one and a half hours chasing around New England with an RV full of like-minded friends, in a successful attempt to climb the high points of all six New England states in one continuous, pointless madcap scramble.

My favorite story involves a midnight crossing of Long Island Sound in an eight-foot rowboat. Steve and a friend set out from Long Island—each manning an oar—armed with a gallon of water, a couple of peanut butter and jelly sandwiches, a compass, and a flashlight. They were nearly run down by a submarine. Bluefish whumped headlong into the gunwales of the boat, which amounted to little more than background thumping when a larger fish slurped by. Apparently Frank Mundus has missed a monster or two.

"The shark was way bigger than the boat, twelve to fifteen feet," Steve told me. "From where we sat in the rowboat, the fin came up over our eyes."

The crew concluded their voyage by hauling ashore at a private shooting club, its members firing a fusillade of live rounds in the direction of the water. "We were just heading for the nearest point of land. We heard this sound like carpenters doing nails . . ."

What I like most about Steve's stories is that at the end, after he's told about rowing in under a rain of heavy fire or slamming the car door in the face of a slavering grizzly, Steve will pause, as if reconsidering the experience anew, nod, and say something like, "It's a privilege to be able to do things like that."

Perhaps wisely, Steve makes little ado of the things he's done.

"People like us are different." He shrugs. "It's not something that's meritorious, it's just a fact."

※

AND SO STEVE proved the perfect playtime companion. It had been several weeks since I paddled the kayak. All the fireside chats I'd had in warm living rooms and overheated boat cabins had left me feeling sluggish and a bit removed from winter. True, it was getting decidedly uncomfortable outside. Not only was it snowing more, but temperatures were dropping off the thermometer. But writing about winter without going outside seemed to me like cheating, and prissy to boot.

I was itching to plunge into winter waters, and Steve was more than game, though on the morning of our planned kayak venture, when I poked my head outside the cottage to regard an icicle-cum-thermometer that read seven degrees, I had second thoughts.

By noon it had warmed somewhat; precisely how much I don't know. I was afraid to look. But as we headed for the water with Steve's kayaks atop his car, the sun shone brightly, causing the

ice-glazed masts of the boats in Mystic Seaport to reflect a pretty
sheen. Great chunks of ice shone somewhat more dully in the Mystic River.

We had no real plan, other than to paddle in the Long Island
Sound. Steve needed to check the wind and chop first.

He had paddled in winter plenty of times before but was still
excited by the prospect. "Connecticut is the place to be for boating.
In the summer the sound is jammed," he said. He flashed me a
Huck Finn grin. "One of the appeals of winter is to be out there
without all the stinkpots."

Pause.

"But it's also kind of unnerving. If you get into trouble, it's nice
to have other boats around."

He peered through the frost-edged windshield, then brightened
again. "It doesn't look like there's much wind out on the sound. You
know it just wouldn't occur to many people to do this on a day like
today. I can pretty much guarantee you there aren't any other kayak-
ers out in the entire Long Island Sound. That's the beauty of winter.
It's like stepping back in time. You get to see how a place existed a
hundred years ago."

Steve wheeled the car into a snowy turnout in Noank, at the
edge of Palmer's Cove. Snow covered the shoreline, but the cove
was free of ice. The sun sparkled on the water, a string of ducks paddling merrily through the glint.

From inside the car it looked like a pleasant scene. But I now
knew how ducks feel about weather, and these ducks, sadly, looked
damn happy, perhaps because the ice-free water was thirty-four
degrees.

Steve had had the foresight to don his gear before leaving
home. Not only that, he was wearing a lot of it—polypropylene
long johns, Gore-tex shell pants, neoprene booties over heavy wool
and nylon socks, two polypropylene turtleneck shirts, a waterproof
neoprene and nylon jacket, and a balaclava expedition-weight
hood. I had a swimsuit and a wetsuit, and they were in the trunk
of Steve's car. Let me just say here that stripping nearly naked in
the snow is a privilege that shouldn't be missed. It wasn't missed

by any of the alarmed diners in the glass-fronted restaurant across the street.

We pushed out into the water, Steve in his yellow kayak, me in red.

Here is the place where I should rhapsodize upon the lovely winteriness of the scene—the gray waters of the sound, the snowy, bare-treed shorelines, the enervating slap and whop of the wind, the kayaks lolling easily over the swells, the slick-black heads of harbor seals popping from the water to regard us. But the truth is, I was too damn cold to enjoy it. As soon as I slipped inside my kayak, my toes—neoprene-booted but sockless—began to go numb. The rest of my body beat them to the punch. It's true I was encased in neoprene, but the wind and the splashing wet wormed right through it. My fingers ached. My face, which poked out of my neoprene hood, burned and then, ever so slowly, went rigid. I have never been seasick in my life, but I felt that was about to change.

Still, I tried to put on a happy face for Steve, who had gone to some trouble to get me here and was now brandishing his paddle like a majorette, proudly indicating the beauty of his local waters. At least I think he was. I could make out Steve shouting, gesturing enthusiastically in the direction of many things, but for the most part I couldn't hear a thing he said. It was as if my brain, mouth, and ears had been stuffed with cotton.

Now and again the wind would bring me a phrase or two— "Look! Seals! They're very wary!"—and I would shout something equally enthusiastic back, which must have made sense to Steve because he would nod happily, though my reply sounded in my ears like *Moonaapppph meeegrup gonnnup.*

Once when our kayaks drifted close, trying hard to keep the whine out of my voice, I was able to articulate the phrase "Are you cold?"

"No!" shouted Steve. "It's the power of positive thinking! I tell myself it's July! It's July! It's July!"

July in Antarctica.

It was beautiful, but frankly it wasn't over soon enough. By the time we pulled our kayaks back ashore at Noank, I thought I might cry, from relief or the prospect of changing again I couldn't tell. Getting out of my wetsuit proved harder. My limbs moved like the Tin Man's, and my senses had apparently short-circuited. Reaching to pull off my hood, I poked myself in the eye. Trying to remove my gloves with my teeth, I bit deeply into a finger, and it surprised me that I felt almost nothing.

Steve must have sensed my addled state.

"Here, I'll lay down a towel," he said gently, and I peered gratefully down to my bare feet standing on ice.

THAT NIGHT at Steve's house, over dinner with his wife, Lisa, and their son, Thomas, I learned two more things about Steve. One: when it behooves him, he can be a poker-faced liar.

He raised his wineglass, tilted it in my direction, and beamed. "You conducted yourself well today for a Californian."

I also learned that Steve is an ardent admirer of Henry David Thoreau. "I loved *Walden*," he said. "The elegance. That someone could derive so much pleasure from simplicity. He saw the beauty in Nature, and man's proper place there."

That night, beneath a blessedly warm pile of down, I dreamed of dark bird clouds that banked against cold winds while below them seals thrust their heads from the icy water and barked a chorus of happy approval. I felt my paddle dip, and the mainland fell away, and I was alone on a vast plain of gray, in a place beyond man and time. I believe I drifted in the direction of wakefulness, long enough to register the black room and the thought that I would willingly do it all over again.

BUT STEVE HAD another plan for us. Two days later, when the morning reading outside my cottage was an enervating two degrees, we went cross-country skiing; but we didn't head for the mountains, we headed for the shoreline. What had shut down airports and quashed West Virginia chickens had provided us with rare opportunity—the chance to ski beside the salt water's edge.

Steve took us to Bluff Point Coastal Reserve. Bluff Point is a thumb of Connecticut woodland bordered by the Poquonock River, Mumford Cove, and, at its thumbnail, the spread of Long Island Sound.

The reserve, Steve told me, is the result of a hard-fought battle by local preservationists, and a rare piece of land, some eight hundred acres in all. "It's the largest undeveloped peninsula between New York and Boston," said Steve. A sad claim if you think hard about it, but far better than the alternative.

We skied first along a snowy path paralleling the Poquonock River. Well, Steve skied and I performed a mincey shuffle, and then Steve stopped and waited for me. The path was lovely, a tunnel of trees whose boughs had traded leaves for drapings of snow. The air stung my lungs, but the effort of skiing generated blessed heat. Today I was comfortable and fully conscious.

"One developer had planned a sort of Coney Island adventure here, complete with a Ferris wheel and a boardwalk and bath-houses," said Steve when I caught up with him. "I don't ever come out here without realizing how grateful I am for the people who had the foresight to preserve a place like this. It would be pretty easy for this to be a subdivision or a huge shopping center."

I thought of Winston Perry, the stately Murrells Inlet shopkeeper down in South Carolina, and his blank-check-carrying friends.

"This time around people realized that there were other genera-tions to come," Steve continued. "But in our culture it's very easy to see how we lose things like this."

We gazed out at the Poquonock River, as white as ivory and nearly as solid. Beyond the river I could see flashing lights at the Groton–New London Airport and past that an enormous smoke-stack issuing gray billows of smoke. But here the world was quiet, its honkings and wailings smothered by the snow.

Steve shook his head. "I can't remember this river freezing up like this."

"Is it completely frozen?" I asked.

"Yeah," he said. "Though I wouldn't necessarily try and ski across it."

Steve schussed off. I minced along, absorbed in snowy silence. Ten inches of snow had fallen within the week. It parted beneath my skis like butter. As I neared the sound, the blessed smell of brine came to me. I awkwardly climbed a short rise, my crossed ski tips clacking.

Steve and I stood quietly at the very edge of Bluff Point, looking out at Long Island Sound. It was like being on the prow of a boat. The day before, the sound had been a fury of wind and whitecaps. Today its waters spread before us, as smooth as a carpet. They sparkled prettily, running off toward the smoky blue outline of the northern end of Long Island. Far below us water slurped gently over rocks covered with milky ice. To the west a long spit of sand made an empty boomerang curve to its end at Bushy Point.

My heart soared. I wanted to sing, shout, and hop madly about, do something plainly idiotic, so drunk I was with my own unimportance in this panorama and the absolute blessing of being here. It was the same joyous upwelling I experienced while paddling amid the ghostly sea smoke off Murrells Inlet, meeting Uncle Sam in the mangroves of the Keys, walking the virgin beach on Hog Island, standing in the silent, snow-stacked Men's Sunyard in East Hampton. Things were starting to string together and connect, like pieces of a jigsaw puzzle that was meant to be.

"Crowded, isn't it?" I said.

Steve smiled. I could see spittle frozen in his mustache. "What makes it even better is knowing that not five miles from here tens of thousands of people are shopping, driving their cars, sitting at their computers, going about their lives. And here we are. We might as well be Columbus."

"Escape really isn't all that difficult," I said giddily.

Steve wasn't as inebriated as I was. "No. Of course, you have to be like a horse with blinders sometimes, too." He nodded at the shin-high brown grass in front of my feet. "There were homes out here at one time."

I looked down. Slowly, tiny square blocks, little bigger than a hand, appeared in the grass.

"These were probably foundations," said Steve. "The rest of the homes were washed away by the 1938 hurricane."

❧

HURRICANES HAVE BUFFETED most of the East Coast, but none took a place more by surprise than the hurricane that roared ashore along Rhode Island and Connecticut on Wednesday, September 21, 1938. From Mystic, Connecticut, to Narragansett, Rhode Island, more than a thousand houses and cottages were destroyed, and more than 130 people died. This was just a narrow stretch of shore, a microcosm of a fury that, in the end, raked the coastline from South Jersey to Boston and, in death, injury, and destruction, outdid the Great Chicago Fire and the Great San Francisco Earthquake of 1906.

"More destructive hurricanes have bombarded U.S. shores," reads an account of the storm in the October 3, 1938, issue of *Time,* "but never has a hurricane struck a region so thickly populated and unprepared."

There were opportunities for advance warning. On Monday, aboard the Italian passenger ship *Conte di Savoia,* bound for New York from the Mediterranean, Rev. Ernest Gherzi, an Italian Jesuit who had served for twenty-three years as a meteorologist at an observatory near Shanghai, came to the ship's bridge. "One of my children will be around in about three days." Another warning came from right at home. On Wednesday morning several Westerly, Rhode Island, schoolchildren told their teachers a hurricane was coming. They were told to sit down and forget that foolish talk. The children had read about the hurricane sweeping up from the Florida coast in their own morning newspaper.

By Wednesday afternoon the approaching hurricane was sending out its own queer signals. Residents reported having a strange feeling in their ears, as if they were ascending quickly in an elevator, the effect of plummeting barometric pressure. Mrs. Geoffrey Moore, in a letter written later, reported that "the clothes had to be pinned doubly on the lines to keep them from blowing away." Another resident, hosting a luncheon, noticed that the sea appeared restless and was hung with a strange yellow light.

Then the wind came up like the rising roar of a siren, and they had no more doubt about what was upon them. The winds reached 150 miles an hour in nearly a blink, with gusts estimated at 200 miles an hour, though this was mostly guesswork since the measuring instruments followed Dorothy's house to Oz. Rooftops and walls disappeared within seconds. A tidal wave scooped up the remains. Seaweed was found in the rain gutters of homes five miles inland.

One afternoon in the Ledyard library, I pored through personal accounts of the storm. There were dozens of them, each documenting someone's long moment in hell. Amid the large-scale terror, it was the minute details people seemed to remember. A rag doll blown across the bay in a bathtub, her legs rising and falling with the gusts; a kitten sucked from a coat pocket and delivered into the air; the disappearing shoe soles of friends swept away by raging waters.

One man welcomed the storm. On Oakland Beach, in Narragansett Bay, a blacksmith sat and waited. His son had drowned six years earlier. Neighbors tried to convince him to leave, but he shook his head. "He's come for me," he said. "My boy has come for me at last."

The hurricane swept across Long Island, through the heart of New England into Canada, and vanished north of Montreal.

Standing at the edge of the promontory, gazing out over the tranquil sunny waters of the sound, I had no trouble imagining a day little different from this, glorious and serene, while out there beyond the bulk of Long Island something unholy churned forward.

I looked again at the foundations in the grass. This time I noticed they were precisely placed, resembling miniature tombstones.

Later I talked with a Westerly woman who had been a child when the storm came ashore. "I remember about two o'clock we were dismissed from school," she said. "It was a dark day, sort of sticky, and there was a funny feeling in the air. One of the kids said,

'We're going to have a hurricane.' I didn't know what that was. The next day I remember was a beautiful day. Perfectly gorgeous. And they were hauling bodies up from the beach. Nobody took the hurricane seriously. We didn't have hurricanes."

You can rightly lambaste our thick-headedness. It's true—we are often as ignorant as children. Equally true, our species possesses a childish innocence and persistence that makes us resilient, so that we may rise up from near-fatal beatings and start anew.

A month after the hurricane a resident wrote a letter to friends, including photographs from a Westerly Chamber of Commerce publication. The photos showed people sailing, golfing, and horseback riding, and two happy tykes sitting in the damp sand at the water's edge.

"The interesting and peculiar thing about these views is that not one of these activities has been ruined by the storm," wrote the letter writer. "We're all right and will be looking forward to seeing you and the youngsters as usual next summer . . ."

As Steve is also fond of saying, "There just aren't many limitations if you keep your wits about you."

⁂

I, FOR ONE, had never permitted myself to cross-country ski at the beach, but that's exactly what happened twenty minutes later, when we skied down from the bluff, bushwhacked through the snowy woods, pushed through a high stand of marsh grass, and exited onto a fairy-tale white shore.

Technically we were near the mouth of Mumford Cove, but it touched the sound, which was oceanlike enough for me. Where the snow had melted, I saw sand as sandy as on any beach. Seagulls turned overhead, their white undersides reflecting the snow's glow. To bring summer and winter as close as possible, I followed the water's edge as tightly as I could; tidepools of dark rock and equally still water rested inches away from my ski edge as I sluiced along. At one point I shut my eyes. With the warm sun on my face, the tart-iron smell of marsh and sea in my nostrils, and the sound of gently lapping waves massaging my ears, I could have been walking the beach in summer, only the wind was too cold and the beach crunched beneath me without lodging between my toes.

It was strange and wonderful, this odd coupling. I felt as if I had cheated convention, pushed between the curtain folds that normally separate the seasons, and stepped onto a hidden stage that snubs normalcy.

Steve stopped ahead of me. I skied up beside him. He was staring across the frozen expanse of Mumford Cove. He had pooh-poohed the thought of skiing across the Poquonock, but he wasn't one to miss out on adventure. I knew exactly what he was thinking.

"I keep looking out there and thinking how tempting it is to zip right across the head of the cove," he said, more to himself than to me. And then, "I don't think it's terribly deep." And then, "I wouldn't do it if I thought there was a remote chance we could go in."

Steve sidestepped easily down from the bank onto the ice and looked up at me. "Worst-case scenario, you go in up to your knees."

What is thin ice to a man who has nearly been one with berries and bear scat?

Steve schussed smoothly away across the icy expanse, his voice drifting back to me: "If you break through, it shouldn't be any more than knee deep." Pause. "I doubt if it would be waist deep."

I followed because I had no choice. To turn back meant another woodsy bushwhack, not easy on annoyingly long skis; the first go-round had seen me pitch forward on my face more times than I care to tell. To refuse to take to the ice also flew in the face of the credo Steve and I now shared: it was a privilege not to be missed. Plus, the way I saw it, Steve would fall through the ice before I did if I stuck to his path like a finger to Braille.

It was windier out on the ice, and tomb-quiet. The ice seemed to stamp out sound even more effectively than the snow. A flock of geese rose into the sky a hundred yards away, without a cry or the snap of a wing beat. Then a single blast rent the solitude, a distant Amtrak train, steel-cloistered commuters whipping past to New York or Boston.

Steve had already reached the opposite bank. Just before I

joined him, I schussed past something oddly familiar, a wooden pal-
let jutting from the ice at a slightly skewed angle. After a second it
came to me: a platform for swimmers.

I waited until I had sidestepped onto the bank before I mentioned what had occupied my mind for the past ten minutes.
"Whew." I hissed out my relief. "I wasn't ever sure if the ice was
thick enough."

Steve nodded. "I saw some deer tracks that went across the ice,
so it gave me a little confidence," he said. Pause. "Not everyone
would appreciate the elegance of this."

He briefly surveyed the ten-foot-high thicket of bramble we now
faced.

"The destination isn't the purpose of the journey, it's the experience along the way," he said, then plunged into the bramble.

15
RHODE ISLAND
Peter Pan Lives

IMMATURITY. *Webster's* defines it as "lacking the emotional maturity, sense of responsibility, etc. characteristic of an adult." But *Webster's* is by definition too definitive for me, though in the case of immaturity Mr. Webster is also impossibly vague. Who, except perhaps my wife, can say what falls under the heading "etc."? I prefer the geological definition—"worn down only slightly by erosion"—or, not far different, F. Scott Fitzgerald's thought: "Growing up is a terribly hard thing to do. It is much easier to skip it and go from one childhood to another."

That was part of the reason why, in Rhode Island, I sought out Peter Pan.

Pan, for those who are not surfers, is a surfing legend, though like most legends, he draws mixed accolades.

"Just because you say you're a legend doesn't mean you are one," a famous surfboard shaper once sniped. "Peter Pan lives an illusion of himself." (To which my thought was, *Who doesn't?*) Greg Noll, a famous big wave rider, dubbed Pan "the greatest cold water surfer on the face of the earth." A young surfer I met at a restaurant in Westerly, Rhode Island, screwed up his face in disgust: "The guy is a complete kook. They had to save him from *drowning* at a contest in Hatteras."

This last statement is true. Pan later told me so himself. "It was pretty big, around ten-foot and really sucking out. I wiped out and couldn't swim too well, so a friend had to dive in and save me." Pan shrugged. "I definitely practiced up on my swimming after that."

I knew of Pan because the surfing magazines sporadically interviewed him, largely because they never knew what he would say.

Magazine: Do you do martial arts?

Pan: I've taken tae kwon do for twenty years . . . Use martial arts only as a last resort, but if you do, try grabbing the genitals.

I was entertained by what Pan spouted, but, more important, I was amazed by what he did. When the surfing magazines didn't have him on the phone, he was out in the water, surfing some of the cruddiest, coldest waves on the planet. He surfed on days when the wind chill screamed at negative thirty-five degrees, the water was twenty-nine, his eyelashes froze, icicles hung from his neoprene hood, and bigger waves pounded the sides of a three-year-old's bathtub.

Most surfers hold six-inch waves in disdain. Fewer still will brave meat-locker conditions to ride them. Pan is different.

"The problem is, if you wait for good waves, you can wait forever," he told me one day. "I get the most waves because I have the lowest standards."

⁂

I ALSO LOOKED up Pan because I wanted to go surfing. In my twenties I was rabid enough to surf in winter myself. Though New Jersey's winters are not as harsh as Rhode Island's, I knew cold; I had surfed on days where the ocean's edge was margarita slush. But twenty years had passed, and with it the precise memory of how painfully cold it was. I was ready to try again, and Pan was the man to take me.

I called him from Connecticut. When he returned my call, I asked him, rather stupidly, if the water was cold.

"It is! It's thirty-two!" said Pan.

Suddenly a sound came from the receiver, as if a donkey had just been made the beneficiary of a stupendous joke.

"Yaaaahhh-ha-ha-ha-ha-ha-ha-ha! The colder the better!"

⁂

THE NEXT DAY I drove up from Ledyard. When I stepped inside Pan's Gansett Juice surf shop in Narragansett, a man was standing there. I knew it wasn't Pan. Pan is only five foot five, and even when he's wet, he weighs only slightly more than Kleenex. This man was tall, his face craggy and weathered. He introduced himself as Dave.

When I told Dave I was hoping to go surfing, a slow smile spread across his face. "It's crap today," he scoffed. "You should have been here two days ago, after the snowstorm. It was overhead. A lot of people couldn't get out in the morning."

"It was so big they couldn't paddle out?" I asked, surprised. Rhode Island is not noted for Hawaii-size surf.

"No, they couldn't dig their cars out."

Dave looked hard at me. Surfing is often territorial. Strangers are not always welcome. But Dave's look was kindly, almost concerned.

"This is the coldest it's been around here in a long time," he said.

Pan bounded into the shop a few minutes later. In the three days I spent with him, I came to see this is how he always moves, like a high-powered CEO continuously hustling to another monumental meeting, only few CEOs have pictures of Goofy on their checks.

Pan is fifty-three, but if you take away the gray flecks in his dark hair, he can easily pass for thirty and, at a quick glance, even younger. He is trim, his face boyish and smooth. It's a little eerie, as if the salt and cold have preserved him. He is Narragansett's version of George Melvin, floating on a surfboard instead of a coffin.

We got right down to business, hopping into his car to check the surf. A few minutes later we sloshed into the parking lot at Narragansett Town Beach, peering hopefully over a snowbank toward the ocean.

The waves weren't bad—they were anemic. If I looked really hard, I could see small ripples limping toward shore. The waves that managed to break fizzled as quickly as possible, embarrassed to be seen.

Even Pan was impressed. "Man, it's terrible," he said. He gazed out fondly at the apathetic ocean and cackled. "This is the worst beach break in the world. It sucks. That's why I love it. No one wants to go out, especially now. Winter is my favorite time of year. What's so great about New England is there's a million kooks. They're afraid of the cold. They just stay inside and play Nintendo games. The weather chops the crowd factor down to nothin'. And that's right where I like it."

A car with two surfboards on top pulled up beside us. The driver took one look at the water, made a face like a child presented with beets on his dinner plate, threw the car into reverse, and was gone.

I turned to Pan. "Do you ever travel anywhere else for surf?"

"I don't like to go anywhere else. We have the best waves in the world right here."

I said nothing. You don't dine with the Queen of England and tell her that her guards dress funny.

Pan's eyes continued to scan the water expertly. Where other surfers saw hopelessness, Pan saw a silver lining.

"That's another good thing about New England," he crowed. "The waves are so inconsistent, everybody gives up. That's what I hope for! Hahahahahahahaha!"

Pan gave me a tour of his town, which is to say all the surf breaks. Rhode Island's craggy coast is pocked with rocky reefs and points that can produce excellent surf on the right day. Today wasn't that day. Everywhere the ocean lay immobile. I'd seen more rise and fall in sidewalks.

We drove south, pulling into Matunuck Beach. The parking lot was empty, and the ocean was parking-lot flat. Just off the beach, said Pan, lurked four perfect reef breaks. He scowled. "This place is disgustingly crowded in the summer. Every asshole in the world goes out here. This whole parking lot is filled with kooks. They'll go out in the water and start fights. They think they own the place."

Surfers are usually portrayed as mellow and cool, but the real truth is most surfers are greedier than Midas and, like any three-year-old, would rather poke you in the eye than share. The funny thing about Matunuck is, many of its pugilists are actually surfers from Connecticut.

Nobody was fighting anybody today, discounting two seagulls tugging at a yellow wrapper.

Pan shook his head. "Localism is the biggest pile of shit. Nobody owns the ocean."

Driving back to the shop, Pan admitted he was a little worried about the peripatetic waters. Today was Friday. On Sunday he was supposed to host his annual New England Midwinter Surfing Championships. He hated contests ("too fucking subjective"), but after thirty-one years as a contest director, the habit was hard to break. Plus the winter contest, not surprisingly, was his favorite.

Pan suddenly turned to me. "Hey! You should do the contest!" He gave this a moment's additional thought. "How old are you?"

"Forty-three."

He grinned. "You're going to be in the final. You're lucky if three people will show up in your age group. You'll go back to California with a trophy."

He appreciated the humor in this

"I'll lend you a board," he cackled. "That way you can feel the cold water."

⁂

OF COURSE, he isn't really Peter Pan. For one thing, Neverland was never so damn cold. Pan isn't really his name. His real name is Panagiotis. At a surfing contest in Newport in 1967 the announcer couldn't pronounce his name, so he said Peter Pan, and it stuck. Pan had grown children of his own and a wife, too.

"She says I always smell like rubber." He grinned.

Like the real Pan, plenty of people give him advice: "You should stay out of the cold water, it will make you sick." "You should get a real job, make some real money." "You should grow up."

Pan had tried real jobs, but they took him away from the ocean and he couldn't stand it.

He wasn't overly impressed with money, either: "The more money you make, the more you spend on stupidity."

There was no Tinkerbell in Pan's world, no Lost Boys, and, discounting the grown-up finger-waggers, no evil Captain Hook. But there was real magic.

How can a man ride a board in a world of howling wind and slushy sea with a heart bursting with joy? "It's the solitude. It's just Nature. It's perfect," said Pan.

I drove up to see him again on Saturday, but the sea was flat again. The only change was that the weather was worsening. Instead of belching snow, the skies issued sheets of freezing rain. Pan decided to call off the contest.

For a moment even he seemed defeated.

"This winter's been bad," he sighed. "Really bad."

⁂

Long ago I learned that Nature has a sense of humor. When I walked into Gansett Juice on Sunday morning, Pan was already there. His buoyant self again, he wasted no time on civilities.

"We're goin'," he beamed. "To K39. It's breaking perfect."

We drove to his parents' house to change. It was near the surf shop, plus Pan had his own clubhouse off the garage, complete with a shower, couch, and neat piles of surfing magazines. A poster of Peter Pan hung on the door. The room was filled with surfing trophies. "Just junk." Pan grinned.

I pulled on my wetsuit, boots, gloves, and hood. I was sweating and my hands were shaking, and once, hopping about on one foot to yank on a bootie, I nearly fell over. In my chest I felt the familiar swell of near-desperate excitement when waves are breaking and all that stands in the way is time. Conjure back the honeymoon moment, when mere ticks separated you from union.

Pan handed me a jar of Vaseline. "Throw some on your face," he said. "It'll keep it warm."

My memories of winter surfing were returning—I slapped it on thick. As we left, I glanced in the mirror. I looked like an exhibit from Madame Tussaud's Wax Museum, after the janitor has left the heat on all night.

The sheeting rain had stopped. Narragansett's streets were foggy-frigid. Cars moved through the mist. As we neared the beach, all signs of life dissipated. We drove along empty streets, lined with lifeless cottages, mist rising from the snow. It looked like some apocalyptic vision.

Pan turned down a final smoky street. In the summer, with waves pumping, the street would have been gridlocked. Only three cars sat at the end in the mist. Their surf racks were empty; their drivers were already in the water. Pan cackled. "It doesn't matter how much technology has improved the wetsuits. Most people still don't have the chops to go out."

I was sweating inside the cab of Pan's truck, but as soon as I stepped outside, the frigid temperature got my attention. We pulled our boards from the back of the truck and crunched through the snow between two houses.

"Hahahahahahaha," said Pan. "I love this!"

On the beach the mist, prodded by the cold water, turned to thick, bona-fide fog. Somewhere behind the curtain a foghorn moaned. I stared hard. There were waves. Seventy yards out I could see their ghostly forms as they marched shoreward, lovely smooth gray walls, slightly darker than the mist. Now and again black figures morphed out of the fog, racing across the waves. My heart raced with them.

As I waded into the water, I felt the neoprene squeeze protectively around me—and then the Atlantic seeped in. Wetsuits are called wetsuits because you get wet. They work simply: the water seeps in and is trapped between your body and the neoprene. Your body warms the trapped water, achieving a degree of comfort until you are crushed by a wave and a new dose of freezing water rushes in.

I generated additional heat by paddling out as fast as I could, trying not to be squashed by the incoming sets. Blind luck saw to it that I wasn't. A wave rolled out of the mist. I spun the board, took four quick strokes, hopped to my feet, and slid down its face. Every surfer knows the feeling. Everyone else will have to imagine what it's like to win the lottery while simultaneously achieving orgasm.

I was nearly frantic with glee. I caught wave after wave after wave. Had this been summer, the water would have been choked with "kooks," but on this day I was the only kook I had to contend with. I stroked greedily into the feathering waves. I must admit, for a time I lost all control. I would have run my own mother over. It wasn't pretty, like watching a starving man eat, and pretty much the same thing.

After a time I calmed slightly. The waves kept coming, more

than enough to go around. I shared them with three other surfers, who were friendly.

"What rubber are you wearing?" one asked, a mistimed and highly personal question, I thought, until I realized he was looking at my wetsuit.

A younger surfer said, "You should come here in the summer. It's completely different." I grinned maniacally at him and thought, *No, this is exactly when and where I want to be.* He grinned just as maniacally and paddled away.

Now and again Pan stroked out of the fog, cackling. Sometimes, while paddling back out, I would see him, crouched and oddly silent, sliding across a wave.

Once I shouted stupidly at him, "I'm not cold!"

Pan nodded casually. "This is tropical," he said, and disappeared on a wave.

Sitting alone in the mist, it suddenly occurred to me that, with a few minor brushstrokes, this could just as easily be a foggy summer's day. Salt graced my lips, the mist delicately moistened my face, small wind-blown ripples jostled and nudged the board, and the Point Judith Lighthouse issued its timeless moan. The palette changes, but the heart surges to the same thrall and joy.

Pan's was an endless summer, skewed only slightly to meet his solitary needs. His words came back to me: *The only thing that ruins waves is humans.*

I heard someone cackle. I looked for Pan, but I was alone.

16
CAPE COD
Ghost Ships and Shores

ON CAPE COD another world is buried beneath the sands, and when winter's storms claw into the dunes, it might be a lantern, an aged barometer, or even a ship that sets sail.

I arrived on the cape toward the end of February. The snowfall that had paralyzed much of the East Coast had of course laid a downy blanket of snow across its shore. During the day the snow lay silent and bright on beach, dune, and ice-choked marsh. At night, beneath a silver moon, the snow grew quieter still and glowed blue, hung with drowsy serenity, like standing in a sleeping child's nursery. It was damn cold, too. One afternoon near Eastham, as a raking wind blew snowy contrails from the tops of the dunes, I watched a heavily bundled couple, bent nearly double, plod slowly to the top of the dunes. At the summit they spun as one and sprinted back for their car, aspiring members of the Eskimo Olympic team.

"Thrust forth as it is into the outer Atlantic, the Cape has a climate of island quality and island moderation," wrote Henry Beston in *The Outermost House.* "Low temperatures may occur, but the thermometer almost never falls as low as it does on the inner Massachusetts coast, nor do spells of cold weather hang on for any length of time. Storms which are snowstorms on the continental mainland turn to rainstorms on the Cape, and such snowstorms as do arrive form but a crust upon these Eastham moors."

Beston's book, documenting the year (from the fall of 1926 to the fall of 1927) he spent on the cape's dune edge living in a cottage he dubbed the Fo'castle, is an astonishing work of poetic observation, but in this meteorological matter Beston erred. On the cape this year there was no rain, no thin snow crust, and no moderation, either in the weather or in people's reaction to it.

"If we get any more snow," said a Hyannis grocery clerk, "I'm going to drown myself."

❧

HAD THIS YOUNG clerk been born 150 years earlier, he could have easily accomplished that aim. Few shores rival Cape Cod's history of unholy winter storms and harrowing shipwrecks.

In the 1800s most coastal commerce was moved by ship, it being difficult to stack much lumber into a horse-drawn wagon. Nearly incomprehensible numbers of vessels sailed along Cape Cod's outer shore, passing to and from Boston, New York, and ports around the world. In 1849 some 16,000 vessels sailed east around the cape. The operative word here is *sailed*. The ships, great and small, relied on the wind, and when the wind became unreliable, they were at its mercy. With sad frequency, storm met sail, and when it did, sail often lost. By one estimate, a sailing vessel caught in a northeaster off Cape Cod's shore had a fifty-fifty chance of reaching port safely. Any child who has sadly watched a toy boat sail out of sight understands the physics.

An official tabulation from 1843 to 1859 recorded more than eight hundred shipwrecks on Cape Cod. In the 1870s the cape averaged a wreck once every two to three weeks. Cape lore holds that if all the shipwrecks off the island's shores were placed bow to stern, they would make a continuous wall from Provincetown to Chatham.

Trivia and numbers are antiseptic. Men, women, and children died in maelstroms of shrieking wind, splintering timber, and thunderclaps of shredded sail. Some died fast, swept overboard by enormous waves that crushed them in a black, burning cold fist. Others climbed into the rigging and froze slowly with land in sight; still others fought their way to the beach and froze to death there. Nature's hand was merciless and efficient. An October 1841 gale deposited more than a hundred bodies along Cape Cod's beaches. Her sense of humor was black, too. In February 1918 heavy ice fields pinioned the *Cross Rip* lightship and wrenched her from her moorings. The ship was last seen flying a distress signal, her crew of six on deck, shrinking against the horizon.

Henry David Thoreau, who walked and ruminated along the cape's great shore during the 1850s, stared out at the ocean and described its menace rightly enough: "The ocean is a wilderness reaching around the globe, wilder than a Bengal tiger, and fuller of monsters," he wrote in *Cape Cod*.

For Thoreau the topic was abstract; his odds of drowning at his desk were roughly the same as his odds of being consumed by a Bengal tiger. For those who made their lives on the water, however, it was not at all abstract. Walking the beach one day, absorbing the pleasurable sounds of the sea, Thoreau happened on an old man, nearly blind, sitting quietly, facing the water. Thoreau assumed the man was also enjoying the sea's symphony and remarked as much in a neighborly manner. The man barked back that he did not enjoy the sound at all; his son had been lost at sea in a storm. Thoreau was smart enough to require but one lesson. "I found," he wrote later in *Cape Cod*, "that it would not do to speak of shipwrecks there, for almost every family has lost some of its members at sea." The gale of 1841 killed fifty-seven men and boys from Truro; all of them lived within two miles of one another.

Opined one Cape Cod sea captain, "Any man who would go to sea for pleasure would go to hell for a pastime."

※

IN THE CAPE's treacherous waters, death came in many forms. But most often winter's raging nor'easters shoved the sailing ships rudely toward shore; their keels caught on the shallow shoals, and the waves splintered the vessel to pieces. Plenty of those pieces are still there, entombed beyond sight in the cape's hummocks of glacial moraine. Responding to this horrific loss of life, in 1871 Congress approved the funds that gave birth to the U.S. lifesaving service. Stations were built all along the East coast from Florida to Maine, but no stretch of shore needed the lifesaving stations more than Cape Cod. The first of the cape's stations were built and manned during the winter of 1872.

One afternoon I walked the beach with Dick Boonisar, a collector and historian. Dick's obsession is the surf lifesavers of Cape Cod, the brave men who, from 1872 until roughly 1930 (when they were replaced by the Coast Guard), risked their own lives to keep the death toll along the cape far lower than it would otherwise have been. Their credo: "You have to go, but you don't have to come back." At its peak the cape had thirteen lifesaving stations along its outer coast, each manned ten months of the year by lifesavers who lived up to their name. "From 1872 until 1930 they saved over 200,000 lives," Dick told me. "Considering the small population back then, that's an impressive number."

A retired bank president, Dick speaks with a declarative bark, and his knowledge of the cape's shipwrecked past is encyclopedic and not to be doubted. He knows the details of every wreck and the intimacies of each piece of rescue equipment the surf lifesavers used, from Lyle gun to surfboat. Over the years he has acquired all these pieces for his own unrivaled collection. Dick doesn't think small—he owns an entire lifesaving station. He lovingly restored it and, Henry Beston–like, spent eighteen months living in it and wandering the beaches of Gurnet Point near Plymouth, something of a life-changing experience.

"Up until that point, I'd never really paid attention to Nature," he said not long after we met. "I never really looked at the beach. I always rushed too much. Now I love to hear the sleet on the windows and the sound of the surf."

Part of his revised outlook came from reading *The Outermost House*. He had been deeply impressed by Beston's solitary year and the resultant observations on life and Nature. Since time immemorial, solitude has been linked to all manner of spiritual and intellectual awakenings, but Dick wasn't so sure the experience was entirely beneficial.

"Can you learn from solitude?" I asked as we drove to Nauset Beach.

"Yeah, you can," said Dick, "but it can also drive you nuts. When I moved into the lifesaving station, one of my neighbors welcomed me warmly. She said, 'Oh, by the way, did you see the flying saucer when you were coming down the beach?'" He shook his head vigorously, as if hoping to shake the memory free. "You can go a little cuckoo," he said.

Dick was practical and clear-sighted. Plus he was the perfect beach guide, able to see both the present and the past.

On the day we met, the weather had been schizophrenic. It had snowed off and on all morning, fitful squalls that came and went suddenly, so that the cape's dunes, cottages, and woods disappeared and reappeared from behind a curtain of smoky white.

As we walked Nauset Beach late in the afternoon, the snow returned. A cold north wind herded the flakes down the beach as if they rode in a river's current. They dipped, lifted, feinted left and right. Those that didn't affix themselves to my lashes or sting my cheeks swept southward in a locust swarm. As the snowflake river waxed and waned, a foggy-pale sun disappeared and reappeared.

"Weather like this could cause the skipper of a schooner to lose his way," said Dick. "Get in too close to shore and suddenly find himself in serious trouble. This beach was pretty active for shipwrecks. Take a look."

He pointed out at the gray sea. I swiped a flake from my eye and looked to where he was pointing. Offshore a line of small breakers coalesced in a mishmash of foamy white.

"That's the outer bar," said Dick. "That's where they ran aground."

The sandbar was about two hundred yards off the beach, an appreciable distance certainly but, it struck me, not an impossible swim.

When I said so to Dick, he gave me the same look he likely bestowed on his UFO-addled neighbor. "You'd have about a minute and a half to survive out there," he said brusquely. "Then the cold would kill you."

As we walked the beach, Dick gazed toward the sea, but it was the dunes that seemed to interest him the most. His eyes scanned their high fortresslike walls. I looked at them, too, and saw sand

curving up toward the sky like a great breaker, the dune wall liberally pocked with long stringy clumps of brown grass, so that, with
not much imagination, they resembled a line of hoary, bearded
faces, coastal gnomes perhaps, long-dead sailors, or maybe the guitarists from ZZ Top.

Life always outdoes the imagination.

Dick spoke casually, as if he'd been expecting to see it all along:
"Up there. Looks like some wreckage coming out."

We walked to the dune wall. About six feet up an enormous log,
obviously crafted by man and splintered at its end, jutted out.

Dick's eyes ran over it appreciatively. "Yep, that's been exposed
by the storm. Looks like a big old ship timber. Washed up here years
and years ago."

He was unfazed, but I was stunned. I had seen historical relics
before but was held distant from them by glass or suspicious
museum guards. This was like walking down the sidewalk in Boze-
man, Montana, and stepping in triceratops dung.

I tried to maintain a cool journalistic mien. Dick, I already knew,
appreciated professionalism. "Is this not uncommon?" I asked.

"Nope," said Dick. "Not uncommon at all. Especially in the
winter."

Dick must have seen the expression on my face.

"It *is* pretty amazing," he said, smiling. "You can still see parts of
ships from the nineteenth century that were wrecked here. You
never know what the sand will throw up."

This is irrefutably true. As children, we are certain that the hot
sands contain wondrous possibilities, secrets to the world until we,
the famed treasure hunters, scoop them into daylight. As we grow
old, we forget that magic, though it just as surely exists. On Tangier
a crabber had handed me a prize inadvertently scooped up with a
lick of crabs. I held in my hands, nearly as heavy as lead, the curved
tusk of a woolly mammoth.

Standing with Dick, I suddenly saw Nauset Beach in summer-
time, its sands a patchwork jumble of umbrellas, blankets, and coolers. This took no imagination. The cape holds a special place in my
heart; I have vacationed there several times with Kathy, Cullen, and

Graham. We had played on this very beach, digging deep holes so that Cullen and Graham could crouch in them and peer out over the edges like sand crabs.

I turned to Dick. "Do you think summer folks give any thought to what they might be lying on?"

He scoffed. "They have no clue."

I saw our fingertips making a final scrape at a summer hole's coarse-grained bottom, stopping, a skein of sand away, from the top of a ghost ship's mizzenmast.

Sure, you say. And when the vessel rises from the sands, it will be manned by gnomes and bearded dune sailors, and maybe Budweiser girls will even throw their coolers on board, and everyone will sail merrily forth, gyrating to the beat of La Grange.

It is not fantasy I am discussing.

One winter night during a storm, Henry Beston ventured outside his Fo'castle and walked the high dunes, a wise path given the entire beach was a frothy flood of angry tide. Sleet hissed past his ears, sand stung his face. Looking north, he saw something that at first must have caused him to rub his eyes. As he watched, the tide crumbled a wall of dune. Like an apparition, the past appeared.

". . . there crumbled out the blackened skeleton of an ancient wreck which the dunes had buried long ago," wrote Beston. "As the tide rose this ghost floated and lifted itself free, and then washed south close along the dunes."

A word of advice, children and children-at-heart. On Cape Cod, winter is the true treasure hunter's season.

"If these dunes could talk," said Dick.

※

I SPENT A WEEK on the cape. I hadn't intended on staying that long, but I found myself retracing old footsteps and reliving memories.

One gray morning, as the traffic of downtown Hyannis sloshed behind me, I stood for an unknown length of time in front of a merry-go-round that Cullen and Graham had ridden when it was a summer swirl of light and shriek and color. The ride was still and horseless now, the horses having been wrenched out and pastured in a place sequestered from the elements. I sought out a beach path my sons and I had walked twenty times a day one happy summer. I walked its snowy length just as many times, and as I did, it slowly went sun-dappled beneath a canopy of leafy trees, and heat rose from the loamy sand, and two small boys in bathing suits ran ahead of me and stopped by a bush and stretched on tiptoe, small fingers plucking juicy blackberries. I walked to the end of a jetty and crouched where we had crouched for hours, dangling strings with chicken bits and hauling up the same crabs again and again, their stomachs far larger than their brains. Closing my eyes, I felt the string jerk, a crab's weighty tug as it pinwheeled slow circles, rising slowly from the barnacled darkness into the hot sunlight. I may have even heard little-boy voices. *Got it, gooooooot it, slooooooooow now, come awwwwwnnnn.*

Someone clinically minded might conclude that nine thousand miles of solo travel had transformed me into the caretaker in *The Shining,* but I don't think so. The past, we all know, can be conjured in an instant by a smell, a voice, a song. For those whose fortunate lives have been touched by salt water, add to that conjurer's list the sea.

Squatting on the jetty, my back turned to the snowy beach, it could have been any season, the pleasant salty tang, the faint mulchy-iodine whiff of rotting sea grass, the sibilant slurp of water rising and falling between the rocks, and before me water to the horizon, and more beyond that.

What the sailor dreaded, a palette remorseless, uncaring, and changeless—"Ten thousand fleets sweep over thee in vain," wrote Byron—is also a gift, a constant backdrop against which past and present stand equally real. Cocooned in winter's cold press, as I watched my young sons jostling bony elbows in their haste to reel in a new crab, I knew they weren't there. But in a life so ephemeral, who would begrudge a parent such pleasurable hallucinations?

Still squatting, I watched a flock of geese lift from the water with a throaty trumpeting and swing away in a unified arc. Just before I stood up, something caught my eye. I reached down into rocks and plucked up the small piece of string.

⁂

IT WASN'T MEMORY alone that kept me on the cape. There is no finer place for briny vistas than Cape Cod, and those vistas are made even lovelier by a fairy-tale glaze of snow and ice.

One evening just before sunset, I drove to Gray's Beach, which is in the town of Yarmouthport. Situated at the western edge of the cape, it looks out on Cape Cod Bay. The beach itself is only a small sad cusp of sand, but the marsh that sweeps out and away from it is grand, a vast spread, as evenly topped as carpet, stretching like prairie beneath the sky.

What makes Gray's Beach so much fun is its long stretch of raised boardwalk. It runs from solid land far out into the marsh, ending in a neat little square where you stand, like a sailor in a crow's nest, surrounded by marsh on all sides.

The marsh is etched with creeks and tidal shallows, and in three seasons these waterways rush and ooze happily, following the draw of the tides. This evening the water was almost entirely frozen. I walked to the boardwalk's end. Below me the creeks and channels were milky white, and up on the marsh itself great chunks of ice lay scattered about, as if someone had cracked opened a giant ice tray. The tide was ebbing. The little water that wasn't frozen flowed through the cold silence with the faintest faucet tinkle. As the sun touched the horizon, the ice turned pink.

It was the perfect place to be alone.

In recent weeks I had noticed an odd transformation. In my early travels I had been intensely interested in the people I met, curious about every detail of their lives, anxious to engage in conversation at any turn. Now I preferred time alone with the landscape. I began to seek places where my path wound unaccompanied. I started my beach walks in evening's gray-pink gloaming and kept walking long into the cold night, when sane people hunkered inside and the surf erased my snowy footsteps beneath the thousand-fold stars. During the day my walks, which seemed absent-minded at first, always took me out over the water, usually as far out as I could go—to the end of a jetty, a sand spit, a boat dock—a place where the ocean washed around me and the wind washed over me, where I was cocooned by the elements and, on honest reflection, removed from all else. The waters murmured; the wind occupied my ears like a jealous lover. I lay in their arms, content. If someone engaged me in conversation during these walks I was polite, but I only half-listened. Their voices sounded louder, jarring. I resented humanity's noise and intrusion. The snowy beaches were mine. I saw these misanthropic tendencies clearly. I knew I was acting like a petulant child. But like a child, I was certain of my course. Solitude was *my* friend. Gautama Buddha once said, "You cannot travel on the path before you have become the Path itself." Buddhas aren't known for being literal, but I found I was becoming like the snow and ice, still and quiet.

Suddenly I saw a jogger coming down the long boardwalk. My heart sank. I braced myself for her arrival, searching my brain for some convivial comment that would allow for friendliness but not encourage prolonged conversation.

She beat me to the punch.

"Beautiful, isn't it?" she said cheerily.

I noticed happily that she continued to jog in place.

"I love this time of year," she continued. "You get it all to yourself."

"I'm sorry to clog the place up," I said. I wasn't being sarcastic. I meant it.

"Oh no!" she said. "It's not that I'm antisocial. It's just that sometimes I like to be alone."

It was the perfect explanation, an echo from my own heart. For a mad moment, I thought I could marry her. We stood at the end of this boardwalk pronging into the marsh, the only two people in the world.

She consulted her watch and spun on her heels. "Enjoy, enjoy!" she said, and off she ran.

The sun went down. The ice sat silent. For a long time I didn't move.

✿

MOST OF THE people I met on the cape thought winter lovely, but for others it was wearing thin.

When I asked a Brewster man if he was looking forward to summer, he snarled, "Only the candyasses come here in the summer," and, perhaps recognizing me as a candyass, left abruptly.

Other folks were civil, though distracted. At a Yarmouth drugstore I listened as a cashier and her teenage friend engaged in a melancholy volley.

"It's way dead here," said the cashier, a dark-haired girl with lime-green fingernails.

"There's nothing to do," said her friend.

"I miss the tourists," said lime fingernails.

I waited patiently, hoping to pay for my gum.

"I miss the traffic," said her friend.

"I miss summer," said lime fingernails.

I missed the part where I turned invisible. The girls looked at each other, sighed, and stared sadly at the gray outside.

I thought about balancing the gum on the end of my nose, but I have enough experience with the fair sex to know that, once focused, they are not easily distracted.

"Maybe I should change my nails," said lime green after a fat pause, then deigned to let me pay for my gum.

But change and hope were afoot. While I was on the cape, the calendar advanced to March. Nature didn't register the flip of the page—it was still bitter cold—but man's timing rarely parallels Nature's.

"The blue-hairs have already started to show up, coming back from Florida," a cape resident told me. "You can tell by all the silly driving."

The next day I watched a Cadillac bump a wheel onto the sidewalk. A woman sprang out, bustled quickly to the mailbox she'd almost dented, and, just as quickly, returned to the warmth of her car.

She had blue hair. She also had a tan.

17
MAINE
Arriving at an Answer

LIKE TALL TALES everywhere, those that originate in Maine may or may not be true, but they are often representative.

In Bar Harbor, a town long inhabited by the impossibly rich and famous, a local told me a story about a media icon who lived in town, a woman with a reputation for throwing her weight around. Said icon was in a local store and wanted to use the phone.

"Sorry, miss," the proprietor replied. "Phone isn't for customer use. But there is a pay phone just outside."

"Do you know who I am?" came the icy reply.

Given time, the proprietor would have answered frankly. But a voice behind the woman cut in.

"Miss," said David Rockefeller, "I've never been able to use that phone, either."

⁂

NOT EVERYONE in Maine is a Rockefeller, Astor, Vanderbilt, or Martha Stewart. At Old Orchard Beach, I met Richard Duhamel.

"Duhamel!" he barked. "Like Hamel. With a Du in front of it."

Actually, the introduction came well into our conversation. First came the part where Richard waved his arms and barked non sequiturs, and everyone else on Old Orchard Beach stared straight ahead and walked quickly past us as if they'd just been summoned suddenly to a meeting in the Oval Office.

They might have had to sit next to Richard.

When I smiled and asked him how he was, he got right down to business. "I'm waiting for some of my friends. Tiger Woods is one of 'em. Dick Cheney, too!"

Richard's conversation took surprising turns, but he still had two more friends in Maine than I did.

He paused to root around in the trash can between us, pulling out several cans and depositing them carefully into the plastic grocery bag he had plucked out first. The pause was brief. Richard had likely seen listeners sidle off when he delayed too long.

"I should have been a pro golfer!" he said. He screwed up his face. "I don't think I'd want to be Dick Cheney."

✳

WE TALKED for a time. Well, actually Richard talked and I listened. I learned that he was a lifelong Mainer, that he had served in the navy, army, and air force, that he was running for governor, and that in the interim he was waiting for the Marlboro man, though he suspected it might be a long wait.

He leaned in close to me. "They killed the Marlboro man, didn't they?" he whispered.

Shaking his head sharply, he answered his own question.

"No. I think Nicorette did."

It was a glorious March morning, sunny and bright blue, the temperature in the sun well over forty. Maine was in the throes of a one-day spring thaw, and Old Orchard Beach was, if not crowded, amply populated. People celebrated the nearly tropical conditions by strolling the edge of the dark blue Atlantic, throwing bread bits to ravenous seagulls, and watching the icicles on the pier drop to the sand.

It was obvious that all of Richard's mornings hadn't dawned so pleasant. I glanced at his fingers. They were bright red and raw; the skin looked as if it had been manicured with a cheese grater.

Richard was observant. "I don't spend much time inside." A little of the shout left his voice. "I collect bottles. It ain't so good in the winter, but in the summer it's a pretty good job." He recovered his bark. "I'm a Mainer through and through!"

Another voice rose suddenly in my mind, this one from inside the dim recesses of a twilight mangrove in Key West: *I'm an American. It's my country, too.*

Not everyone comes to the beach for a holiday. I asked Richard if he would accept some money.

"Sure," he said. "I don't like it, but I haven't had a job since 1995."

I looked in my wallet. I had three dollars. "How about two dollars?" I said, somewhat embarrassed.

I would meet many people in Maine, but it was Richard who cemented my opinion of Mainers. He carefully counted the bills I had handed him.

"Hey," he said. "Did you know you gave me three dollars?"

⁂

MAINE'S COASTLINE is magnificent, and you get one hell of a long look at it by driving U.S. 1 and its rural offshoots, which fork toward the water in countless thready veins. You could spend several lifetimes exploring Maine's edge and not see it all. The coast stretches a mere 250 miles as the crow flies, but those who aren't crows have some 3,000 miles to explore. Maine's coast juts, pokes, folds, turns, twists, and backtracks, sculpted apparently by someone who attached a cookie cutter to the end of a jackhammer. And then there are the islands. Hundreds of them dot Maine's coast like scattered birdseed—granite bumps with pine crew cuts—exactly how many hundreds no one seemed to know. Two thousand, states a geological blurb on my roadmap. Thirty-five hundred, a Mainer told me. Four thousand, said another. On the sly, the things seemed to be breeding like rabbits.

These islands were a powerful siren call to me. Once, enticed but sorely lacking common sense, I put the kayak in the water and tried to paddle for an island that couldn't have been more than a half-mile offshore. I was back in the van in ten minutes, screaming expletives and pawing the air like a suckling child rent from the breast, begging my senseless sausage fingers to turn the heater on. The wind that had coursed over the water was beyond cold. It had burned me like a brand. Had it actually been a brand, it would have read "Idiot." Maine's coast, I learned later, is prone to tidal fluctuations of eighteen-plus feet. I could have easily returned to shore and been unable to locate my heater or my van. This is not exaggeration. While paddling off Bar Harbor, a kayaker once spied a shiny-tipped antenna poking from the water. The antenna ran down to an equally shiny Ford Explorer that had been parked there earlier in the day at low tide.

I made a mental note that I wasn't in Key West anymore and put the kayak away for the last time.

Unfortunately I didn't make a note to avoid hiking, and so on a rainy Sunday morning I drove a few miles outside of Stonington, along the tip of the Blue Hill Peninsula, parked the van alongside the road, and ducked into the snowy woods.

I had arrived in Stonington the night before, after several days of aimless driving and countless rugged coastal views. As I drove Maine's convoluted coastal roads, hauled over regularly by magnetic sweeps of sea and sky, it was impossible to gauge any arrival time accurately. When I pulled into Stonington, it was night. Black, black night. Stonington is a fishing and tourist town. Being winter, there were no tourists. Being night, there were no fishermen. It was like driving into a crypt.

Main Street was so quiet, I could hear the ice in the harbor making a soft rustling sound, like someone rolling over in bed. The motel and bed and breakfast I located were both dark. A sign outside Boyce's Motel said they wouldn't be open for another week. The sign on the office door of the Inn on the Harbor said they were closed for the day.

This was disheartening. Actually, it was worse. For a brief moment I thought I might cry. There are few things more depressing than being helpless in a strange and frozen town, though I would discover one of them the next night.

Fortunately the Harbor Café was open, the only light on Main Street, and after the five diners in the place looked me over, a friendly waitress named Miranda made a few calls on my behalf. In ten minutes Vickie Hardie was cheerily unlocking the front door of the Inn on the Harbor and showing me a clean, cozy room that would have cost me $115 in the summer but that I could have for $60 now.

I booked the room for two nights, maintaining a businesslike demeanor during the exchange of cards and paperwork so that I wouldn't throw myself to the ground and hug Vickie around the knees.

There would be muffins and hot coffee in the morning, said Vickie. If I needed to stay longer, it could be arranged. "Your room is available the next night, too," she said, and laughed. "We have quite a few openings."

Vickie left. I repaired to my room, where I turned up the heat and did a jig in my underwear. Outside the wind keened. The Harbor Café was dark. Its sign rocked in the wind.

✤

WHEN I WOKE Sunday morning, I could see the harbor, blocks of ice edging its rim, and fishing boats, their bows pointed out toward several foggy islands. Now and again a pickup truck sloshed down Main Street. The sky was smeared with an uninterrupted ceiling of dark clouds, as if a peat bog had taken up residence.

I walked down to the water. A fisherman, parked in a pickup, regarded the same sky. He rolled down his window and nodded to me. "It's been a hell of a winter."

I had to agree.

We shared the silence.

"I think I'll head home," he said after a time. "I'm not too excited to go out in the wind and the rain."

I should have followed his lead. I should have gone back to my room and spent the day staring ruminatively out at the harbor through rain-streaked windows. But it wasn't raining yet, and I foolishly felt the familiar urge to get outside and explore. And so, blithely ignoring both the sky and several other obvious omens, including a fishing boat named *Clueless,* I drove out of town, turned down Goose Cove Road, and found my way to a parking lot that didn't allow parking, filled as it was with four feet of snow.

Firm now on my path of wanton stupidity, I parked the van at the edge of the road, ignoring a last subtle plea. "If parking lot is full," read a sign, "please return another time."

It began to rain steadily.

I chose to hike through the Barred Island Preserve because, consulting a map the night before, I saw that it led eventually to Barred Island. If I timed my hike correctly—low tide—I could walk across an exposed gravel spit to the island. My reasoning was quite sane. In weather this foul I would have my own private Maine island, and I wouldn't have to paddle to get there.

At first the woods were lovely, oddly warm and dry. The canopy of spruce and balsam fir blocked out most of the rain, and the raincoat I was wearing sloughed off the rest. As I trudged through three-foot snowdrifts, my long underwear and a clothing rack's worth of fiberfill and down saw to it that I was soon actually sweating.

The woods were dreamlike and quiet; all sound, other than an occasional gull cry, was damped out by the snow and the mossy, bearded trees. The snow, as smooth and unmarked as ivory, gave off a faint ghostly mist. There was, as I had surmised, no one else around. Now and again I could see the water in the distance, silent and shrouded in its own fog.

As Thoreau, Henry Beston, and countless other Nature lovers have discovered, being truly alone provides the opportunity to observe delicate nuances that are overlooked in ordinary life's clamor. Pausing beside a bare pine twig, I watched a lovely parade of tiny water droplets, perfect crystal balls, move slowly, single file, down the twig's length before dropping, one at a time, off the tip like polite shipwreck victims. I noticed something else, too. The raindrops that had run down my raincoat earlier were now bouncing off like popcorn.

I hiked back to the van as fast as I could, but I wasn't fast enough. The freezing rain had spread an icy glaze over Goose Cove Road. On the first hill I encountered, the tires spun vainly for purchase. For a brief spellbinding moment I was driving backward. Then the van's back end performed a sickly swing and plunged firmly into a ditch. In a blink, solitude went from enervating to unnerving.

For an hour I tried to get the van out on my own, succeeding only in getting myself thoroughly soaked. Having finished glazing the road, the rain now happily morphed between liquid and solid state, both of them equally frigid. I had a cell phone, purchased specifically for this trip, with just such potential stupidity in mind. It merrily informed me I had no service. I sat in the van, wet and cold. The rain drummed harder.

My life has been filled with good fortune on many fronts, which has endowed me with what many would see as childish optimism. Childish it may be, but it is also true that the successful traveler must have a kind of bravado. Without it, the world's harsh realities would crush his spirit, and he would barricade himself inside his house.

I believed someone would eventually come down this lonely rain-slashed back road, and sure enough he did. Bill Baker had a truck with four-wheel drive and snow tires and a phone that worked. While I stood, dumbly grateful in the rain, Bill called AAA.

He rolled down his window. "They should be here by four o'clock," he said.

I wiped the rain from my watch. It was three-fifteen. I was speechless with relief and gratitude.

Bill, however, didn't know this. He looked at me intently. "Are you warm enough? You're not hypothermic, are you?"

I assured him I was fine.

And then Bill said an odd thing: "Don't worry, someone will come. If they don't, just walk to the nearest house."

By ten P.M. I was fairly certain no one was coming. I had wiled away the past six hours with various activities. First I kicked myself. Then I did my best to dry my wet clothes. Normally I would have had a bag filled with dry clothes in the van, but on this evening they were back in Stonington enjoying the warmth of their own harbor-view room. I read. I pulled out my map of the East Coast and slowly retraced my route, circling each of my stops with a pen, visions rising and drifting away in my mind. I felt the toaster-oven Key West sun, the pinch of salt drying on my bare back. I scraped shooting-star barnacles with Erik, packed fish with Cotton, walked Ocra-coke's beach beneath the flooded heavens. I saw George Melvin riding the currents off Hog Island, long hair wafting about him.

Every now and then I turned the heater on, but I was spare in its use. I didn't want to run down the battery. I pulled on my jacket and the fur cap with the beagle-ear flaps I had once mocked. As the night wore slowly on, I wrapped myself in everything I could find, including the down comforter, which thankfully I hadn't unpacked.

After exhausting my recreational activities, I sat and stared out the windshield at the Maine woods.

Thoreau called Maine's woods a place of "standing night." Judg-ing from the phrase, he made this observation in daylight. At the risk of waxing poetic, I'll say that the Maine woods are a lot darker at night. I stared out the windshield only because I faced that way. All was ink. For all I knew just across the road flying saucers were spit-ting forth an exploratory expeditionary force. Perhaps they would happen on me and turn on their heels, convinced there was no intel-ligent life worth vanquishing.

Solitude was what I fervently sought, and I had found it in spades. In the silence I grasped a single great truth: if you die out here it will be your own asinine fault.

Truth is, I was never in any great danger.

I had the down comforter. But I could see my breath, and my feet tingled, and when I shifted, the damp parts of my jeans felt unusually stiff.

I'm not sure when I fell asleep, but when I woke to an odd grind-ing sound, like sandy cobblestones being tousled by waves, it was just past dawn. The grinding sound came from the City of Deer Isle sanding truck moving slowly up the road.

I got out of the van and moved stiffly toward it. The rain had stopped, but it was colder than it had been all night.

The man on the passenger side rolled down his window. From inside there poured something that felt vaguely like heat.

I started talking, babbling perhaps. I must have made some

sense, because the man's eyebrows went up. "You spent the whole night he-ah? No one came?"

Hearing his words, it occurred to me that I could be irate, but all I felt was silly. "It's my fault I'm out here," I said. I formed my words slowly, as if I were learning English. "I should never have been out driving in weather like this."

"You'd be a shut-in if you waited around here for good weather," said my new best friend.

"They shouldn't have left you out here all night." He called AAA. Then he said roughly the same thing Bill had said: "If no one comes, we'll be back in an hour."

No one did, and they were. Again I walked up to the truck.

This time my friend dispensed with AAA. He left his window down halfway, perhaps so I might enjoy some heat.

"Hey, Ron," he said into his phone, "this is Paul. Yep. Hey, listen, we got a guy that's been down here for over thirteen hours."

Paul paused while Ron said something, then resumed talking. "I've sanded it twice for you now." He peered at me. "Looks to me like he's getting pretty cold."

He hung up and smiled at me. "Ron's station is just around the corner," he said.

I nodded noncommittally. I was interested, but not overly so. This didn't strike me as odd.

"They should be here any minute," Paul said. "You understand?"

As best I could, in a land where time stood still.

I got back in the van. Through a narrow sliver in the windshield, I watched the day come, the sun slowly working its way from the top of the pines down to the road.

The next truck I saw was a tow truck. The driver was young. I think he introduced himself as Robert. I felt as if events were unfolding inside a block of Jell-O.

"You got a scraper?" he asked.

I had bought an ice scraper in a Wal-Mart in South Carolina. Back then, it had seemed a novelty. It seemed useless now, the cheap thing it was. I couldn't get the damn ice off the windshield.

Robert spoke kindly. "The ice is on the inside," he said.

He hooked up the van and hauled it out of the ditch. Riding back to Ron's Garage in Stonington, he was chatty. "I was listening to the scanner yesterday," he said. "There were rollovers and everything. It was pretty bad. You can have all the winter driving experience you want, but it don't matter much when the roads turn to ice. It's like drivin' on marbles."

Later I would hear on the radio that a tow truck driver had been killed, hit by a truck while trying to pull an SUV out of a ditch.

It may have been my imagination, but when I walked into Ron's Garage, Ron Gross appeared to take a step back. "Have some coffee," he said. "You were out there all night?"

It was a question I had grown used to answering. I told Ron how I really felt, that I had been fine, that I had gotten myself in trouble through my own boneheadedness, that I was just damn happy to be in a warm place drinking hot coffee from a styrofoam cup.

Ron shook his head. "I wish we'd gotten you last night. You could have bunked with us. The kids are in school." He jumped my dead battery for free and handed me another cup of coffee for the road. "You know," he said, shaking my hand, "I expected you to come in here both guns ablazin'."

Not after I'd already shot myself in the foot.

Back at the Inn on the Harbor they were relieved, too. While I tucked into the best blueberry muffins I'd ever eaten, Christina, the inn's owner, shook her head.

"We thought you were the quietest guest we ever had," she said. "I didn't even hear a toilet flush. After a while somebody said, 'I hope he didn't die up there.'"

❧

No doubt, stuck in a ditch in the Maine woods, Bob Dale would have fared better than I did. Bob would have rigged a catapult out of pine saplings, or taken the van apart widget by widget and reassembled it back on the road, but not before turning the radiator fluid into three-bean soup.

It occurs to me now that most of the people I met along the

coast were resourceful. They could jury-rig a compressor, rebuild an engine, lasso a pelican, or find a set of false teeth on the right tide. Unlike many people today, they didn't solve problems by reaching for the phone. America has become a land of service, 24/7, and Americans have become helpless. Not so my coastal denizens. They live in small communities where not every service is available, or they can't afford to pay someone to fix things, or maybe they prefer the job done right and so they do it themselves.

Still, even amongst the salty self-reliant, Bob Dale has elevated life beside the water and self-sufficiency to high art. Not that he would admit to competence. Like most highly competent people, Bob is quiet. He is one of those people you walk by at a bus stop, who you would never know was once a fighter pilot who nearly dropped a nuclear bomb on Canton, China.

I met Bob at his cabin on Hockomock Island. Friends had recommended I look him up, and when I phoned him, he was amenable. Hockomock Island is one of Maine's innumerable islets, a half-mile long, forty acres in all. In three seasons there's an organic garden and fruit trees and bees that make honey for Bob and his wife, Jean. In all seasons there are chickens, lobster tanks that catch rain, and the log home Bob built by hand, almost entirely on his own, first dragging 150 logs across the water three at a time on an aluminum skiff, then hauling them up onto the island, then skinning and barking them, then laying them astride one another to make a house Craftsman would weep for.

Hockomock Island was not on any map I could find. Bob named it, and in deference to Bob and Jean, it will remain off the map. It isn't easy to get to in winter. I parked off a dirt road, walked down a second steep road through the snowy woods, crossed a frozen pond at a southerly angle, and then half-walked, half-pulled myself, hand over hand, up an icy path, thanks to a rope looping from tree to tree. Take away the snow, and it was like traveling to see Tarzan.

At the top of the path, I paused to catch my breath. In the quiet the trees creaked. The smell of woodsmoke hung in the air, a cheery fire that would burn in the potbellied stove for the entire day I spent in Bob's cabin. Bob and Jean don't have heat as most of us know it. Bob hasn't paid a utility bill of any kind for twenty-eight years. He does own a car, though he allows he could do without it.

"I don't like too much machinery," he said almost apologetically. "It's not that I'm a Luddite. It's just that I don't want to always be fixing things. I like a simple life. A lot of people say, 'Oh it's just escaping,' or, 'Living on an island is too remote.' But it's not." He smiled. "I'm not a hermit, but this place is my sanctuary."

Bob is slender and slight, the perfect physique to wedge into the tight confines of a cockpit. He remains fighter-pilot handsome, but now he wears a beard, and a multitude of fine lines run away from his eyes and mouth, crow's-feet turned to stampede, likely from a lifetime of smiling and squinting into sky and water.

Jean, said Bob, was visiting friends in town. Like many women, his wife is more socially inclined than he is. Bob is content to be alone, and there is always plenty to do. Not that he is a monk. They both regularly see family and friends. They belong to civic-minded groups. Rather than hiding away, Jean and Bob speak out for what they believe in. They recently joined in vigils protesting the war in Iraq. This may seem an odd stance for a career navy man, but slowly, over many years, Bob has come to see war differently.

I spent an entire day sitting inside the cabin visiting with Bob, the sun arcing slowly through the sky, touching the water with various angles of light, while inside the fire crackled and we talked and drank tea sweetened with honey until we forgot about the tea and it went cold, though the tea didn't forget about us, driving us both outside now and again to pee in the snow. "We have an outhouse." Bob shrugged during one such foray. "But my wife is gone, and no one's around."

I was happy to limit my time in Nature to her occasional call. There were cross-country skis pronging from the snow outside the front door and two pairs of snowshoes around the back. The day was cold, clear, and enticing. In different circumstances I might have asked Bob for an island tour. But after my impromptu overnight two days earlier I harbored little desire for the outdoors.

Bob was content to stay inside, too. Though days filled with chores have kept him fitter than most men half his age, he is seventy-eight now and is less apt to waste energy needlessly. "It's labor-intensive living in this kind of place. The power you use is your own power, and I'm noticing now that I have less of it. I'm getting too old to wrestle things around."

He smiled ruefully. It is a strange thing to grow old when your spirit stays young.

"Jean and I are getting to the age where it's kind of hard to live here. But I've got thirty years of my life invested here, and I just don't want to walk away from it. It suits me. If we move into town, I feel like I could deteriorate pretty fast. This place keeps me going emotionally, spiritually, and physically."

The smell of woodsmoke was heavy. Bob smelled it, too.

"I've got to clean the chimney pretty soon," he said.

It was also easy to sit inside because Bob's life has been fascinating. He could have been a pathological liar, but a pathological liar wouldn't have this depth of imagination.

As we sat, ringed by books and neatly mounted kerosene lanterns, Bob recounted his life. He had been a fighter pilot. He had overseen the aviation operations at McMurdo Station on Ross Island in Antarctica's far south, where temperatures, excluding wind chill, can drop to seventy below zero. He segued neatly into work for the National Science Foundation, organizing Antarctic expeditions and helping to see them through, flying into places no one had seen. He helped design an Antarctic research vessel. He spoke Russian. He shouldered a backpack and went off to see the world three times. He mentioned these items without an iota of chest-thumping, in a tone you might assume when reading down the appetizer list.

Bob first saw the waters of Maine in the early 1950s and was stunned and enamored by their tides. "I couldn't believe what I was seeing, they went out and out and out," he said. "I'd never seen anything like that in my life. I was awed. I knew I wanted to be on the coast of Maine."

What interested me most, though, was the flying. Flying, I

learned slowly, has profoundly affected his life, providing Bob joy, then for many years confused anguish, and finally reconciliation and peace.

He joined the navy in 1942 to become a fighter pilot. He stayed in the navy for twenty-four years. He received his wings in early 1945. In November of that year he got a look at the future. "I went to Japan," he said, "when it was just ashes."

This wasn't just the world's new reality, it was Bob Dale's, too. Based on an aircraft carrier during the Korean War, he was among an elite group of fliers tagged to do what the *Enola Gay* had so ruthlessly accomplished. His assigned target was an airfield in Canton, China. The proposed mission called for a night launch; the squadron was to fly in low over the water to avoid detection, then climb quickly to avoid incineration when the bombs dropped.

Ironically, Bob's visual guide for the possible strike was an island near the airfield. "It stood out like a beacon," said Bob. "The computer knew the difference between the island and the airfield."

But the computer didn't make the most important decision. "The countryside was black," said Bob softly. "I could see in the darkness on the horizon the fireballs of the other bombs that were going off as the other aviators dropped them. There were these big fireballs, and these rising orange-red clouds, and I knew that this was the most horrible thing that could happen. And I turned the plane around and headed back out to sea. I aborted the mission."

This, of course, was only a haunting visualization, played out countless times in countless circumstances. Harry Truman, perhaps with similar visions of his own, never ordered the strike.

Had Truman given the order, I asked, would you have aborted the mission?

Bob didn't hesitate. "I would have dropped the bomb. I was a kid. It's like doing what you're told and not thinking about the consequences. The military knows how to manipulate young minds and make you gung-ho warriors."

The kerosene lanterns flickered. Bob sat still as stone.

"If we had delivered a nuclear bomb in Canton, it would have killed millions," he said.

In 1988 Bob went to the very airfield he had been slated to destroy. He found a corner where, ignored by the teeming Chinese, he meditated, ruminating yet again on the potential consequences of his actions and asking forgiveness.

This struck me as odd. It wasn't his fault he had been assigned to drop the bomb.

A log settled with a pop.

"I volunteered," he said.

We went outside to pee. Well, Bob needed to pee. I needed to get outside to shake the vision of a young warrior, heart and mind yet firmly in place, loosing an inferno from which there was no turning back. It was terrifying because history repeats itself.

It felt good to be slapped by the cold. We stood, each straddling our own patch of snow, and looked out to the water. The sun was dropping. The wind had died. The world was nothing but water and wood. It was lovely and serene, real life wrought still life. The water appeared as solid as concrete, without movement on its gray surface, but this was not the case. The tide was drawing out. The dark mudflats rimming Hockomock's edges caught the sun and glowed dull gold.

"It's the prettiest place I've ever peed," I said.

Bob grinned. "Our guests get quite a view from the outhouse, too," he said.

When the time comes, Bob plans on selling his island to his daughter. When the next step arrives, she will scatter her father's ashes across the water, and he will run with the tide he loves, beyond decisions.

⁂

As I DROVE north again, the newspapers were filled with news of winter. Vicious wind chills, high winds, whiteout conditions, horrific traffic pile-ups. Reporters filled their columns with historical comparisons. "On this morning in 1950 it was so cold that Ebenezer DeGroot's cow froze to the side of the barn, and we're only three degrees short of seeing Ebeneezer once again conducting animal husbandry with a paint chipper." I could see the reporters scurrying

288 / KEN McALPINE

outside in their shirtsleeves to consult the thermometer one last time before deadline.

Bob Dale moved at Nature's pace and so saw things differently. Through his patio doors we had watched two bluejays pecking hopefully at a bare spot in the snow.

"Spring's not very far off," he had said. "I'm seeing the change already. I've seen a finch or two. We saw a robin the other day. Some Canadian geese are heading north."

When I left Bob, I knew I was making my final push north. It wasn't so much a conscious decision—I felt it more in my heart. Winter was receding, slowly, by no means defeated but dragged nonetheless in great heel-digging, squalling fits for the door.

Nothing should overstay its welcome; not seasons, not writers, not travels.

I drove north to Ellsworth along roads pocked with ice and edged with snow. I spent the night. The next day it rained hard, and at the Ellsworth Chamber of Commerce Pat Jordan counseled me not to continue north.

"Those little villages up there, they don't get out to clear the roads as well as they could," she said. "I know the area, and the weather can change very quickly. I think you'd be wise not to take chances. I don't really care to drive up there this time of year."

The next morning when I woke, the roads looked no different, but the rain had stopped and the sun was out. I had no good reason to go farther north except that I wanted to, and that was good enough, whatever Pat Jordan had said.

Despite journeying through the Winter of the Century (albeit a young one), I had received only glancing blows. Tornadoes, ice storms, Arctic whiteouts—they had erupted on all sides of me but never directly overhead. Now the kindly weather gods, having watched over me for five long months, bestowed one final favor: clear skies of summer blue.

Still, I drove cautiously, with a knot in my stomach. My pirouette on the ice in Stonington had scared me. Outside Ellsworth a student driver passed me. Not long after that an octogenarian who could barely peer over the dash raised her hand high enough so I

could see her middle finger. I didn't care. I planned on driving to Lubec and back, roughly 160 miles round trip, and I had all day to do it.

As a final destination, Lubec was fitting. In a journey up the East Coast, it seemed only right to finish at our country's easternmost point. Plus I had been told there was a lighthouse nearby at Quoddy Head State Park, and if the day was fine, you could see Canada.

Everywhere along U.S. 1 there were harbingers of change. As I drove north through Sullivan, Millbridge, Harrington, and Machias, tanning parlors offered specials, bright stacks of two-by-fours leaned against motels readying for repairs, and in the icy marshes, vast rippling puddles expanded their reach. A few miles short of Lubec a sign appeared that made me smile for both its chutzpah and promise. It sat nearly buried in a snowdrift: "New Beachfront Summer Rental."

But Maine wasn't out of the woods yet, and neither was I. As I neared Lubec, the roads narrowed, the ice in the marshes crawled hungrily up alongside the road again, and the wind gathered heart. The sky turned from blue to gray and back again as if it still couldn't decide.

When I arrived at West Quoddy Head, the sky had settled ⟨ gray. The red-and-white-striped lighthouse was closed. The sign s⟨ it would reopen on Memorial Day.

But I hadn't really come to see the lighthouse. I had com⟨ always, to see the ocean, and the Quoddy Head Light, adher⟨ lighthouse custom, afforded a stellar vista, this one from the ⟨ a ninety-foot cliff. There was the Atlantic Ocean, running and serene to the horizon. There was Campobello Island. T⟨ Canada.

A woman in a leather jacket and red boots was alread⟨ the view, and when I approached, she turned to me and ⟨ tentedly.

"This is the first time I've seen this place without ⟨ "I've been here before in summer, but each time it w⟨ figured winter was the time to come."

I knew this already.

She sighed. "Look at the ocean," she said. "It's just amazing to be enveloped in so much beauty."

It was beautiful, but I needed something more intimate. It didn't seem right to finish my trip with a tour bus view. I followed a snowy path along the edge of the cliff, slid down a long ladder of icy stairs, and stood on a dark-cobbled beach awash in salt air.

I knew this was the end. I closed my eyes and drifted along the ocean's edge, through the mangrove Keys and the marshes of Georgia, along shores disparate but one; Tangier, Hog, and Ocracoke Islands; Strathmere, Montauk, Narragansett, Cape Cod. Faces swam before me, voices rose again. Tim Marshall whistling, pedaling home to his grandson. Cotton barking numbers. Erik singing under someone else's yacht.

There were no great answers. They had chosen their place. They were content, and I was, too.

The wind came off the gray sea. I stood before this familiar face—a realm beyond us, and within us—and then I crouched and put my fingers gently in the water, as cold as winter and as clear as a summer day.

Snow began to fall.

About the Author

A freelance writer, Ken McAlpine's work has appeared in many national publications, including *Sports Illustrated, American Way, Outside,* and *Reader's Digest.* His travel writing has earned him two Lowell Thomas awards. He is the author of *Diving the World,* which documents the world's best dive spots and critical marine issues and features the work of underwater photographer Norbert Wu.

McAlpine has spent his entire life around the ocean, a lifelong love that has brought him great happiness and caused those around him some concern; at one point he considered professional lifeguarding as a career. He has grown up as best as he can.

Most important, he lives in Ventura, California, with his beautiful wife, Kathy, and their sons, Cullen and Graham.